MODERNISM AND AUTHORITY: STRATEGIES OF LEGITIMATION IN FLAUBERT AND CONRAD

MODERNISM AND AUTHORITY: STRATEGIES OF LEGITIMATION IN FLAUBERT AND CONRAD

MARK CONROY

THE JOHNS HOPKINS UNIVERSITY PRESS

BALTIMORE AND LONDON

This book has been brought to publication with the generous assistance of the
Andrew W. Mellon Foundation.

The Johns Hopkins University Press, Baltimore, Maryland 21218
The Johns Hopkins Press Ltd, London

The paper in this book is acid-free and meets the guidelines for permanence and durability of the
Committee on Production Guidelines for Book Longevity of the Council on Library Resources.

Library of Congress Cataloging in Publication Data

Conroy, Mark.
Modernism and authority.

Bibliography: p.
Includes index.
1. Fiction—History and criticism.   2. Flaubert,
Gustave, 1821–1880—Criticism and interpretation.
3. Conrad, Joseph, 1857–1924—Criticism and interpretation.   I. Title.

PN3491.C63   1985   823'.912   84-21848
ISBN 0-8018-2480-X (alk. paper)

To my father in memory of my mother

Contents

Acknowledgments

I would like to thank both people and institutions, beginning with people. Much of the original intellectual stimulus for the project was given by John Brenkman, and much of its original dissertation form owes to Henry Sussman. Rodolphe Gasché's seminar on Gustave Flaubert worked to crystallize my thoughts on his work, and Joseph Fradin's expert criticism and guidance enforced greater clarity and precision upon my treatment of Joseph Conrad. Gale Carrithers provided needed moral support. Bainard Cowan helped greatly to improve the book manuscript in its early stages. William Sisler was instrumental in facilitating the editorial process at Hopkins, as was Eric Halpern in the final acceptance and production of this book. Christine Cowan did a great job of typing the final manuscript, as did Susan Wilson in editing it.

As for institutions, libraries—specifically the Lockwood Library in Buffalo, New York, the Middleton Library in Baton Rouge, Louisiana, and the New York Public Library through its Wertheim Room—are due some thanks; and so is the Criticism and Theory School, whose members assisted me in making the theoretical facets of my project clearer both to myself and, with luck, others. Above all, I want to thank my colleagues at S.U.N.Y.-Buffalo, whose often casual conversation nurtured my interests in pursuing this inquiry at least as much as formal courses did.

Introduction: Readership into Audience

Ask to whom a writer of fiction desires to make his or her work legitimate, and the answer is implied as swiftly as recto suggests verso. It is, of course, to the reader. Sometimes the reader is oneself, sometimes others, sometimes an "ideal" reader; but writing, like all rhetoric—at least according to Kenneth Burke's version of it—is addressed.[1] It is no longer daring, in this age of "reader response" theory, to challenge the formalist premise that a work of art be autotelic, concerned only with its own inner structure.[2]

Yet that only begins the trouble, for this reader is not easily defined; and when we stalk its path, it easily slips away. It quickly becomes clear that not one but many types of audience are possible, and the actual readership that emerges is only one among many potential audiences. The kind of reader whose responses are shaped by, or inscribed within, a work of art—the so-called ideal reader—is often what is meant by the "reader." Reception theory approaches the reader as the historical public who have actually bought and read a given work of art. There are indeed many readers in criticism's imaginary library.[3]

The kind of reader I propose to assume as the point to which appeal for legitimacy is made is the reader posited by the appeal itself; in other words, the potential public created within the rhetorical space of the text itself, by the relation the writing adopts to its possible reception. In the strict sense, no novelist has a foreknowledge of the public he or she will obtain; the actual future readership does not yet exist, except in two ways. Novelists really operate on two assumptions: one concerning the public their work is likely to find; and one concerning the public desired for their work. The legendary tendency on the part of Dickens to modify plot elements to account for reader mail, or of Richardson's similar experiences while writing *Clarissa*, are exceptions to the rule, no doubt; and serial publication clearly provided a certain avenue for feedback from readers while narratives were still being composed. Nonetheless, I would contend that, by and large, most novelists have worked with far less certain knowledge of the contours of their readership.

To say that a work of art constructs an ideal reader, however, is only to say that any piece of writing—or any communication of any complexity—is by definition addressed to the one who can completely understand and appreciate it. But what is of more interest is the way writers attempt to balance the desire to please an assumed type of audience with the desire to shape and to modify—or in extremis, as with Gustave Flaubert, even to transcend—that audience. The audience one is likely to accrue and the audience one would hope to produce: the writer tries, to varying degrees and in various proportions, to blend these two publics—neither of whom, strictly speaking, empirically exists. The result of this blending is a kind of "phantom audience," its lineaments combining the probabilistic and the utopian, but necessary to help define both the hoped-for ideal and the felt constraints of the historical writing situation. The probable audience is only the forward projection, so to speak, of past audiences; the audience desired—insofar as it diverges from the probable—is more simply a proleptic vision of the future. Hence, in its furthest form, it is an appeal to "posterity." But to obtain the audience one wants, one must appeal to the audience one has; to win the future, one must gain sanction from the past. The phantom audience is a ghost of readers past and future, and it haunts what is written. It haunts authors as they pursue their writing projects, and it should haunt the critics who examine the written results as well, if they are perceptive.[4] In the readings of Gustave Flaubert and Joseph Conrad which follow, the awareness of this phantom underlies much of the analysis.

Can this phantom audience really be fixed clearly, or is it only a matter of gesturing toward it? One gets at this phantom the way one locates any phantom: by its effects. It requires observing the generic, political, and cultural constraints of an author's time and place, especially as it affects his or her probable readers, and then noting how (if in any way) that author's text strains against, modifies, or extends those constraints. Any given work can easily work against one set of constraints while embracing others, as *Madame Bovary* may be said to have shocked its bourgeois readership in one respect, but seems also to have extended the tradition of nineteenth-century realistic prose fiction in another. Though we pursue the phantom of a phantom—our notion of the author's notional audience—this project is no less capable of success than other strategies for interpreting a work. This may not seem in itself immense encouragement; but close reading of texts, against the background of a work's historical and literary contexts, effectively yields most of what one needs for this purpose, with little recourse required to notions of authorial intent as such, or to a great deal of biographical sleuthing.

Assuming this phantom could be designated, why attempt it? Does one's appreciation of the work gain thereby? It is, of course, impossible to answer questions of value with much dispatch, but it would seem likely that if a work of, say, Conrad's is more precisely put into its rhetorical context (for that is what assessing an author's public in this fashion would do), one would have a better sense of it not only as a historical product but also as literature. A more acute appreciation of the historical constraints and opportunities for a text's rhetorical strategy could not but make one's critical assessment more fruitful. It is my presumption that any historically oriented reading ought to open out and to complicate possible interpretations rather than to police or to exclude unacceptable readings.

A kind of, if not policeman, at least overseer, supervises what is written, then; and despite the difficulty of defining it, writers cannot cease attempting to define it and their relation to it. The phantom audience assumes various forms appropriate to its literary and historical occasions; and though this audience lacks the fixity of an object, the type of writing often determines the degree of clarity it may assume. In folk art, for instance, the boundaries between consumer and producer, author and audience, are so blurred that the audience is in effect part producer of the thing it hears. In the case of the artist under noble patronage, the audience is still fairly specific as to its desires and suppositions, is known to the author, and is active in its role.[5] What kind of phantom awaited the heirs of nineteenth-century literature, the novelists?

In many ways, it was ghostlier than ever. Nineteenth-century narrative prose, for reasons later discussed, has few of the certainties either of older forms of folk art or of the patronized high art of preindustrial times. The eccentricity of writer to reader, his or her "outsider" status, seems to have become more acute by this time. This state of affairs is in part revealed in the very structure of the novel form: a bastard genre derived from many different previous forms, with many forebears and no predecessors. Writing, always a lonely process, became even more isolated from reading, as the potential public, growing vaster, grew also more distant, less formed.[6] Many commentators on the novel form choose to see this deracination as part of the novel's subversive potential. There is less recognition, though, of the desire on the part of some of the greatest novelists to win legitimacy for their form either by placing it firmly within the lines of past, aristocratic genres (as Flaubert did), or by trying for sustainable popular appeal as a novelist (as Conrad did). The legitimative desire flows in different directions, but in many novelists it bespeaks the feeling that what is a source of innovation and subversive freedom is also a cause of anomie and desperation. Some of this isolation and oddity spring from the situation of the emergent nineteenth-century middle classes in general: condemned to individualism, they yearned for the social validation they had spurned. But beyond this, there is also a physical—and in some measure psychological—alienation of novelists from the public to which they had to make appeal: alienation caused by the sheer facelessness of the printing-press masses and exacerbated by the conflict over values that increased between author and readership as the century wore on.

Flaubert remarked this in a letter to his friend Maxime du Camp: "It may well be that from a commercial point of view there are 'favorable moments,' a ready market for one kind of article or another, a passing public taste which raises the price of rubber or cotton. Let those who wish to manufacture those things hasten to set up their factories. . . . But if your work of art is good, if it is authentic, its echo will be heard, it will find its place—in six months, six years, or after you're gone. What difference does it make?"[7] What underlies Flaubert's testament here is not only the generalized appeal to posterity, common at the time, but also a suspicion of the reading public as it exists at his time and place, and a tendency, in response to du Camp's pleadings to him to "become established," to conflate literary fame and mass production for the anonymous marketplace. It has been amply remarked that Flaubert's economic smugness may have permitted such high-mindedness: permission denied, for example, to his later, sometime disciple Joseph Conrad, who had to write for publication. Both writers, despite this distinction, share that remoteness from readership which increasingly characterized the serious writer of prose fiction.

Part of my task will be to show how this situation affects not only the novel as such but also the specific writings of Flaubert and Conrad. But in this estrangement of author from readership, it is necessary to re-examine what this phantom audience often becomes concretely for a writer in such a condition. If the conjectural status of any possible audience was especially obvious by the nineteenth century, this is attributable not only to the fact that a writer is read in solitude, rather than listened to in public with others, but also to the increasing remoteness of the values of serious writers and those of their dominant readership. This yields a desired audience, much on the model of the face-to-face audience no longer possible. That audience was very much a part of the patronage that sustained artists of an earlier time, and much of Flaubert's urge for an audience of the happy few partakes of these nostalgic, aristocratic aspirations.[8] In Conrad's work, there is overt expression of the nostalgia for a genuine audience—a group of listeners—in the figure of Charlie Marlow.

The replacement of an intimate audience with a larger, less fixed, and more anonymous group of readers—sometimes called, in an unaware oxymoron, the "mass audience"—results, then, in a harking back to the imagined condition that could have produced a "real" audience. In some cases, such as Flaubert's, there was the urge to banish the readership, to transcend it by instituting a kind of salon of posterity; in other cases, such as Conrad's, the chief urge was to fashion of potential readership into something like an audience. Flaubert tends to flee his likeliest bourgeois readership for the sake of his sense of mission, whereas Conrad's exoticism, by contrast, makes it harder for him to be embraced by the British public he most requires. Although the desired trajectories of the two writers seem opposed, each is contaminated by the contrary movement—and most crucially, each arises from the same eccentric relation to the available, likely public of the day. In varying ways, each author sought to establish some sort of legitimacy for his writing. In their yearning for such legitimacy, they at once affirm the need to present their works to a putative audience and to measure the distance those works must traverse.

The novelist, of course, is not the only user of language who must establish such a claim to legitimacy; all of us, it can be argued, must do that, and it starts quite early—at the inception of language itself. The speaking subject's entry into language situates rhetorical legitimation at the most intimate level (our first audience is our parents) and also at the most universal (something of this process informs almost any entry into communication). It also introduces the strictest problem of legitimacy— that of a child—and in so doing, prepares, by invoking paternity and the law, for a more general treatment of the political dimensions of rhetoric, such as Burke explores. Narrowing the focus of the inquiry, there follows a historically oriented analysis of what specifically political legitimation is—and especially of the difficulties confronting the bourgeois order emergent in the nineteenth century, for whom no convenient paternal metaphor seems to work in making the new nation-state form and its culture a part of any given tradition. The artists of the nineteenth century perceived this legitimative quandary at least as keenly as the bourgeois readership with which they shared it. But in a further focusing, the final chapter of the opening section reprises in more detail the special problems that bedevil the novel, the most middle-class of genres.

The serious novelists of the latter nineteenth century are intriguing to observe because they were always trying, in varying proportions, to legitimate themselves in two ways: as writers, to a specific and available public; and as artists, to posterity's judgment and to that of other artists in more securely exalted forms, such as lyric poetry. But no matter what specific form writing may take, writers seem always to have to do at

I:
Legitimation and Its Discontents

Every statement involves a field of antecedent elements in relation to which it is situated, but which it is able to reorganize and redistribute according to new relations. It constitutes its own past, defines, in what precedes it, its own filiation, redefines what makes it possible or necessary, excludes what cannot be compatible with it. And it poses this enunciative past as an acquired truth, as an event that has occurred, as a form that can be modified, as material to be transformed, or as an object that can be spoken about, etc.—Michel Foucault, *The Archaeology of Knowledge*

If my hypothesis is correct, the primary function of writing, as a means of communication, is to facilitate the enslavement of other human beings. The use of writing for disinterested ends, and with a view to satisfactions of the mind in the fields either of science or the arts, is a secondary result of its invention—and may even be no more than a way of reinforcing, justifying, or dissimulating its primary function.—Claude Lévi-Strauss, *Tristes Tropiques*

1

━━━━━━●━━━━━━

Heirs and Usurpers: Legitimation as Rhetoric

Everyone is, in a sense, born illegitimate. The scandal of one's existence must be explained, given reasons, cause, and legitimacy—much as we may devoutly wish mere existence were, like beauty, its own excuse for being. It is not, however: the type of excuses one finds no doubt depends upon the audience one confronts, but the requirement that excuses be found perdures. Likewise, and by extension, most activities are born illegitimate. Beginnings are always scandalous, impious, while the more sanctified origin is invariably consecrated by virtue of a temporal trompe l'oeil: it is a beginning that erupted in the remote past.[1] What begins now seems always to legitimate itself by reference to what has begun before; and this fatality entails not only a temporal but also a social dimension, as all questions of authority do.

The Oxford English Dictionary, in a philosophical search for origin that mimes what the word itself describes, notes that the Latin root of *legitimate* expresses "a status which has been conferred or ratified by some authority."[2] In the case of the founding scandal—that of existence itself, or birth—the product of that catastrophe is usually given status, and indeed social identity, through the parents, that is, through the fact of their existence and link to the child. Paternity, of course, is never a sure matter, and so parental origin—which is what, in the narrowest legal sense of the term, legitimates the child—is generally presumptive rather than verified: not something the child, or anyone else, was there to witness, but something the parents tell both the child and the community. The discovery by the child of this parental origin comes well after the scandal of birth, and that discovery accompanies another one: that of parental injunction and taboo.

This paradox—that the father who legitimates one's existence is also the source of prohibition—obsessed that analyst of patriarchy, Sigmund Freud, to the point that he argued in the later work *Totem and Taboo* that the constitution of the law through the representation of the Founding Father is itself synchronous with the primal crime of parricide.[3] Certainly on the familial level, Freud saw a synchrony between the emergence of the father as the source of legitimate identity for the child, that of the desire to transgress that very authority, and that of the guilt attendant upon that desire.

Jacques Lacan, the French psychoanalyst, has pursued the idea that the father is the locus of the law (or the "symbolic order"), and he has linked the symbolic order explicitly to the emergence of the infant as a speaking subject. Insofar as the father's law formulates the bounds within which the infant may legitimate a claim to be heard by others (or the potential community of listeners, called "the Other"), the social law he represents also guides the form of the claim, the language in which the claim can expect to be heard. The double meaning of the term *code*—a code of proper conduct and a procedure for the formulation of messages—conveys this dual function. The means by which desire can be formulated and expressed to others is also the means of repressing those desires. Such a contradiction between expression and repression, aggression and guilt, inhabits the very act of giving words to desires and helps to produce what is called "the unconscious." How more precisely does this process by which an uttered wish produces repression and the unconscious work?

This phenomenon Lacan explicator Anthony Wilden locates, interestingly, not so much in the preexistent desires that a person communicates as in the activity of communication itself, for this reason: "Whatever its content may be, no wish is really intrasubjective, nor can it remain intrasubjective." That is, it cannot remain within the individual but must be expressed to others. Usually the parents are the first "others," and the term "the Other" often "refers to the parents," according to Wilden. The parents, as "the Other," are thus also the place of the code itself. They are both the audience to whom this wish is addressed and the bearers or representatives of the code by which that wish is made possible. However, because the "desire to communicate" is never fully exhausted by the "content of the communication," frustration and even guilt will result. The part of our desire that can be transformed neatly into a wish is less of a problem than the dimension of our desires that cannot be formulated. Remembering that the code, flowing from the parents, conflates linguistic and behavioral rules, one senses somehow that the desires that cannot be voiced are, in the narrowest way, unauthorized, as much as those wishes that are voiced but denied. The unspoken part of those desires is repressed, burrowing so deeply into the interior of the subject that even he or she cannot find it.

The unspoken becomes the unacknowledged, and finally the unconscious.[4]

The fall into language that allows children to become speaking subjects also puts them into the position of usurpers, having to justify themselves not only before their parents, but, through them, before the law of society and before the language they use. It is the fact that the unconscious springs from the code itself that gives Wilden leave to say that, like the code, the unconscious as well is "not 'within' the subject" but is "the third position through which the sender is provided with a receiver," and that the unconscious is thus the locus of "the desire to communicate."[5]

Again, the act of communication gives rise to this situation as much as to what is specifically requested: the act of speech by itself calls up the eccentric relation of speaker to code and the consequent illegitimacy of the speaker. For one thing, the unexpressed desire cannot be coincident with what is expressed, both "in the purely formal sense that our choice of messages is limited by the code" and also "in the existential sense that the conscious subject has only a limited control over the content of his messages, and less over their reception."[6]

But beyond these factors, because the code, the legitimate language, is embedded in the family structure, the space of authority created by the language-giving father (crystallized by Lacan into the Symbolic Father or *nom du père*) is also a space of judgment: judgment that presumes guilt and that requires the repression of that which founds the subject's ability to communicate.

The same father who provides the linguistic and legal code for appeal also presents both an obstacle to possession of the desired object (hence the collateral desire to remove the father) and a reproach to that desire, whether or not it is executed (hence the negative injunction). This fact accounts for the dual message of the "locus of the code" and provides a clue to the link between linguistic usage and the unconscious. The same rules that legitimate our appeal before the court of the community also seem to insure that we shall always be found guilty.

The father is still unavoidable, though, both because the law is his to administer and because his name secures a lineage for the child, as guaranteed by the father's name (or *nom du père*). The child may instinctively doubt the father's legitimacy and that of his law—and if he wishes to usurp his father's position, he is even likely to doubt them—but that doubt is checked by the understanding that the father's legitimacy gives the child's own existence and desire social standing, even if he may seem, as bearer of the law, to be condemning both. The father whose name excuses the scandal of birth, then, also establishes, with the code he bears, the infant as a speaking subject: as one who can articulate his or her wishes to others. Even in this discovery, though, the subject realizes, for all the reasons above, that he or she is eccentric to that structure; born into it, the subject must nevertheless learn it slowly, making many mistakes. I have emphasized the relations of the speaker to parents, because they characteristically provide a speaker's first audience; but features of that paradox of guilt and justification—and the way one wears the other's guise—inhere as well in any recourse to language the subject will later have.

All of the elements that are sketched here as part of the ensemble that children experience as soon as they begin to speak are reproduced in the rhetorical situations we confront later on. The gap between the code and the individual who must use it, the placing of oneself within a code (by assuming the father's name, for example) and the alienation from oneself that results, the need to usurp silence by speech and the subsequent need to justify that usurpation, the audience that exists both to call forth the desires of the speaker or writer and also to check those desires—these parameters define any rhetorical circumstance. Insofar as one uses language, one reenacts the conditions that first made language possible; and those conditions, of course, are political in a very close sense. The code is both a linguistic and a behavioral one: rules imposed from above, which are enabling only within certain limits. The speaking subject's relation to the father can be seen as a miniature, then, of all users of language as they make their way through the culture of their time and place, adapting to its codes of intelligibility, by which they make their wishes known, and to its codes of behavior, by which those wishes are channeled and, frequently, frustrated. The position of narrator Marlow in Joseph Conrad's fiction exhibits this dual code, for instance: Marlow both providing a code for understanding (or mystifying, by turns) the stories of Kurtz in "Heart of Darkness" or the title character in *Lord Jim*, and also embodying a "fixed standard of conduct." (His fatherly image profits from this dual status, no doubt.) The fact that most nation-states still draw on paternalistic metaphor to legitimate their political structures is more pointed indication that the complex way we as users of language respond to our first encounters with legitimation and its discontents also informs the more explicitly political dimensions of rhetoric.[7]

As users of language, we may renounce our putative father, either by trying to become our own father or by searching for many fathers.[8] Both moves betray impatience with the constraints of a determinate history and its legacy of guilt and obligation: the Freudian father and the eternal debt in which his mutinous sons are placed. This debt, never remissible, is inscribed twice: for the origin that gives one legitimacy and for the gift of communicable wish. This familial level, though, is embedded within a larger social context, which puts additional stresses upon our use of language. Yet if Freud has said that our parents provide our first love affair, it is equally true that they provide us with our first phantom audience.

It could be objected that even if the infant's situation as Lacan presents it is accurate, it still only applies to one brief phase of a child's life. Certainly, no less of an authority on authority than Richard Sennett has cautioned against "transferring," to use the loaded term, the domestic experience of paternal authority too patly to public, institutional life.[9] Yet the elements of law, authority, and code are set in place to last, and furthermore, these are part of the greater society beyond. With the current interest in matters of rhetoric, it is worthwhile periodically recalling that rhetoric—even when it is supposedly an interior monologue—always implies a greater audience from whom some reaction (usually approval) is sought. In this process, it is often hard to differentiate between what we convince ourselves of and what we convince others of: that old adage that the first person a salesman convinces is himself applies here. After all, if the version of the unconscious sketched previously is accurate, then things we find impossible to express to others easily become things we hide from ourselves.

In *A Rhetoric of Motives*, Kenneth Burke is quite clear how the nature of rhetoric as "*addressed*, since persuasion implies an audience" can apply even to the intrasubjective individual, seemingly removed from the need for an audience.[10] In taking up the question whether rhetoric can be introspective, Burke says that "you become your own audience . . . when you become involved in psychologically stylistic subterfuges for presenting your own case to yourself in sympathetic terms."[11] Thus, the author who may claim, as Flaubert occasionally does, to be writing only for himself—even if such a claim were, strictly speaking, correct—would, for Burke, still not step beyond the realm of rhetorical persuasion. Even the interior monologue replays within itself the patterns that have informed the rhetoric at work among people: "The Freudian psyche is quite a parliament, with conflicting interests expressed in ways variously designed to take the claims of rival factions into account."[12] This observation goes a long way toward explaining why writers weave their phantom audience as much from inner instructions as from those they may impute to their readership. For in making this simile, Burke not only points to the homology between the social and political spheres (the "parliament") and the individual subject (the "psyche") but also hints at the role of that larger sphere in forming the content of those "rival factions" that will battle it out in this interior parliament. This content extends to empirical historical experience and also to the way rhetorical appeals will be taken up and interpreted.

In solidifying a bond of content as well as form between individual psyche and the larger culture of a time and place, Burke resorts to an argument that, but for jargon, strikingly recalls Wilden's:

> Such considerations make us alert to the ingredient of rhetoric in all *socialization*, considered as a *moralizing* process. The individual person, striving to form himself in accordance with the communicative norms that match the cooperative ways of his society, is by the same token concerned with the rhetoric of identification. . . . Education ("indoctrination") exerts such pressure upon him from without; he completes the process from within. . . . Only those voices from without are effective which can speak in the language of a voice within.[13]

This passage takes up and expands some aspects of Wilden's argument that were previously only in germ. Burke's emphasis on the way "communicative norms" match "cooperative ways," on language as symbolic action, reminds one of the wordplay on *code* made by Wilden. The chief difference between the two models is the relative weight given the subject. Whereas Wilden's version of the developmental process stresses the role of the symbolic order in "producing" the subject and even the unconscious, here Burke stresses the need for effective indoctrination to answer to an individual's interior voice. In practice, the two models seem symbiotic, each pointing up a different element of the psyche's dependency on social forms for its very structure. What is more, both society and psyche are equally bound up with rhetoric itself.

The effect of Burke's emphasis is to shift the rhetorical problematic from a strictly epistemological one, having to do with the truth-value or validity of the message itself, to a transsubjective and contextual one, involving the function of address and persuasion as constitutive of a community between speaker and audience. The attempt to establish contact is prior to the concern with epistemological reliability in Burke's scheme, and beyond that, even in situations where a specific action or orientation is not explicitly aimed at, the overriding goal of discourse is—to discourse, to keep the lines of communication open, to transmit for its own sake (i.e., for the sake of addressor and addressee).

Burke calls this phenomenon "pure persuasion," which "involves the saying of something, not for an extraverbal advantage to be got by the saying, but because of a satisfaction intrinsic to the saying."[14] In describing its processes, he cites Bronislaw Malinowski:

> What the anthropologist Malinowski called "phatic communion" might seem close to "pure persuasion." He referred to talk at random, purely for the satisfaction of talking together, the use of speech as such for the

establishing of a social bond between speaker and spoken-to. Yet "pure persuasion" should be much more intensely purposive than that, though it would be . . . a kind of purpose which, as judged by the rhetoric of advantage, is no purpose at all, or which might often look like sheer frustration of purpose.[15]

Burke's example of "pure persuasion" is prayer, in which, to maintain the process of communication, the object of the persuasion must be absent or the thing appealed for must be withheld, or preferably both: "Obviously you would not maintain this form except insofar as the plea remained unanswered."[16] Both "pure persuasion" and the "phatic communion" of Malinowski—unlike in the respect that one is idle, the other purposive—are alike in that both reduce the matter for which persuasion is sought to the discourse itself, and the legitimacy of the discourse itself and of its speaker.

Examples of situations where a flesh-and-blood addressee has been transformed by the act of appeal into an object of prayerful apostrophe are many: Petrarch's Laura may be the most famous. What should be clear here is that what Burke calls "pure persuasion" may be the phatic impulse itself, changed from the initial drive for communication or ground for contact to the telos of communication itself; from the desire to persuade or merely to address a determinate audience to the desire to project into a virtual audience, one that is primordially molded by the rhetoric of the addressor. One thinks of those who write for posterity, a common nineteenth-century claim. Given the rhetorical nature of language, what really would it mean to write only for oneself? The urge for pure persuasion betrays a restiveness with the available sources of legitimation for one's discourse: the attempt not so much to be one's own father as to produce fathers for oneself by calling them forth.

Between the pure desire to communicate and to be taken seriously and the pure delight in the play of rhetoric for its own sake, our speech and writing stage both the bid for what Burke calls "extraverbal advantage" through polemic with an existing community and the project of developing a new community engendered by the rhetoric itself. Thus is the addressee both found and created, both situated and posited; in this way, we see in greater detail how and why it is that the phantom audience, product both of the writer's desire and of his or her felt constraints, emerges.

But this mediate space, between the autotelic omnipotence of prayer and the mere phatic desire for communication in itself, is where the content of utterance, presuppositions, universes of meaning, historical prejudices, and the struggle among factions for material advantage and for recognition all reign. This is presumably why Burke says that "rhetoric is concerned with the state of Babel after the Fall."[17] For Burke, the rhetorical status of language becomes most evident where strife is most likely to be the rule: "We need never deny the presence of strife, enmity, faction as a characteristic motive of rhetorical expression. . . . If men were not apart from one another, there would be no need for the rhetorician to proclaim their unity."[18] But Burke's model of rhetoric is not warfare itself: it is an attempt to persuade others not of like mind, and in this—as in his model for rhetoric as the courtroom and the parliament—Burke is following Aristotle. Where proclaimed unity breaks down and force supplants suasion, warfare itself takes over. As it is, Burke sees warfare as merely the figure for one aspect of the rhetorical activity.[19] Insofar as rhetoric hopes to persuade, it assumes a common ground of understanding and sympathy that force does not.

One engages, in effect, in polemics, whether or not deliberately, because one writes or speaks against a tradition or a corpus of opinion. ("Against" here is meant in both the positional and the attitudinal senses.) One must clear a space for oneself, and the polemical strategy attends this process, however implicitly. At the same time, one must gain the ear and credence of what is often the same corpus of opinion one is writing against. No wonder the rhetoric of justification is such a tangled affair.

Burke makes pointed the polemical features of rhetoric in a way that broadens the scope and enriches the implications of what Wilden has set out. Although his genetic model of indoctrination is similar to Wilden's, he is able to clarify the large-scale political ramifications of the linguistic act. (Not incidentally, Burke is able to show these polemical features of rhetoric at work in literary texts as well, a procedure that gives him some status as a father of this project, too.) Whether discussing Franz Kafka's *Castle* or Castiglione, Burke finds it necessary, like Malinowski, "to describe the customs, social psychology, and tribal organization that were implicit in a given utterance" when he explicates texts.[20] His work is useful to me, then, not only as theory but also as textual practice.

He is also useful as a kind of *argumentum ad auctoritatem*, for as we have come to define rhetoric, it is, at bottom, mostly an appeal to authority. (Burke calls it the "hierarchical principle.") In literary analysis as elsewhere, appeal to the text or to the "truth of experience" is only one legitimative strategy among many. To secure some cachet for one's own discursive status, one may seek a respectable lineage for one's key concept; cite various authorities to shore up the claims made for that concept; perhaps even attempt a line of filiation for the major texts one uses the concept to analyze. All of these strategies this study itself uses in some form. These strategies can be seen, as will become clear in the next section, on the largest cultural level.

The first order of business for a discourse is to establish itself as discourse. It must gain ascendancy over the attention of the addressee.[21] There is an aggressivity in the desire to be heard, a usurpation of silence by speech, that anyone who has endured an overlong seminar paper has surely felt most acutely. It is in this sense that a new piece of language is as much a political act as a change of government is. The very process described by Lacan through Wilden, whereby the speaking subject enters into the code of the culture, is a form of scandal: the infant erupts into the father's language partly (at least) to challenge the father's preeminence. But the infant must master the father's code to do this. With such baleful implications in the offing, it is somewhat shocking that anyone would presume to initiate communication in the first place—especially since, as the child with its father's law, the tribunal set up for our rhetorical self-justification, as soon as we appeal to it, foredooms us to be judged guilty. Yet we nonetheless make bold every day to impose our discourse on others, first forcing open the channels of communication, then justifying the initial violence by establishing various paternal origins (besides ourselves, of course) to which the reader may trace our discourse in the same way the usurper-king attempts to establish a line, however rambling and circuitous, that would legitimate his forcible seizure of the throne.

The macropolitics of a historical circumstance and the micropolitics of a specific textual strategy, then, are similar not only in form but also in content, as a close look at texts such as Flaubert's *L'Education sentimentale* and Conrad's *Nostromo* will reveal. But beyond that, these reflections on the political implications of rhetoric prompt consideration of the rhetorical implications of politics, and especially of that familiar topic of political theory, the nation-state. As sociologist Max Weber has described it, any structure of domination requires some type of legitimation, just as the usurper tries to secure a noble lineage for himself. This means that the urge to persuade is necessary to most ruling groups: a rhetorical necessity as much for them as for the individual speaker or writer. This necessity has several corollaries.

First, it means that the essence of power, in most ongoing social contexts, is linguistic, a matter of who gives the orders. Weber defines *domination* as "the situation in which the manifested will (*command*) of the *ruler* or rulers is meant to influence the conduct of one or more others (*the ruled*) and actually does influence it in such a way that their conduct to a socially relevant degree occurs as if the ruled had made the content of the command the maxim of their conduct for its own sake."[22]

Even though Weber does not define *domination* as the specific command of the ruler(s) in a determinate situation, it is still clear that the structure of a ruling order depends on instilling their "manifested will" in the ruled classes, and instilling it as a code of conduct. Domination is effective when ruler's command becomes underling's maxim.

Second, however, it should not be concluded that this definition cedes all the advantages to the rulers; rather the reverse. The need for domination to make use of rhetoric implies a great deal of "feedback," or "consent of the governed." There are precious few rulers who can merely issue commands and have everyone obey them automatically, any more than Canute could command the sea. (A child may occasionally do something because the parent "says so," but adults usually, though not invariably, require a bit more.) This element of "give-and-take between the strong and the weak," as Sennett calls it, is precisely what defines the need for legitimacy in the first place.[23] Hegemony, to use Antonio Gramsci's term, needs at least the acquiescence and moral credit of those who are dominated.[24] Granted, the reason for this is partly pragmatic: things go more smoothly if people do not have to be continually coerced into obedience. But the desire for legitimacy is practical as well as psychological.

This psychological need for approval from below leads to the third crucial component of rhetorical legitimacy: the recognition rulers often crave from those they govern.[25] If it is true that recognition by others is part of the pleasures of governance—that authority's claim is "always one of personal superiority based on strength"—then the need to persuade oneself of this superiority and the need to persuade others may be the same.[26] It is a commonplace to speak of the loss of power of the ruling classes who ceased believing in themselves.

This need for recognition makes self-mystification something the masters indulge in as much as the servants. An occasional act or statement may simply be a cynical lie or gesture; but there are few political orders that can operate long without evolving ways of excusing, to themselves, their own existence. Writing against Machiavelli's version of power in *The Prince*, Sennett tartly observes:

> This paranoid vision of authorities who know exactly what they are about requires too much genius among the master classes to be convincing. Indeed, it is precisely because the strong believe in themselves and in what they do that they become creditable in the eyes of others. Deception which occurs without a conspiracy to deceive is properly called illusion. Illusions are deployed systematically, in norms of behavior and belief; they can be shared by masters and servants.[27]

What Sennett calls "illusion" others call ideology; but whatever the term, the process is inseparable from domination itself. In the best novelists, a bid for popular esteem which results in appeals to certain cultural codes is hard to distinguish from "sincere" concerns of the author, not only because the evidence cannot be gotten but also because there is little difference between the two, for purposes of putting together a convincing narrative. Similarly, a ruling group's bid for legitimacy in the eyes of others is bound up with its sense of itself, its belief in its own correctness. Burke's indoctrination, which operates on the speaking subject within the family and on the schoolchild, works also upon those members of the ruling group—even if they may control some part of that process of acculturation. When those in charge give the commands, they must also "speak the language of a voice within" themselves; they must believe in their own commands if they wish them to become maxims.

Why is it that rulers have a social or normative urge to validation and not merely a pragmatic one, assuming this urge to be the case? Weber's answer, steadfastly unspeculative on its surface, does nonetheless get at what is perhaps the critical reason:

> The fates of human beings are not equal. Men differ in their states of health or wealth or social status or what not. Simple observation shows that in every such situation he who is more favored feels the never ceasing need to look upon his position as in some way "legitimate." . . . This same need makes itself felt in the relation between positively and negatively privileged groups of human beings. Every highly privileged group develops the myth of its natural, especially its blood, superiority.[28]

Weber stresses the favored man's desire "to look upon his position as in some way 'legitimate' "—not merely the public relations requirement that others so regard it, but the need so to regard it himself. Beyond that, another aspect of the need for legitimacy presents itself: the desire to see the outcome of chance not as fortuitous but as foreordained, occurring not as the result of external forces but as the recognition of intrinsic, superior merit. This desire usually expresses itself in a temporal key. The advent of new power must always be consecrated by appeal to what is prior and established. To legitimate a chance occurrence is to give it a cause, to institute for it a chain of logic.[29] William the Conqueror, for instance, appears to have forged a link to the past in more than one sense when, upon usurping the British throne, he solemnly pledged to observe the "laws of St. Edward" and then quickly proceeded to have those laws drawn up; and this is only an extreme instance of the way newly won power legitimates itself by being inserted into a line of succession which will make it foreordained rather than fortuitous.[30]

The appeal to tradition is a strong component of the legitimative urge, for both the consumption of others and for one's own peace of mind. This results, by its own particular logic, in a need to consider the appeal to tradition one of the most characteristic necessities when power invests itself with authority. As the historical focus is narrowed to the bourgeois nation-state, the question will arise as to how and why any given ruling group situates itself within a cultural and political tradition; and whether legitimacy without appealing to tradition—unthinkable before the advent of parliamentarism—is ever truly attainable, even for today's political order.

2

The Bourgeois State: Remembrance of Legitimacy Past

When the fortunate man justifies his luck by arguing his superior stock, the appeal to tradition is not far in coming. The myth of "blood superiority," to which Max Weber alludes, is a primitive version of the line of succession a king would use to justify his own reign. It is true that Weber gives tradition as only one of three major modes of legitimation, the others being the "legal-rational" and "charismatic" modes.[1] But it is probably the most overarching, since even legal-rational and charismatic appeals usually rely upon long-standing common values, at least, or upon established custom and precedent. It is most difficult to prove this point with charismatic leaders because they generally come to the fore at a time when "normal" institutions are in a legitimation crisis of some type. But even these historically reach into deeper, often populist sources of validation that appeal to the mythical past.[2] Those in power must always, in various ways, perform the double task at once of usurping the tradition and of appropriating it to their own suasive requirements. Whether the appropriation be cynical or innocent, can a nation-state, a society, or a ruling group ever get on without looking to the authorizing past for its validity?

Legitimacy must always come from some other source than the act of seizing itself, usually a source already established. This source of legitimacy may be quite irrelevant to the actual power that has appeal to it, but that does not often matter. Here is the place, incidentally, to make plain the distinction between established authority and the process whereby authority is vested in (or sought by) power. *Legitimacy* may be said to refer to the posited source of value that renders power as authority. But *legitimation* is the act or rather the ongoing process of positing that value: the struggle to associate the source of authority with the thing to be authorized. A given source of authority must always be posited, enunciated into being, and yet it is always posited as prior (a kind of metalepsis). In various ways, the legitimating urge always eddies back to an event, a founding, a fixed date, for its truth of being, however remote. Much in the manner of the infant, a nation-state must often justify itself in terms that are alien to it.

It is the paradox that Friedrich Nietzsche speculates upon in the famous section of *The Genealogy of Morals* in which, in remarking on the institution of punishment, he says that "the actual causes of a thing's origin and its eventual uses, the manner of its incorporation into a system of purposes, are worlds apart."[3] The concepts of origin and of purpose are here cleanly separated, and the process reveals that, for Nietzsche, the long arm of the law is no more a given of nature than the eye or the hand. Whereas people assume that "the eye is made for seeing, the hand for grasping," and that therefore punishment is simply "an invention for the purpose of punishing . . . [nevertheless the] 'evolution' of a thing, a custom, an organ is not its *progressus* toward a goal. . . . Rather, it is a sequence of more or less profound, more or less independent processes of appropriation, including the resistance used in each instance."[4] By calling attention to what is discontinuous in the evolution of custom and law in general and of punishment in particular, Nietzsche undoes the comfortable tautology by which culture becomes nature; by which the institution of community can claim a smooth causal flow from a founding authority; and by which any current custom or practice is seen as the handmaiden of immutable destiny. Current purpose may not be ancient origin, and whether a given law or custom has been turned to novel use is less a question than how it has been appropriated.

By doing violence to the standard interpretation of custom, Nietzsche gives us to glimpse the founding violence of custom itself: "All pragmatic purposes are simply symbols of the fact that a will to power has implanted its own sense of function in those less powerful."[5] In recurring to the social hierarchy or "rank of souls" he so often invokes, Nietzsche here means to celebrate this state of affairs, though his acute sense of the falsity in appeals to originary legitimacy may lead errantly to latter-day historians such as Michel Foucault, whose *Surveiller et punir* takes a rather different approach to what Nietzsche chooses to approve.[6]

The insight Nietzsche affords us is extensible to society and nation as a whole, which hark back to an origin to "implant their own sense of function" in their members. Whether the process is quite as cut-and-dried and amoral as he would have us think is another matter: the molders of these appeals to origin—whether hereditary lineage or theory of parliamentary procedure—often become captives of their ideologies as much as "those less powerful" are. What concerns us more narrowly is the form this search for legitimacy seems to have assumed in bourgeois civil society. This engages for at least two reasons: (1) we are ourselves currently living under one of the many versions of civil society; and (2) the novelists I treat are, in both theme and relation to readership, especially sensitive registers of the strains peculiar to civil society's search for origins.

Most observers who have cared to probe the matter have come to sense that the modes by which bourgeois social and legal institutions legitimate themselves are in some way quite distinct and discontinuous from most previous modes. What varies is the tone taken by any given observer toward this new development. Hans-Georg Gadamer, for example, views the developments of recent years (or rather centuries) quite darkly. Much of his magisterial *Truth and Method* is devoted to refurbishing the Viconian meaning given to the term *sensus communis*, whose degradation he sees as a symptom of the post-Renaissance loss of both social cohesion and continuous tradition (they often go in tandem). Its modern variant, common sense, is a poor substitute for its earlier, stronger meaning—a sense or meaning commonly held or determined:

> The main thing for our purposes is that sensus communis here [in Vico] obviously does not mean only that general faculty in all men, but the sense that founds community . . . the sensus communis is the sense of the right and the general good that is to be found in all men, moreover, a sense that is acquired through living in the community and is determined by its structures and aims.[7]

It is clear that for Gadamer the gap in the philological line of *sensus communis* marks a similar gap in the experience of what the term denotes: "The concept of sensus communis was taken over, but in the removal of all political content it lost its real critical significance."[8] The collateral loss of the humanist tradition itself has been therefore inevitable according to this scheme, which allows Gadamer to contrast Giambattista Vico's time, which afforded him a place within that tradition from which he "had only to reassert anew its ageless claim," to that of us poorer moderns, who "must feel our way back into this tradition."[9] Much of Gadamer's own attack on the hypertrophy of scientific method has its own legitimation in the desire to restore this term to active philosophical use; but its chief use for him is in measuring the remoteness of our own age from its proper sources of legitimacy, to which we can at most "feel our way back."

It is probably true that the bourgeois nation-state relies less on preindustrial tradition and lineage than just about any previous form of social governance: its sheer novelty was perhaps too conspicuous to allow it to rely on these things. Yet, as can be seen in its authors, the bourgeois age does hark back to precapitalist and predemocratic forms of legitimacy; at the same time, the age has evolved its own positive and specific, and sometimes contradictory, modes of legitimation. This was necessary to do, for the quasi-patriarchal forms of both theological tradition and genealogical lineage could not subsume bourgeois democracy, or, perhaps more crucially, the capitalist political economy. For capitalism to "take off," it became key that the older prohibitions—against usury, free trade, the expropriation of church-held land, and so forth—be overturned. Whether the break was clean (as in France) or gradual and still incomplete (as in the United Kingdom), the dismantling of the old order by the new has proceeded apace.[10] According to Jürgen Habermas in *Legitimation Crisis*, this dismantling has produced both a profound split between the political system and the capacity to legitimate it for social and moral acceptance, as well as a search for new legitimative strategies.

For Habermas, the possibility of legitimation rests neither on mere brute force nor on some contractual arrangement among parties. Both models propose either too much or too little voluntarism. His model relies heavily on what he construes as the nature of discursive language itself, and the fiduciary metaphor of claim and redemption:

> [We] cannot explain the validity claim of norms without recourse to rationally motivated agreement or at least to the conviction that consensus of a recommended norm could be brought about *with reasons.* . . . The appropriate model is the communicating community [*Kommunikationsgemeinschaft*] of those affected, who as participants in a practical discourse test the validity claims of norms and, to the extent that they accept them with reasons, arrive at the conviction that in the given circumstances the proposed norms are "right."[11]

Habermas's model, then, implies a polis almost in the classic sense (it is a gemeinschaft, not a gesellschaft), and the polis is one that comes, through discussion and quasi-parliamentary disputation, to the consensus that certain norms or practices proposed for the polis are in fact valid as claimed, are "discursively redeemable." It is not a matter of contracting somehow with individuals in a multiplicity of transactions, or of simply bludgeoning them into submission. Rather, the community, to continue the fiduciary metaphor, extends a tactit line of credit to those in power.

This model is related to the precondition of discourse itself, since the process of testing the validity of these norms is, for Habermas, only an extreme form of ordinary linguistic practice: "In taking up a practical discourse, we unavoidably suppose an ideal speech situation that, on the strength of its formal properties, allows consensus only through *generalizable* interests."[12] The center of gravity for Habermas's argument concerning legitimacy is the argument itself. Both Gadamer and Nietzsche, in different ways, attempt to describe what is closer to a society in which argument does not even begin. To Gadamer, all of society must assume certain basic concordances (a fellow-feeling or intuitive communion of some sort) before it can divide on other issues; to Nietzsche, the ruling elites establish the parameters of discourse so powerfully that the rest will generally take the elite's presumptions as its own. Habermas would probably disagree with neither proposition, but takes as his primary interest the subjection of claims to rational argumentation by a group.

The shift in emphasis in Habermas has much to do with the phenomenon he is describing. The world of bourgeois democracy is increasingly one where "normative-validity claims" are brought up for argument and adjudged. Indeed, capitalism itself, if it was to provide itself with a congenial political atmosphere, had to produce a situation in which values as such have no assumptive moral priority. Habermas makes the best of the situation by calling attention to the *"generalizable* interests" that allow consensus as part of the "fundamental norms of rational speech." But the gap between generalizable interests, whether or not built into an "ideal speech situation," and anything like moral or ethical legitimacy is a large and perhaps unbridgeable one.

What remains is the parliamentary model, wherein any and all values are constantly open to assessment and disputation, and Habermas exploits the advantages of this model to the fullest. It is surely true that the domains where bourgeois society has been forced to draw clear moral imperatives constitute major concessions: the legal status of the person and the concomitant opposition to serfdom; freedom of speech; commitment to parliamentary forms of government and extension of the electoral franchise. In a sense, these forms can be seen as the duty the new regime has had to pay for a society that is, to a larger extent than any previous society, value-free. The increasing emphasis on free agency and the establishment of deliberate forums where anything could be discussed and where no viewpoint held presumptive authority were in part ways of governing a society that had, on its face, abandoned previous systems of social restraint, both secular and religious, and that had no coherent mode of positing a source for its validity that would effectively supplant the sources it was discrediting.

The earlier feudal structure had the ratification of the Christian religion, the seniority of extensive lineage, and the patriarchal ideology of noblesse oblige. For capitalism, by contrast, the claim to lineage was not available. The ideology of noblesse oblige, having been killed off to a large degree by the nobility itself, would not be given a second trial by the bourgeoisie, notwithstanding the occasional corporate paternalist or philanthropist. The ideology of capitalism, despite all sorts of help from Protestantism, was in the final effect an aggressively secularizing force, unable to appeal to God for kingly anointment (though often it certainly tried).

These circumstances meant that the new order was singularly incapable of gaining proper legitimacy from the sources of authority that were available to the *ancien régime*. But circumstances also pushed it to form parliaments and to democratize its political arrangements, because in the absence of a validating consensus it gradually became necessary to evolve a stage on which all forms of legitimation would have the formal, if not practical, ability to be presented, debated, and acted upon: this to be accomplished in the name of the abstractly negative ideal of political liberty.

Strangely enough, this democratization has occurred while the many social and economic events have been to varying degrees withdrawn from moral judgment and public understanding, coming to seem like forces of nature:

> While in traditional societies antagonisms between social classes were mediated through ideological forms of consciousness and thus had *the fateful objectivity of delusion* . . . in liberal capitalism, class antagonism is shifted from the intersubjectivity of the life-world into the substratum of this world. . . . Economic crises thus . . . acquire the objectivity of inexplicable contingent, natural events.[13] (Emphasis Habermas's)

Of course, there is a kind of apologia for capitalism that explicitly emphasizes its productivity, whose teleology is displayed by the explosion of goods, services, and people that capitalism has brought about. Even this appeal tries to downplay the traumatic novelty of the system by stressing its status as an evolutionary stage in a long-standing desire to overcome scarcity. Further, there has also often been, especially in Europe, a nervous backward glance to precapitalist and aristocratic forms of justification for the new order: a glance whose implications *L'Education sentimentale* and *Lord Jim*, for example, are concerned to explore. The point is that since the inauguration of a political order has violence in its very nature, and since the synoptic view that clarifies what is of fullest value in any epoch is not available to a nascent political order (Hegel's owl of Minerva), the process of legitimation is usually a conservative one. This is as true of bourgeois civil society as of previous ones; and in some respects, the establishment of bourgeois society by means of the "self-regulating market" was singularly violent in its social effects. In *The Great Transformation*, Karl Polanyi emphasizes the artificiality of the so-called free market, its imposed character, and points out that attempts to regulate it came about quite spontaneously from diverse political quarters, as if by a social reflex of self-preservation.[14]

But there remains the competing and more open-ended claim that Habermas isolates, grounded not in appeal to a genealogical line or to divine ordinance but rather in the very suspension of any final appeal other than one procedurally springing from the civic participants themselves. Parliamentarism, free speech and assembly, and the rest of the so-called political liberties have this for a rationale: their necessity in the process Habermas describes whereby all claims can be openly, even endlessly debated. The process itself is its justification, which is the ingenuity of bourgeois democracy.

However, when the state under bourgeois rule has felt the need to legitimate itself by appeal to positive values, it has looked to older patriarchal and feudal modes.[15] Sennett is, once again, helpful in this respect. While acknowledging that public authority has historically assumed one or another vaguely patriarchal model, he still distinguishes both patriarchy, where the male family head is the central figure of the government, and patrimonialism, where property passes solely through male relatives, from paternalism, which essentially appropriates the image of paternity for a power relation that has few of the real elements of a family.[16] Sennett notes the way John Locke applauded the gradual death of primogeniture and so of patrimonialism as "the way to curb the power of kings," since the king could not then "base his power on the rights of family inheritance."[17] Indeed, kingship seems an extension to sovereign rule of the principle of legitimate inheritance on the ordinary level. Sennett is sensitive to the failure of Locke's hope that with primogeniture would go patriarchy: "What he and other liberal idealists did not anticipate is that what could be materially destroyed could be imaginatively rebuilt: metaphor linking fathers and bosses, fathers and leaders. Paternalism attempted to accomplish by a new means what patrimonialism had accomplished: a legitimation of power outside the family by appeal to the roles within the family."[18]

In Joseph Conrad's fiction, for instance, Kurtz's priestly aspirations, Charles Gould's kingly aura, and Lord Jim's pretensions to a kind of barony all imply the attempt to inscribe authority within a paternalistic line. In "Heart of Darkness," *Nostromo*, and *Lord Jim*—where these characters emerge respectively—noblesse oblige is powerfully reintroduced, but always as metaphor.

It is clear that this was not a merely personal quirk on the part of Conrad's characters, but a need of the nineteenth century as a whole to revivify fatherhood as a metaphor for the new, more impersonal structures of the authority of the time. But why? Sennett does admit the form of legitimation Weber calls the "legal-rational" as possible, too.[19] But he nonetheless argues that for the nineteenth century, the source of authority to regulate many if not most of life's transactions—the marketplace—was completely anonymous and impersonal: "The market idea, as Adam Smith proudly announced, banishes the authority of persons; it is a system of exchange which is legitimate only as a system." He even notes that Smith's "invisible hand," the most famous appendage in economic history, is a way of personifying what is really the impersonal force of a purely mechanistic market.[20] Yet, this personalistic image itself indicates that a system whose main pragmatic appeal would seem to rest upon an infinite future potentiality has still recurred often to the past and to tradition for moral justification.

That novels should concern themselves with such a matter as the search for legitimative origins is no surprise. The form of the novel has been, as no other, characteristic of the bourgeois epoch and its readership, within and against whose special strictures the writers under discussion were compelled to work.

3

---◆---

The Case of the Novel: The Fatherless Genre

If there is one continuous strand running through the various attempts to define the novel form, it is the reliance upon other genres against which to define it. Georg Lukács does this in *The Theory of the Novel*, taking the epic form as a parental genre for the novel; Walter Benjamin, in "The Storyteller," works a similar process, comparing the novel to the folktale tradition; Marthe Robert, in *Origins of the Novel*, entitles her first chapter "An Undefined Genre" (she then proceeds to try to define it); and so forth. Part of this tendency may be accounted for by our need to define any relatively recent thing by its predecessors: the "novel," as its English name attests, is fairly new by the standards of literary tradition. Some of this tendency, however, is also the desire to grant the embarrassing and untidy newcomer a pedigree. John Fletcher sums up the state of affairs well in *Novel and Reader* when he calls the novel a "parvenue genre" and "genre of parvenus."[1]

Critics seem constantly to worry that the novel, so devilishly similar to so many other literary forms, is not only different from but defiantly contradictory of those forms. Robert, in fact, is fascinated by precisely this defiance the novel form has historically displayed, to the point of arguing that the novel form partakes uniquely of the Oedipus myth for its structuring principle. Of particular interest to her is the French colloquial expression *faire un roman*, which has "two distinct meanings: either 'to capture the heart of a person of higher social standing, as in a popular love story,' or 'to report events otherwise than they occurred.'"[2] In focusing on this colloquialism, she is preparing her argument for an oedipal interpretation of the novel form; but more crucial for our purposes is the linking of fiction, and specifically novelistic fiction, to illegitimate or arriviste social standing.

In her chapter entitled "Telling Stories," Robert adapts Freud's notion of the "family romance" to the novel; in doing so, she distinguishes the "foundling" story, where the child believes its legal parents are not its true ones, from that of the "bastard," where, in truer oedipal fashion, the child believes only that its legal father is not its true sire.[3] The clean separation she makes between these two myths as modes of interpretation of novels may even be too clean and arbitrary altogether. Still, the recurrence of both motifs throughout the novel form and the suggestion of a general obsession with illegitimacy are convincing.

It is important for Robert's argument that the foundlings and bastards that litter prose narrative from the late eighteenth century on be seen as the sign of willed illegitimacy, since she is taking the Oedipus myth and its family romance as a model. Yet, what is chosen illegitimacy with regard to one's immediate family—even granting her model some degree of explanatory power—may be the desire for legitimacy with regard to one's society or time as a whole. In other words, if Heathcliff in *Wuthering Heights* begins as a foundling and ends as an admittedly unconventional member of landed gentry, this progressus may indicate that, for the plebians, having no definable origins is better than having definitely lower origins. To imagine oneself illegitimate is perhaps to feel that one's official social-standing is not legitimate enough with one's legal parents in tow. Therefore, what Robert sees as a defiant illegitimacy is also the expression (on the part of a parvenu class) of the desire for greater social legitimacy. The term *faire un roman* works not only to describe the family romance and the transgression of social place; it also describes the yearning for permanent pride of place, but on a higher social plane, and the desire to be able to give a different account of one's origins to the world.

Tony Tanner remarks this yearning for stable and valid identity among readers and writers of nineteenth-century novels in saying that "the bourgeois novel inevitably concerns itself more with problems of tenure and maintenance. The ideal aim of the bourgeois family, as of bourgeois society, was simply to maintain the structure it has established, to rescue it from the contingency of its origins and invest it with permanence."[4] He also remarks, elsewhere, that "bourgeois society, more than any other, sought to establish its own stability within history."[5] But for all his stress on the importance of tenure and maintenance, Tanner ends up saying that in a sense "the novel has never really been interested in genealogical continuity" and that "its real, if secret, interest has been aroused by the weak points in the family, the possible fissures, the breaches, the breakdowns."[6]

Coming from very different "optics," Robert and Tanner approach similar insights about the novel form, and specifically about the oddly subversive tendency in the novel, at least vis-à-vis the family. Yet both also are obliged to admit the conservative side of the novel form and do not seem to know what to do with that fact. Robert scarcely hints at this aspect of the novel, noting that the likely outcome of the oedipal story is supposed to be assuming the father's place; Tanner is more straightforward in accounting for this conservative side. Since both critics restrict their ambit largely to the bourgeois family itself, it is difficult for them to deal with the "fissures," the "subversion" that both see as crucial to the novel's habitual thematics. Tanner, for instance, quotes Max Horkheimer on the nineteenth-century family: "In the bourgeois golden age there was a fruitful interaction between family and society, because the authority of the father was based on his role in society, while society was renewed by the education for authority which went on in the patriarchal family."[7] But if this symbiosis is so perfect, whence come those fissures, those breaches that are the "secret" subject of fiction?

Drawing on theories of transgression given their greatest currency by the French writer Georges Bataille, Tanner points to "how marriage ceased by the nineteenth century to be basically a secular contract and was . . . 'sanctified' into 'holy matrimony,'" a process that "increases the possibilities for effective blasphemy or desecration."[8] The point is as tempting as the forbidden fruit of which it speaks, because it is so neatly paradoxical. Yet even if partly true, it is close to an argument to human depravity, and the imp of the perverse can carry us only so far. More solid leads are provided when Tanner alludes to the tension between the family's role as a part of the larger society and its more intimate role as what Christopher Lasch, and Tanner in citing him, call a "haven in a heartless world."[9] But this insight must be strengthened and made more fully historical by sketching in with more clarity this shadow boxer that puts increasing strain on the bourgeois family: the larger society.

One way to sketch in these figures is to return to the question of the parvenus of this parvenue genre. To legitimate their origins, the men on the make had also to deny them to some extent. Tanner insightfully commences his treatment of the novel with a consideration of the famous shift in the nineteenth century that was labeled by Sir Henry Sumner Maine as being "from Status to Contract," that is, from the assignment of social roles based upon lineage and genealogy to the appropriation of roles on the basis of agreements freely entered into. Since the emergent middle class was on the cusp of this shift in the basis for authority, it became possible for those in the age of the "career open to talent" to advance beyond their fathers' status. This possibility bore two difficulties: (1) the rejection of one's origins was cause for guilt, the genuine identity rebelling against the assumed one; (2) if successful, one knew that one was a sort of fake, and also that one's own arrival in the favored circle suggested the status itself to be not as pure as it seemed on the outside. Robert shrewdly notes the relation between the attraction to novel writing and the desire to overreach one's station: she even cites Honoré de Balzac's admission that an aristocratic marriage was more important to him than the success of *Comédie humaine*.[10] Yet this curious status of the bourgeois attempting to insinuate himself into the upper reaches without abandoning the past (or else feeling guilty if he does so) accounts for at least as much of the obsession with illegitimacy as what Robert attributes to the family romances of foundlings and bastards.

Walter Reed takes up this point most forcefully, applying it not only to subject and theme, but even to novel form. He states that "the novel is the literary genre which gives the greatest weight to those human fictions . . . which lie beyond the boundaries of the prevailing literary canon."[11] Claiming the novel to be contestatory in its essence, Reed directs much attention to the fact that it is, above all, written and read in private, though publicly printed and circulated: "This peculiar technology of communication on which the novel was originally based, itself continually reaching out to new masses and in toward new privacies," sets the stage for other, more overt aspects of "the novel's ongoing critique of literary tradition."[12] He uses this feature of novels especially to chide semioticians such as Roland Barthes and Tzvetan Todorov for conflating novel and oral folk forms, because they ignore "the inherited notions of literary form against which the novel has struggled" and hence fail to "grasp the novel's dialectical nature."[13] Like Tanner and Robert, Reed highlights the Peck's-bad-boy role of the novel as a kind of spoilsport to previous aristocratic genres. Nevertheless, he also notices the novel's frequent need to authorize its own existence, appealing in the process to unstable models: "A novel reads out the conflicting codes [within its thematic and semantic structures] according to protocols of its own fabulation."[14]

Reed understands the ambiguity of the novel's status vis-à-vis past genres. But he may overstress the free play of the novel, its "potential freedom from the authority of tradition," at the expense of its very real enmeshment in the power shift of its own day.[15] Furthermore, although the central paradox in the novel's relation to its audience as language consumed in mass isolation is mentioned by Reed, he seems to draw back from the implications of that strange remoteness. He expresses doubt about Ian Watt's reliance on the reader as the ground for his theory in *The Rise of the Novel*: "Watt provides an explanation by referring to the author's 'obligation' to 'satisfy' the reader's need. Too much depends on these elusive commitments and desires."[16] One hesitates to deem such obligations more than elusive. But an elusive obligation can be as deeply felt for all that—perhaps more so by virtue of its vagueness, of the inability to fulfill it. There is another side to the "freedom from the authority of tradition" celebrated by Reed as a part of the novel form. For this freedom also implies the anxiety of solitude; a novelist freed for the kind of uncertainty that afflicted writer as well as reader in the nineteenth century would be forgiven for feeling not so much emancipated as somehow disinherited, orphaned.[17]

As mentioned previously, then, the foundling comes to loom large in the novel, and for good reason. Clearly, in a time when authority is less sure, along with the social cohesion that provided its ground in simpler times, the foundling becomes an object of particular solicitude. *Tom Jones*, of course, is "about" orphanhood, but later novels such as *Wuthering Heights* and *Great Expectations* feature orphaned figures who achieve prominence through a variety of fair and foul means. The condition of Defoe's central figures, such as Moll Flanders or, more radically, Robinson Crusoe, approaches that of the fatherless child. And the great "metanovel" of the eighteenth century, Laurence Sterne's *Tristram Shandy*, can be read with little distortion as an amazingly loquacious parody of the appeal to genealogical line or paternal origin, and thus of the novelistic project of constructing a legible line to give one's story causal paternity. In what way is this concern for paternity or for the absence of paternity of interest?

Like the social conditions it describes, the novel found its nurture, paradoxically, in a situation for which the metaphor of orphanhood is appropriate. The readership of the novel was a class paying for its arrival to wealth and station by an anomic loss of social identity and by an increasing isolation and distrust of others. Watt, who chronicles as well as any the features of the nascent English reading public, makes a remark that bears upon this development: "It is . . . paradoxical that the process of urbanisation should, in the suburb, have led to a way of life that was more secluded and less social than ever before, and, at the same time, helped to bring about a literary form which was less concerned with the public and more with the private side of life than any previous one."[18]

Delete the words "in the suburb," and Watt's remark on Richardson's works can apply to the universal condition of the novel's audience from the turn of the nineteenth century onward. On the evidence not only of its works—such as *Robinson Crusoe*, to which Watt devotes considerable attention—but also of its other public documents, the turn of the nineteenth century was a period in which social atomization and the loss of identity accelerated: most critically in and around Paris and London, but also, in part, for industrializing society in general. (The French and British novel-reading public, to say nothing of the novelists themselves, tended to be urban.) One who has done some crucial spadework in the social psychology of these new cities is Richard Sennett, who has analyzed the altered psychology of the public audience in Paris and London as an effect of this larger alteration of city behavior. Sennett's discussion of nineteenth-century cities explores ground similar to Benjamin's unfinished project on Paris, to which it is heavily in debt; and it bases much of its insight on its definition of the "urban situation" as "one in which strangers are likely to meet routinely" and on its concern "with the social psychology of encounters between strangers," because, in the nineteenth century, "this social psychology came to apply to a brutal demographic issue."[19]

That issue was the rapid influx of strangers into the urban areas, the disruption of older neighborhoods. The increased social mobility of the nineteenth century, along with the alarming increase in sheer population density, combined to make the public sphere in the city a more fearful place. Whereas earlier periods offered an established repertoire of roles to act out in the public sphere (Sennett points out that in the eighteenth century occupation, class, rank, and even neighborhood could usually be read from an individual's clothing), the more fluid and foreboding cityscape of the nineteenth century encouraged a certain reticence in public as well as a certain voyeurism, because one's clothes, speech, and behavior were increasingly read more as signs of the psyche rather than of class: "The material conditions of life in the city weakened any trust people could place in the 'natural,' routine labeling of others by origin, family background, or occupation. The effort to color one's relations with others, the attempt to give these social exchanges a form, was an effort to create a meaningful sense of audience."[20]

Sennett links the increasing opacity of behavior and uncertainty of life in the urban public realm to the audience for theater and music that evolved in the nineteenth century, especially in its cult of the artistic personality as one who could somehow "express himself" in public. These linkages go far toward explaining Watt's paradox that the nineteenth-century urbanization produced more insularity and alienation rather than less. Indeed, *L'Education sentimentale* and *The Secret Agent* take as their own the cityscape shadowed forth by Sennett and Benjamin: the *theatrum mundi*, where the actors seem to have forgotten their lines, where characters from other plays begin wandering in, and where the proscenium arch separating the public and private realms becomes ever harder to locate.

This approach, however illuminating, accounts more for the salient aspects of the subject matter of certain novels than for developments within and readership of the form itself. Sennett concentrates his attention more on explicitly spectacular art forms, such as the opera, the theater, and concert halls, and less on the novel or other written literature. We get a glimpse of the problematic peculiar to the novel by returning to Watt. In an antithesis very similar to Lukács's between epic and novel in his study *The Theory of the Novel*, Watt stresses the novel form's bondage to the bourgeois individualism of what for many is its inaugural moment, in *Robinson Crusoe*:

> For, just as there is a basic congruity between the non-realist nature of the literary forms of the Greeks, their intensely social, or civic, moral outlook, and their philosophical preference for the universal, so the modern novel is closely allied on the one hand to the realist epistemology of the modern period, and on the other to the individualism of its social structure.[21]

The nominalist tendencies of empiricism, for Watt, parallel both the privatization of literary space itself and the social atomization that literature increasingly takes for its subject; parallel as well the urge to verisimilitude that informs the tendency of the novel.

It is in the novel that the need for verisimilitude becomes most urgent, and it is in the novel that narration—the simulation of contiguous events occurring in a causal series—becomes a high art. Obviously, narratives existed before the novel. But these earlier forms repeated stories already familiar and, in many instances, generally believed to be true; also, the focus had not yet narrowed to one or two characters and their lives. As a result, and more significantly, the novel relies for its impact on the credibility of the events it relates and on their inner coherence rather than on the allegorical grid of meaning to which it alludes. The clearest examples of this latter tendency occur in the epic poems such as *The Faerie Queene*, *Paradise Lost*, or those of Dante, which tended to rely on a reading-in (or allegoresis) of the paradigmatic meaning levels that form their substance. The events narrated in these works, even if they never happened, are ways of disposing semantic givens of the culture and specifically religious concepts that are somehow being illuminated or demonstrated in the narrative. Like medieval painting, these narratives set up iconographies through which can be read the "real" story, in itself inaccessible without the embellishments of those narratives. A well-defined cultural nexus and a relatively stable, small and literate audience initiated into the iconographic mysteries produced a tighter relation between the production of allegory and its comsumption, or allegoresis. Once the paradigms were known, the chief pleasure would consist in the tapestry that could be woven from them. Indeed, Michel Foucault has argued that the world in these earlier times, particularly during the Middle Ages, was assumed by and large to be a text waiting for its proper allegoresis.[22] The affective force of a work of literature, its capacity to teach a lesson and its cachet within a universe of discourse—qualities that the now rather faded term *edification* once summed up fairly aptly—all entailed the relation of the work to a grid or grids of allegorical meaning which could be read through it, a "vertical" relation to a transcendental signified, shared by a community of readers.

The novel continues to have allegorical components, of course, just as the earlier counterparts of the novel proposed to narrate a sequence of events. But with the novel, the axis swings radically toward metonymy: the ever-increasing requirement that the narrated events be somehow their own interpretation, with internally justifiable causality. A recognized component of literary art, at least since Aristotle's *Poetics*, gradually assumed overweening importance. Whereas the rather outlandish events of *Sir Gawain and the Green Knight* troubled no reader of that tale—nor (because we are aware of the condition for its reception in that day) do they trouble us—nevertheless, were similarly inexplicable things to occur in a nineteenth-century novel, they would generally be viewed differently. The novel has made such a virtue of the inner necessity of its narrative to gain its effects: on a "horizontal" relation among elements fashioned expressly for the work, rather that the "vertical" relation to a preestablished allegorical pattern that the work somehow follows.[23] This, by the way, is true even of most of the works written nowadays to which is affixed the term *novel*.

The metonymic structure of the novel form resulted from the same processes that altered other fields of social practice. The novel of the eighteenth and nineteenth centuries was an extremely popular form, at least by comparison with earlier modes. Watt admits that, while "not, strictly speaking, a popular literary form," the eighteenth-century novel was "closer to the economic capacity of the middle-class additions to the reading public than were many of the established and respectable forms of literature and scholarship."[24]

Because the novels were generally addressed to a wider readership, because the shared assumptions of a potential audience were beginning to unravel, and perhaps even because events in society had become improbable enough that no supernatural intervention was needed to evoke a certain wonder—for all these reasons, the metonymic bias of the modern narrative found nurture and encouragement.

Milton's goal in constructing a narrative of lost paradise was to justify God's ways to man, but the novel's task is to justify men's ways to themselves and to each other. If everyone believes in the God one proposes to justify (and even the nature of Milton's project implies that a few did not), that task is by far the easier. More crucially, the common fund of value that accompanies this belief cluster is understood: it does not have to legitimate itself from the very start. In a sense, Robinson Crusoe's situation mimes that of the novelist in the eighteenth century, just as Don Quixote's story in some way was the tale of the medieval romance. Novelists, like Robinson Crusoe, are very much their own persons, forced to construct in relative isolation, far from the insular warmth of a cloister or a court, a world sufficient unto itself, one that is sustainable through time, one that "works," one that is in some way familiar to them or reminiscent of the larger world from which they have (temporarily) exiled themselves. They also have the task, not one of Crusoe's but surely of his creator's, of making this world credible to another observer in three aspects: as internally consistent (through appeal to logic), as representing something like reality (through its correspondence to an experienced or imaginable world of the reader's), and as affectively significant for the reader (through an implicit synecdochic link between the characters or events of the text and the reader's desires or fears for self or community).

It would be mistaken to leave the impression that the novel somehow jettisoned all iconographic elements or culturally shared thematic assumptions from its practice. Quite the contrary: the novel's "Robinson Crusoe" project for its potential readers, particularly insofar as it purports to be affectively significant, necessitates the retention of allegorical strands. And indeed, part of the attempt in these pages is to show how crucial these culturally shared thematic assumptions are to novelists in question. However, it is still the case that, addressing a less cohesive audience in an increasingly secular age, the novelist must especially labor to suggest the desired allegoresis (or, decoding) of those assumptions by constructing its ground of allegory from the immediate materials of one's narrative. That ground cannot nearly as readily be assumed. "Borrowing on margin," as it were, from a vaster fund of narrative in which all one's readers believe themselves to be participating to gain resonance for one's specific narrative is less and less profitable. The search for realistic social milieu; a believable character one can "identify with" or from whose life's destiny one can draw counsel; the insistence that to play fair novelistic effects should have verifiable causes, whether material or psychological—all spring in some measure from this loss of common ground.

Obviously, the need for allegorical structure often conflicts with that for narrative logic, and in fact *Lord Jim* is treated below largely as the result of this conflict. This could mean that in *Lord Jim* the need for verisimilitude has disconfirmed a tenet of the British idea whose resonance Conrad attempts to use in the narrative, or simply that there has arisen an inner contradiction in the imaginary world that the British idea creates for itself. In either case, the verisimilar imperative in the novel creates new challenges for the allegorical structure of a text: a structure that, though functioning primarily as a part of the work's effect, still must, despite itself, carry a heuristic baggage of Wisdom in tow. Whether or not designed for the purpose, all narratives are implicitly counsel or have counsel as an inescapable aspect of their impact on a reader.

Small wonder it is, then, that the great novelists produced by this process soon became painfully self-conscious and given, for instance, to much rewriting. The cult of novelistic craftsmanship ushered in by Flaubert presents us with the heroic, dutiful figure of the artist working sentence by meticulous sentence to build his edifice, and consulting vast numbers of books to solidify his work, whether on ancient Carthage or on the commonly remembered events of his own day. In the same way, it is small wonder that novelists, increasingly worried that they be read correctly, take to writing prefaces that often are meant to provide powerful clues to the "right" allegoresis. Henry James is perhaps the most notorious, but his admirer Joseph Conrad has a number of famous prefaces to his credit, the most famous among them that to "The Nigger of the *Narcissus*." Is it Conradian irony that the opening lines of what is clearly an exercise in self-justification present as aesthetic that seems to deny the value of such an exercise? "A work that aspires, however humbly, to the condition of art should carry its justification in every line. And art itself may be defined as a single-minded attempt to render the highest kind of justice to the visible universe, by bringing to light the truth, manifold and one, underlying its every aspect."[25]

Thus, Conrad's preface very nicely conveys the fresh sense of illegitimacy that compels the novelist to seek justification in the first place, whether in the work's every line or in its preface. A recurrent word in the preface is *appeal*, but the nature of the appeal is interesting: "Fiction—if it at all aspires to be art—appeals to temperament. . . . Such an appeal, to be effective, must be an impression conveyed through the senses; and, in fact, it cannot be made any other way, because temperament, whether individual or collective, is not amenable to persuasion."[26] Conrad here means logical persuasion, because appeal implies the desire to persuade; but the persuasion works not by discursive argument or by a common symbology one purports to illuminate, according to Conrad, but by the resonance somehow latent in the things themselves. This yields Conrad's famous statement of purpose, and the implicit pedagogy that goes along with it: "My task . . . is, before all, to make you *see*. . . . If I succeed, you shall find there [in the novel], according to your deserts, encouragement, consolation, fear, charm, all you demand—and, perhaps, also that glimpse of truth for which you have forgotten to ask."[27]

It is, then, the constant labor of the novelist, by presenting a vivid scene and making the reader "see," that both textual effect and wise counsel are produced. The intended result is consensual: "fellowship," "unavoidable solidarity," and other terms that dot Conrad's preface make clear the synecdochic ambition here and with it the desire that readership become audience. Yet, it proceeds from what is generally perceived, perhaps rightly, as the least stable of grounds: the appeal to "temperament." Conrad seems to acknowledge the chanciness of such an appeal. He ends his attempt at justification with a lengthy analogy of the writer to a workman in a field whose "failure," if we are "in a brotherly frame of mind, we may bring ourselves to forgive. . . . We understand his object, and, after all, the fellow has tried, and perhaps he had not the strength—and perhaps he had not the knowledge. We forgive, go on our way—and forget."[28] There is also the chance of success for Conrad's workman, available to a very few; but the analogy may be more than disarming modesty. It may indicate a sense of how herculean the novelist's labor has become and how hard it is to achieve a sense of "unavoidable solidarity" solely by appeal to temperament, whether collective or individual.[29]

The self-reflexive overtones of Flaubert's text suggest the plight of one who must fall despite himself into the clichés of the dominant ideology to "connect" with the readership, whereas those of Conrad's text suggest the dilemma of one who, despite his best efforts to translate his material into fully communicable form, fails even so to "connect" to the extent he would want.

Everyone is born illegitimate, and certainly that goes for every text as well. The task of legitimating one's discourse is unceasing: truly it can be said that a good audience is hard to find, and harder still to found. These writers are of interest because of the specific pressures, the particular strictures applied to narratives of the recent past, and the unique ideological web in which each is implicated. The authors were chosen for two additional reasons that bear on the larger interests of this project: first, because they are acutely aware of their delicate positions in the culture of their time, and, second, because—above all in their works that are discussed here—they help make connections between their own micropolitical positions as authors with readers and the macropolitical social elements they portray in their narratives. Each author's will to phatic communion with his audience redoubles and responds to larger patterns of community and struggle, because the legitimation of his own position as author is intertwined with other struggles of a similar sort in his time and place. Certainly some writers are more thorough than others in exposing this intertwining, and the authors considered here are possibly among the most thorough of all.

Within any text a curious inversion takes place, where the great forces of historical conflict become strangely miniature: tactical maneuvers in a strategic game plan involving the author and reader in which, during the time of reading, the text itself is the great thing at issue. Yet the game plan always assumes that what the author folds into the enclosed pages of a book can be unfolded, can be "read" properly, by the reader. For reasons already indicated, it becomes increasingly difficult to assume (it was always impossible to know) the difference between what was meant to be folded in and what just happened to end up in the book more or less on its own. The best that can be done is to unfold as many of those resonances as possible and to arrive thereby at a tentative allegoresis, not of the book as an isolated totality, but rather of the text as a response to larger processes of cultural legitimation to which it is at once inevitably attracted and, for all that, still irreducibly eccentric.

The indifference as to its use, the lack of attachment to any individual because it is unrelated to any of them, the objectivity inherent in money as a mere means which excludes any emotional relationship—all this produces an ominous analogy between money and prostitution.—Georg Simmel, *The Philosophy of Money*

The greatest discrepancy between idea and reality is time: the process of time as duration. The most profound and most humiliating impotence of subjectivity consists not so much in its hopeless struggle against the lack of the idea in social forms and their human representatives, as in the fact that it cannot resist the sluggish, yet constant progress of time; that it must slip down, slowly yet inexorably, from the peaks it has laboriously scaled; that time—that ungraspable, invisible moving substance—gradually robs subjectivity of all its possessions and imperceptibly forces alien contents into it. —Georg Lukács, *The Theory of the Novel*

4

The Muse and the Marketplace in Early Flaubert

There exists, no doubt, a line between Flaubert's youthful and mature writings, but it is not a straight one. The justification, therefore, for resorting to Flaubert's *écrits de jeunesse* at the outset is partially pragmatic (since Flaubert's letters, so numerous on *Madame Bovary*, are much scantier on *L'Education sentimentale*), and also partially philosophical (since many of the concerns that motivated the young Flaubert to take up his pen are insistent in his later work as well, and not only because *L'Education* itself has been a continuing project). After this detour, the argument will treat the text proper of the second *L'Education*.

Best suited to our purposes, both for simplicity's sake and for its clues to the thematic texture of *L'Education*, is a little-known piece from Flaubert's early writings entitled "Les Arts et le commerce." Written in 1839, the article is of interest largely because the problematic of this otherwise unexceptional essay resonates so powerfully in Flaubert's later work.

We see in this piece a young Flaubert confronting the stolid bourgeoisie of his day, but the form in which he does it is itself symptomatic of later concerns. The first sentence reads: "The uselessness of the arts and the usefulness of commerce have become commonplaces [*mots banals*] throughout society."[1] At the outset, Flaubert's disapproval of the valorization of commerce is disapproval of *mots banals*. We know immediately that the fact that the utility of commerce is taken as a commonplace will condemn it in Flaubert's discourse, and so he doubles his distaste for commerce with a disdain for the common coin of language. Because the artist must make use of this common coin of language, this double gesture in Flaubert's opening sentence exfoliates into a larger problematic: the inextricability of art and commerce. What word exists that could escape the banality of the marketplace and its shopworn clichés? The trail of this sentence could well be followed all the way to the *Dictionnaire des idées reçues*.

But for the moment it does not. The interesting thing about the remainder of this early essay is that it ignores the way language itself becomes a commodity. The purple rhetoric of the piece is directed squarely against the idols of the marketplace and opposes to those idols a purity of spirit, unsullied by that marketplace. This passage is typical: "I gladly leave to you opulence, commerce, industry, the ports and factories, the raw materials and the metals, but leave me . . . my reveries, my futility, my empty ideas; your common sense bores me, your matter-of-factness [*votre positif*] horrifies me" (p. 185). This dualism of art / commerce is also the classic one of spirit / matter. Whereas commerce reigns over the brute material of the world, the arts take refuge in the world of the spirit. On the conquering of Greece and Rome, he remarks: "indeed, the conqueror can destroy the ports, burn the fleet, demolish the factories, divert the rivers, stop up the canals and put the people in chains, but the spirit? Where would you find chains that could hold down this Proteus who speaks with sounds, rises up [in resistance] with stone, and expresses himself and thinks with words?" (p. 185). In a formulation reminiscent of Epictetus, both language and the spirit, in turn, are on the side of freedom. The artist is indestructible because he presides over the realm of the spirit and because he uses words—the two here are linked. This Proteus is unconquerable. Yet, the spirit and language, it becomes clear, not only resist conquering by others; they are themselves means of conquering. This dual status will prove an irritant to the progress of the argument.

For the moment, the spirit and language only operate as the guarantor of the singularity and purity of true works of art. For the development of the argument, despite this distance of art from the world of those who "build and destroy, who haggle and who deceive," it is art that wins. Flaubert renders it this way: "The poets are like those statues one finds among the ruins; people forget them, sometimes for a long while, but then one recovers them intact in the middle of a now nameless dust [*une poussière qui n'a plus de nom*]; everything has perished, these only have lasted" (p. 186).

The test of endurance, finally, is the test of posterity, which may retrieve the poets like statues, intact while the earth around them lacks a name. That to survive intact for Flaubert is to retain one's proper name is worth noting, since part of the opposition Flaubert sets up is that between the singularity of the world of art and the anonymity and interchangeability of the goods traded in the marketplace, and by extension the people who trade the goods. (If the market is protean movement, then it is surely a sinister parody of the Proteus of the spirit.)

The poets live after their culture has lost its name because, logically if not temporally, they were always already prior to it. In Flaubert's view, art wins out because commercial relations depend upon ideas, on the stuff of the soul; though different from commerce in some profound way, art also founds that commerce: "With us [modern peoples], the trade relations establish the political relations, but, before all that, there are relations of ideas [*les rapports d'idées*]" (p. 186). In the example of Europe and Asia which follows, Flaubert tries to show that the ideas must first penetrate new markets before the goods can. In fact, the goods are themselves little more than counters of these *rapports d'idées*. It is interesting that Flaubert does not consider the possibility that the ideas can themselves come to be items of trade, that they participate in a system of exchange very like the economic structure they seem to stand apart from. Flaubert alludes to "two centuries of combat between Europe and Asia, between Islam and Christianity" before trade could commence—a trade that recurs in *L'Education*, where the motif of the Orient is strong. This example also becomes critical for the rest of the argument here.

The port at which the East and the West exchanged their goods in the time of the Renaissance was Venice, and Flaubert pairs it with Carthage as another city that gained its prestige primarily through the exchange of goods. Even though he admits that both attained "something colossal and superb" in their heyday, nonetheless he adds: "Is there, in all of modern times, a sadder throne, a gloomier and bloodier glory than this city of Venice with its spies and hangmen, and is the name of Carthage not full of horror and cynicism to us?" (p. 185). Carthage, of course, will provide the setting for a later Flaubert novel, *Salammbô*, and much of the thrust of that novel will be indirectly aimed at the commercially minded society of Flaubert's own day; Venice will play a somewhat similar, though subordinate, role in *L'Education*. But, again, the curious fact is that, in discussing Venice, Flaubert neglects to mention that for which Venice is more famous than for its spies and hangmen: its art. Though Venice can be said to be only one specific example in an argument here, it is still another instance in which the political entanglement of the realm of art in economic exchange is elided in the analysis. Art and commerce are the two facets in the historical memory of Venice at her height; one wonders if Flaubert's idealistic scheme simply did not permit him to acknowledge one facet of Venice in discussing the other.

A spiritualistic conception of language is the companion of this desire to separate art from the toils of getting and spending. It relies on a notion of language that ignores the way in which the language is embedded in social and economic (material) structures. This spiritualization of language allows Flaubert to put his own chains on Proteus: it is free from the constraints of the commonplace, but it is faithful to the call of individual artistic genius and its will. Despite this, the materiality, the timebound nature of the poet's language is acknowledged, insofar as that materiality (as French, German, or English, say) will confirm a language's conquering role over other languages. For Flaubert in this essay, poetic language functions very much as the idealist counterexamples to the mercantilist balance of payments. It is the nation's truest wealth, and its surest means of conquering other nations. Poetic language is the rhetorical negation of both trade and war, and the fact that it performs a parallel conquering role to these only underscores the radically different way in which it conquers. Of France Flaubert writes: "This France, frivolous, foolish and gay, . . . has already conquered Europe by its literature before Napoleon vanquished it with his sword, and what remains of our Emperor's sword? . . . The Emperor and the empire are dead, but our poets live, Corneille lives, Racine lives, Voltaire reigns forever, and in all the courts they speak his tongue, that tongue so pure and clear, as he made it" (p. 185).

Like the crossing of ideas that founds material trade, this puissance of the French language is both better than and other than the more conventional means of gaining dominance through conquest or trade. It is as much the identifying mark of a nation as its goods, and it is not subject to the corruption to which goods are subject. Just as the language is a nation's guarantor of singularity among other nations, so the poets' language is the guarantor of their unique genius among other users of the same language. In both cases, influence and dominance are established by more legitimate means than force or economic pressure. By extension, then, the poets become a synecdoche for the singularity of the nation's linguistic wealth, because in Flaubert's analysis the poets' use of language is not only singular (that is, proper to each poet) but also exemplary (an inalienably national possession). Hence the argument that "Corneille and Racine did more for France than Colbert and Louis XIV" (p. 186).

It is ironic in an essay entitled "Less Arts et le commerce" that Flaubert seems consistently to evade the question of the relation between these two things, even in places where the structure of his own argument would make the question a logical one. The exchange of ideas makes the exchange of goods possible, but the two processes are in no other way linked by Flaubert: the French language conquers more surely than the French empire or high finance or trade, but that language, pure and pellucid, does not partake of these political or economic forces. It conquers despite itself, the way Greece conquered Rome, "with her orators and her artists" (p. 185).

The language that the individual artists use is the mark of their defiant singularity and bears no relation to the *mots banals* of the marketplace; yet a nation's artists become a solid indicator of cultural identity when it confronts those of other nations. The process by which singularity and protean defiance become exemplary of the culture as a whole is not really elaborated in any way. That it might have something to do with the distribution and acceptance of the artists by the culture (which is a commercial process, or is becoming so by Flaubert's time)—this possibility is not raised. Again, in international relations it is somehow the *rapport d'idées* that must precede the exchange of goods, yet that *rapport* is inconceivable without, and may initially be a by-product of, the interaction that trade necessitates between countries.

These blind spots in Flaubert's discourse lead one back to the notion of language on which the rest of the distinctions are grounded. Language cannot escape the grounding intention of spirit, precisely because it is synonymous with it. Nothing could be a starker contrast to the process of economic exchange, which is predicated not on qualitative uniqueness but on quantitative interchangeability and which promotes not the retention by individuals of their powers or property but rather the alienation of their powers and the circulation of commodities. The contrast has its value, but what the young Flaubert's rhetoric seems to lack and what *L'Education* possesses to a greater degree is the suspicion that language, too, can be bought and sold; and further, that the exemplary status Flaubert assigns any artist cannot be clearly separated from that artist's understanding and deployment of the common currency of a nation's clichés. (We know from scholarship that Flaubert employed his *Dictionnaire des idées reçues* to write *Bouvard et Pécuchet* and even parts of *L'Education*; in this connection, the dictionary could almost be seen as a kind of capital formation of clichés—though in this case, of course, to satirical purpose.)

Flaubert's rhetoric tends to isolate the work of art from its place, its nation, or region, while all the same contending that it is the truest and most characteristic product of its place; in the same way, his rhetoric argues a motive role, perhaps *the* motive role, in historical processes for art, while denying art's extrication in historical processes. The statue has survived the passage of time because it is fundamentally other from the dirt that surrounds it; but the statue has remained, throughout the centuries, exactly as it was when it was first made.

As the essay progresses, the elaborate process involved in the exchange of commodities has been relegated to the level of eating and sleeping. Insisting that spirit has always directed the body, in history as in individual life, Flaubert says: "Are not pictures, scenes, laughter and tales what is needed to nourish a child? It is only later, when the flesh speaks in him, that his body feels pain, that he becomes greedy, possessive and carnal, that he dissembles and deceives [*qu'il ruse et qu'il trompe*]" (p. 186).

The first need of the infant, according to this analysis, is for stories, laughter, and pictures—things of the spirit which are the chief sources of nourishment. It is only later in this scheme that the infant desires good food. Quite apart from this order or priority for an infant's needs, the very fact that Flaubert describes the flesh as speaking in the infant suggest that language is, conversely, also a thing of the body. Even if one were to argue that the infant requires the stories as much as the physical nourishment, the corollaries would then be that the language that provides this nourishment partakes of a material economy (as does food) and that these needs can be catered to by commercial interests and even exploited (as that for food can be). Yet Flaubert does not draw these corollaries. To maintain the initial opposition, it is necessary to treat the realms of art and commerce as separate, making the former an agent of the spirit and the latter part of brute nature. The intriguing problem of how language and nourishment may be entangled is never addressed.

History, politics, and commerce are all a part of the body, which *ruse* and *trompe* as the spirit does not. To be inviolable, art cannot partake of matter's mutability or permeability any more than it can of the interchange of commodities or the shifting fortunes of merely practical interest. The mature Flaubert does not assume this kind of inviolability for art, and with reason.

Despite this, of course, the essay is in some profound if partial sense true. Its "truth" here lies less in any specific statement than in its implicit assessment of the grave dangers presented to the nineteenth-century artist by the demands of commerce: dangers whose magnitude, if not nature, was unprecedented before that time. The great fear that animates the essay—the fear that the acquisitive mentality cultivated in nineteenth-century industrial capitalism was trivializing and degrading the arts—must be granted its force. Says Flaubert: "They [his contemporaries] see nothing in art, really, other than an after-dinner pastime, an amusing recreation, a refreshing game, and they consider plays the police's best invention ever to keep the masses off the streets [*pour fixer les masses en lieu sûr*]" (p. 184). A serious artist (which Flaubert was, even at this early stage) could not but regard these uses of art as a perversion or at least a pale and pathetic reduction of the more essential functions of art. To display the contradiction in Flaubert's position is not to deny the force or the validity of the perceptions that underlie it. The force of this perception, in turn, comes from an acute sensitivity to the historical moment, much as his scheme of art seems to reject the processes of history. How is it possible that art could, after all, be traduced in the very way eloquently described and deplored in the essay?

Since art and artistic language have no traffic with commerce, politics, or the body, while on the other hand founding the possibility of each, it is hard to account for the low estate to which these pursuits had fallen in Flaubert's time. Thus it should not come as a surprise that he does not account for it. One must retain the sense that art is not food, or political advantage, or industrial strength to appreciate what attends its misuse by bourgeois society; but the process of that misuse is understood by exploring the problematical relation between art and its larger culture.

L'Education is neither an elaboration of this early essay nor a reply to it; still, there is shadowed forth in its pages a far clearer enactment of the arts' entanglement with the messiness of their time and place than one gets in this early context. The generic difference between a brief essay and a novel of hundreds of pages may alone account for a greater complexity in the treatment. It is probably more than that; but whatever its cause, it remains to show how the art that is inviolable in "Les Arts et le commerce" becomes all too violable, all to vendable, in L'Education. Indeed, the irony will be that the dreams that seem the most intimate, and for that reason the most sacred, are somehow the cheapest of all. But this is not an irony with which to be easy. For just as the commodity, despite its implication in a seemingly impersonal process of social exchange, is invested with the aura of uniqueness by its owner, so dreams and art, in spite (or perhaps because) of their circulation in the common traffic of the culture of one's time and place, remain dreams and art. The infant, after all, will claim his nourishing due, and his dreams' impact will not be the less his own despite their banality or fragility, despite perhaps even their falsehood. That Flaubert may not have wished to acknowledge the illusory character of art—its reliance on the common currency of cliché for its very claims to exemplary uniqueness—is understandable. Nobody is quick to admit the mutability of his or her illusions, products as they are of the human spirit. Yet the Flaubert of L'Education can rest easy in one respect with the Flaubert of this early essay. Both depict a world in which the things of the spirit—language, art and dreams—are indestructible. For in the world of Frédéric Moreau (unlike that of Emma Bovary, for instance), even if nothing is learned in the course of the story, neither are any illusions lost. One could well argue that, for Frédéric, they are transposed from the future to the past, but they retain their original power nonetheless.

In 1839, the young Flaubert can write of Italy: "Doesn't anyone who has the soul of a poet or painter wish to wander through this sacred ground of art, where the stones have immortality, and the very debris still holds the future?" (p. 185). In L'Education, the sacred ground of art shares the mortal clay that surrounds it: the place of art is, for better or for worse, finally a commonplace. But for all that, the capacity and the desire to invest the debris of one's life with an aura—the will to illusion, in short—is inexhaustible. The common stock of cultural inheritance is appropriated by each individual as his or her own, particularized by the force of subjective desire. No doubt, whatever immortality art can hope to attain lies in this very weakness: that people will continue to make illusions for themselves, even when they know them to be illusions, and even after bearing the cost in bitterness and in disabused hope.

5

L'Education sentimentale:
The Political Economy of the Sign

The Myth of Paris

The Flaubertian project in writing *L'Education sentimentale* can be viewed as the unsuccessful attempt to legitimate Paris as a myth—or rather, to inscribe the ways in which Paris would be legitimated, either as the proper forum to realize the dream of love (through Frédéric Moreau's designs and through his subjectivity as well) or as the stage on which a collective, utopian vision could be brought into being (not only through Frédéric's sometime partner Deslauriers but also through the larger sociopolitical backdrop that dominates parts 2 and 3). *L'Education* takes the cultural investment that the readership of the time placed in Paris, whether it concerned the dream of love or of utopia, and reveals by Flaubert's dual method how, by the workings of the codes themselves, these investments do not yield a return. The economic metaphor is advised for, in the absence of any libidinal return, only the calculative investment remains. As a result, Paris becomes by degrees the marketplace: the stage where lives, careers, things, love, and labor are bought and sold.

This tendency in Flaubert's treatment of Paris (and by implication of the French history it stands for) presents us with an irony. This irony contains two parts: (1) The emptiness of the cultural codes does not diminish their power within the narrative; rather, the codes assume an independent status as such and are maintained by a mechanism that will be described later. (2) The exposure of these cultural codes as empty forms by Flaubert means that the writer's own text reveals the need to ironize its own irony. To one who sees a world where language itself has been debased into the service of the marketplace, to communicate in itself may be viewed with a certain aesthetic (if not ethical) suspicion. Against the many "little ironies" of Flaubert's novel, which rely for

51

their ironical character on some satiric point, one can see at the same time the more cryptic irony of self-effacement or *impassibilité*, in a way the direct opposite of satire in that it aims above all at not communicating a point, at refusing to conclude. The constant tension between the satire of the larger canvas, an inheritance from the Balzacian tradition, and Frédéric's subjective vision with its misty view of Paris are symptomatic not only of a contradiction in the representation of Paris but also of a need of the text simultaneously to evoke a perspective of Paris and to forestall any clear and distinct ideas about it.

As shall be observed in detail, Flaubert's Paris is often a harlot. Yet, Paris as a harlot has its history in past texts (Balzac's most famously), and by invoking this Paris, Flaubert has recourse to another cultural given of his age and probably of ours. But what he proceeds to do beyond that is to inscribe explicitly the various modes of representing Paris as so many fictions or semantic products, neither true nor false in themselves. The Paris in one's head, the reflector of individual or collective fears or aspirations, is no more or less a cultural artifact here than the Paris of buildings, bridges, cafes, and cobblestones. Frédéric's moods call forth a different Paris for each occasion, it seems; and this changeling city is capable of accommodating these shifts. Indeed, the various guises and myths of Paris are so numerous and so salable that in addition to being a marketplace for other commodities, the city itself becomes one of the most precious commodities on display.

But the fact that for Flaubert Paris is the city of fictions—not of illusions or dreams *tout court*, but of fictions, that is, objects created according to those dreams—means that Flaubert's own invocation consciously takes its place among those fictions of Paris. His is perhaps the most fully elaborated and detailed rendering of the social and environmental milieu of Paris within that space up to that point, filled with verisimilitude and historical fact, its power relying to a great degree upon its consonance with those facts. Yet, the text shies away from drawing a moral from its story, perhaps because to do so would be to barter in commonplaces with its readership. The changeling Paris Flaubert invokes, as it shifts within the shifting narrative consciousness of the novel, may be one strong way of presenting in convincing clarity a city in all its attributes, while maintaining the tentative equipoise, the tactful refusal to conclude, that permits skepticism over any construction that a limited perspective may want to place on such complexity. These two goals of presenting a detailed, historical city and still suspending judgment on it are not as conflicting as at first they may appear, for the Paris of Flaubert's day was a more baffling place than it had ever been before.

Paris in Flux

There is a Balzacian element in *L'Education*, as mentioned above. Like Balzac, Flaubert takes as part of his purpose giving a kind of *physiologie* of Parisian types: a vast table of the many and varied categories of people that occupy the Paris scene. Where Balzac uses a Rastignac or Lucien de Rubempré provincial to serve as the filter for the various Parisian characters and their machinations, Flaubert uses Frédéric, at the edge of every group and a part of none, as a filter for his own spectacle. Walter Benjamin, surely one of the more astute theorists of Paris, has described the function of *physiologies*: "They assured people that everyone was, unencumbered by any factual knowledge, able to make out the profession, the character, the background, and the life-style of passers-by. . . . With such certainties Balzac, more than anyone else, was in his element."[1] As the pace of change in the Parisian cityscape became increasingly dizzying and incomprehensible, the need for these tokens of readability was more acute than ever. The epistemological function of the *physiologies*, then, is inseparable from that of reassurance.

In *L'Education*, the Balzacian impulse to construct a catalogue of types is very strong, and the various background figures, such as de Clay, Hussonnet, Mademoiselle Vatnas, the actor Delmar and others, threaten at times to overwhelm the supposedly central figures of Frédéric and Madame Arnoux. At the same time, *L'Education* complicates the Balzacian formula by dramatizing the unstable nature of these signs, the unease of reading them, and the quicksilver nature of many who adopt them. Jacques Arnoux begins as the proprietor of L'Art industriel, reappears as a manufacturer of wine labels, then as the purveyor of religious articles. Hussonnet becomes the editor of a paper that changes title and political slant frequently. In a milieu where roles are exchanged with such dizzying velocity, the actor Delmar recurs with sinister regularity; but though every major party and gathering seems to gain his presence, that presence does not provide reassurance. His face, "intended, like a stageset, to be viewed from a distance," appears throughout part 2 in various roles, and even his name reflects changes of identity and role: "His name being Auguste Delamare, [he] had originally called himself Anténor Dellamare, then Delmas, then Belmar, and finally Delmar, altering and improving his name in this way to match his growing fame."[2] If part 2 has a constant, it is the fluidity of role, the quick change of costume and fashion that Delmar signals.

The party Frédéric attends in the opening chapter of part 2 inaugurates this movement: "This dizzy, whirling movement, growing ever faster and more regular, produced a sort of intoxication in his mind, filling it with other pictures, while the women passed him in a single dazzling vision, each with her distinctive beauty exciting a different emotion" (p. 126). Since the many women at this party have adopted a variety of disguises, it stands to reason that a multiplicity of roles would be needed to win them; it is fitting that Delmar should dominate the proceedings. This first chapter reveals not only the erotic possibilities of Paris but the proliferation of its disguises, roles, and costumes as well. Many of these roles will be picked up and discarded by Frédéric as the book progresses, which is why Delmar is Frédéric's opposite number: not because his identity is similar to Frédéric's so much as that, properly speaking, he has no identity. Like Delmar, Frédéric picks up a role and lets it drop, moving with agility from one identity to the next, never inhabiting any role he plays. This fluidity of persona is the characteristic of almost all the major characters in the text to varying degrees; and it marks as major a shift as between Balzac's Paris and Flaubert's. The *physiologie* form is retained in *L'Education*, but it effloresces to the point at which the "certainties" of which Benjamin speaks are virtually nonexistent. In Balzac's world, there are admittedly characters who alter personae as the situation changes, but they tend to be criminals such as Vautrin. In this novel, there are few characters who do not change identities, whether out of boredom (Frédéric often) or out of expediency (the many bourgeois who embraced the 1848 Revolution, after it occurred, and whom Flaubert ridicules). Ironically, despite these changes of identity, most remain types nonetheless.

There are critics who view this Paris as merely one manifestation of Flaubert's epistemology. Christopher Prendergast argues this in general terms about Flaubert: "What is known as the 'true' or the 'real' is, fundamentally, a matter of *forms* of intelligibility, of constructions which, as is witnessed by the evidence of cultural difference and historical change, are not immutable, natural entities, but are based entirely on convention, articulated through conventional codes of knowledge and understanding."[3] Flaubert was especially sensitive to the conventionality of codes, no doubt; it is also surely the case that the Paris of Flaubert's novel and of his time was a stage on which roles were exchanged with more rapidity than on Balzac's. If it is symptomatic of an epistemology, it is also a historically determined one.

Paris always assumes a dual aspect in French novelistic texts: at once the creator and the destroyer of illusions, the realization and the degradation of youthful ideals. From Crébillon *fils* onward, it seems the provincial in Paris has inhabited a bifurcated city. The scene at the dinner party at the opening of part 2 promises Frédéric the same multiple fulfillment Lucien is offered in the theater in *Illusions perdues*; but the nature of this promise is betokened by the frenzied anonymity of the situation in which it is offered. Many women become one, and individual women are fragmented into partial objects at the party. The scene refracts in a subsequent dream of Frédéric's: "He felt slightly dazed, like a man disembarking from a ship: and in the hallucination of his first sleep he saw passing to and fro before him the Fishwife's shoulders, the Stevedore's back, the Polish girl's calves, and the Savage Woman's hair" (pp. 133–34). The women at the party have no stable identities, not only because they wear costumes, but also because Frédéric cannot retain an integral image of any one woman. Rather, like Proust's Marcel who constructs a goddess from the most fondly remembered fragments of various women he has known, Frédéric recalls only the most striking fragments from the giddy cascade of female flesh.[4] The women at this costume dinner-party have clearly put themselves into circulation: they whirl about, putting Frédéric's thoughts into a whirl as well, and both thoughts and women participate in a sensual bazaar with a hint of prostitution. When the scene is repeated at another class level at Madame Dambreuse's party later, the hint is even more insistent: "This gathering of half-naked women suggested a scene in a harem; a cruder comparison came into the young man's mind" (p. 164). The ensuing catalogue of beauty, mentioning English, Norman, and Italian women, is a profusion recalling what the Maréchal's party sets in motion. In both parties, there is something erotic in the very profusion and fluidity of women, in the rush of images and the dissolution of personal integrity. It is at this party, which begins part 2, that Frédéric's interest in the Maréchal becomes strongest, and it is very much Rosanette's Paris that is on display.

The constant, hectic movement of Paris is always obtruding on the narrative in a ceaseless flux, which, like the traffic, the crowds, and the Seine itself, can be invigorating and saddening by turns. Rosanette, with her flighty shifts of temperament and her fleeting but intense passions, personifies this Paris. It is in the midst of another whirl of activity, this time of traffic, that Frédéric experiences a great sadness over Rosanette. The context of that meloncholy reflection bears some scrutiny, for it bears on his own abrupt change in mood. At first the traffic is brisk, and the people cheery: "Shouts of 'Good afternoon!'— 'How are you keeping?'—'Fine!'—'Not so bad!'—'See you later!' were exchanged from a distance; and face followed face with the rapidity of magic-lantern slides" (p. 210). Meanwhile, Frédéric and Rosanette, riding in the same carriage, exchange no words, absorbed in what is happening all around. But when the traffic is stalled, the gaiety dissipates; pleasantries exchanged from a distance are replaced by less edifying spectacles:

> Now and then the files of carriages, packed too closely together, would all stop at the same time in several lines. Forced to remain for a while side by side, everybody stared at his neighbour . . . eyes full of envy gleamed in the depths of cabs; sneering smiles replied to heads held arrogantly high; . . . and here and there some pedestrian in the middle of the road would suddenly leap backwards to avoid a rider galloping between the carriages before succeeding in making his escape. Then everything moved off again. (P. 210)

All is well as long as the traffic is moving with the "rapidity of magic-lantern slides"; it is only when it slows down and the passengers are forced for a long time to look at each other closely that the goodwill begins to dissolve, only to be restored when the pace again quickens. It is here that Frédéric reflects on his relationship with Rosanette: "Then Frédéric remembered those days, already distant, when he had longed for the ineffable joy of sitting in one of these carriages, next to one of these women. He now possessed that joy, and he was none the happier" (p. 210). Like the people in the traffic, Frédéric and Rosanette avert an undercurrent of suspicion and possible violence largely by rapid movement: movement that can be as misleading as it is reassuring.

The Parisian social whirl is, then, Janus-faced: its appearance often dazzling, its motivation frequently hollow and vicious. Just as a moment's respite in traffic may spark latent animosity among carriage-goers, so a peek at the machinations backstage makes the stage of Paris less inviting. The ambivalence toward Paris in flux derives from the disparity between the seductive, multifaceted appearance of Parisian society and the destructive dynamic driving it. The demonic component in the eroticism implied by this world of society is suggested also in Frédéric's dream, in which he envisions the Maréchal "digging into him with her golden spurs" (p. 134). But in the destructive element he immerses all the same.

The sinister dynamic behind the flux of society is a feature of Paris that, as mentioned, is not uniquely Flaubert's: Balzac also shares this insight. What is particularly dangerous in Flaubert's view of this flux and its ever-increasing velocity is not so much that this quick-change social world conceals machinations, but that it is more and more difficult to read the social signs properly and so to make one's way through. This milieu's increasing unreadability is itself the destructive element. People cynically adopt the roles required by the stage of Parisian society, but the roles outstrip the ability of players or audience to understand or control them. Frédéric's experience at the costume party is mirrored by his experience as a would-be candidate for public office; and while it is impossible to tell who is genuine and who is "phoney," it is apparent that the roles themselves have taken flight: an astonishing bazaar of personalities with roles fluctuating like stock-market trends. The rapidity of movement among these roles is as enticing as a shop-window, though as the figure of Delmar indicates, this fluidity is generated by a commodity-relation between people as well as to oneself. (An actor, quite literally, sells himself on the basis of his ability to assume the role needed at the moment.)

In such an environment, Flaubert's hero Frédéric would have to flourish. From the beginning he is posing: "A long-haired man of eighteen, holding a sketchbook under his arm, stood motionless beside the tiller. . . . And soon, as Paris was lost to view, he heaved a deep sigh" (p. 15). A man whose inherited wealth allows him to play at numerous occupations such as writing fiction, painting, and practicing law, Frédéric is a chameleon whose identity is determined largely by the fashion of the moment and by his own whim. (They generally coincide.) He is very much the figure of the *flâneur*, of which Benjamin, in his study of Charles Baudelaire, writes so famously: "Because he did not have any convictions, he assumed ever new forms himself. *Flâneur*, apache, dandy and ragpicker were so many roles to him. For the modern hero is no hero; he acts heroes."[5] The constant alteration of identities is crucial, as Benjamin points out, because the market demands novelty: "Novelty is a quality which does not depend on the use-value of the commodity. . . . It is the quintessence of false consciousness, of which fashion is the tireless agent."[6]

Frédéric is himself a very chic young man, as Flaubert remarks, and a product of the nineteenth century as much as Baudelaire. Freed from the necessity of work like his fellow coupon-clippers in the *bohème*, Frédéric inhabits a world where commodities and commodity-relations float suspended in the unreal ether of Paris, their shifts dictated only by chance or fashion. The critic Jeanne Bem has called *L'Education* "less the novel of the accumulation of wealth than the novel of monetary exchange, of the circulation of signs."[7] The social psychology outlined by Benjamin thus applies strongly to both Frédéric and his Paris.

The *flâneur's* ultimate truth, for Benjamin, is the truth of the commodity, since he argues that the "man of letters" of that time went "to the marketplace as a *flâneur*, supposedly to take a look at it, but in reality to find a buyer."[8] To the extent that Frédéric initially goes into the marketplace at all, he goes to buy: more directly, to secure Rosanette as his mistress. But the structure of the situation is such that Frédéric becomes himself more and more of a commodity. To maintain his place in society, he takes up with Madame Dambreuse in a relationship that bears close resemblance to prostitution on his part. His actor's ability to change characters along with his wardrobe proves valuable. But in so doing, he is fragmented like the women at the costume party, and the roles he adopts take on their own life, ceasing to be the servants of his interests and becoming, instead, the masters.

In manipulating his identity to gain a commodity, Frédéric gradually yields his identity to the role and becomes a commodity for Madame Dambreuse. It is only when he sees his ideal degraded—as his mistress purchases an intimate possession of Frédéric's true love Madame Arnoux at auction—that Frédéric sees the specular figuration of his own degradation. The casket that Madame Dambreuse purchases thus operates a dual metonymy: (1) Because it has belonged to Madame Arnoux, it indicates that she can be bought, at least in fragments; thus she is not altogether different from the women at the costume party. (2) Frédéric associates the casket with his first passion for Madame Arnoux (he sees it during his initial visit to the Arnouxs); its sale suggests how easily that passion has also been sold, betrayed, simulated. As shall be seen, this casket opens out in several dimensions. For the moment, one knows simply that Frédéric leaves Madame Dambreuse, having become angry with her and with himself, after she makes her purchase.

The Marketplace of Love: Sacred Fetishes and Profane Commodities

The auction scene enacts the conflict between an ideal of love and its counterpart in the marketplace and in that way is useful for reminding us that in addition to the Paris of commodities, which generates the marketplace of love, there is also another Paris for Frédéric: the locus of an erotic ideal that transcends barter. Throughout his bemused adventures in the *demi-monde*, Frédéric carries his almost talismanic ideal with him, an ideal he links firmly with the city. Instead of the dizzying circulation of libidinal investment occasioned by the multiplicity of stimuli, this ideal is one of stasis, serenity, and eternal fidelity.

Indeed, the very first time we glimpse Madame Arnoux, the "apparition" comes in vivid contrast to the scene of movement on the previous pages: the flowing water of the Seine, the noisy boat traveling upon it, and the sweaty, milling crowds aboard. She alone sits quietly, Apollonian amidst the turbulence of the surrounding humanity. But she herself, as the necessary counterpart to the bewildering circulation of commodities in the Parisian marketplace, is nonetheless Paris for Frédéric, despite her singularity in his affections. And what is true of the ideal is also true, finally, of the role Frédéric adopts toward it: it is an agent of stability in identity, a role consistently played.

Despite his later glimpses of her, Madame Arnoux's sex remains hidden "in a mysterious darkness," and even her eyes are imagined with greater clarity than seen. The dream after the costume party that inaugurates part 2 has its contrast in the vision of Madame Arnoux, again melding into a vision of Paris, which occurs toward the beginning of the chapter. As Frédéric espies a rather forlorn Paris through the mist, he sees that "a fine drizzle was falling, it was cold, and the sky was pale, but two eyes which meant more to him than the sun were shining behind the mist" (p. 110). These eyes and indeed the sex of Madame Arnoux are figments of Frédéric's imagination, at least as much a construction of his interior desire as Paris.

Though initially in vivid relief against the backdrop of the "real" Paris represented on the boat, Madame Arnoux comes, then, to be merged in Frédéric's mind with an ideal Paris, one that somehow stands behind the apparent whirl of day-to-day Paris. Flaubert puts the point as clearly as possible:

> In the flowergirls' baskets, the blossoms opened for her to choose them as she passed; in the shoemakers' window, the little satin slippers edged with swansdown seemed to be waiting for her feet; every street led towards her house; and the cabs waited in the squares only to take him there more quickly. Paris depended on her person, and the great city, with all its voices, thundered like an immense orchestra about her. (P. 78)

The babel of Paris—and its traffic and its commodities—are given form and meaning only as the ensemble can be related to Madame Arnoux; only by virtue of her presence can the mayhem of Paris become consonant, an orchestra. This passage must be viewed ironically, considering Frédéric's search for Madame Arnoux's house at the opening of part 2, where in fact all roads lead him to every place but her door—including into the path of a funeral procession. Such reflections are in themselves part of the point of identifying Madame Arnoux with Paris. After all, Frédéric is equally unable or unwilling to conquer one as the other, and it can be said of Paris as of Madame Arnoux that the illusion is never totally dispelled. It can be ceaselessly reconstructed because the reality behind the illusion (assuming such a reality exists) is never confronted.

The illusionary charm of Paris, as of Madame Arnoux, is thus resurrected again and again in those celebrated descriptive passages of the novel that provided such technical resources for successors like Emile Zola. These views of Paris are naturally refracted through Frédéric's consciousness, and they draw their luster from that consciousness.

Yet Paris is not Madame Arnoux, and this is precisely the reason that the process by which the two are conflated is an interesting one to pursue. To examine how this happens, one must return to the "great orchestra" of Paris that thunders around Madame Arnoux. The means by which the city of Paris yields Madame Arnoux are its commodities:

the shoes, the streets, the cabs are "intended" for her. It is through them that Frédéric can imagine her best. His vision of Madame Arnoux also has the effect of sanctifying the commodities by uniting them to a private experience. The Paris of love, even of ideal love, is also always the Paris of commodities—a Paris evoked very well by Benjamin.

An object of desire is itself necessarily a commodity, and as a result the image of Madame Arnoux is indissolubly linked to the cultural codes her image comes to embody: codes, as vendable as goods, that provide the valuative basis on which goods of any kind can be traded. Frédéric may not follow out the implications of this complicity between her image and the cultural codes and commodities that make it possible, but he does live those implications despite that.[9]

His ideal is in one sense identical to Paris, but it must also be protected from contamination by the "real" Paris: hence the peculiar poignancy of the furniture auction where, despite Madame Arnoux's leaving Paris, the thing that most horrifies Frédéric is that her intimate possessions, his fragments of her, are now reentering the circulation of commodities. Her image has all along been inseparable from those possessions: "Frédéric [loved] everything connected with Madame Arnoux—her furniture, her servants, her house, her street. . . . Her comb, her gloves, her rings were things of special significance to him, as important as works of art, almost endowed with life like human beings" (pp. 65–66). Frédéric's love for these objects endows them with life like that of human beings, setting in motion a process more or less inevitable from Madame Arnoux's close linkage with her belongings. The bond between Madame Arnoux and her possessions is shattered by the auction. This rending is particularly chilling because it brings to the surface the commodity character of the things he associated with her and suggests their role in engendering her allure to begin with.

Frédéric leaves Madame Dambreuse when she buys Madame Arnoux's casket because this insult is both a violation of her memory and a cruel reminder of his subjection: Frédéric simply cannot believe that both he and his dreams are so easily bought. For the casket is surely a crucial commodity, perhaps the central commodity, of the narrative, and it is the appropriate locus for the dilemma in Frédéric's attitude toward Madame Arnoux. It embodies both exchange value (as an expensive luxury item) and intimacy (as the gift from a lover or relative—in Madame Arnoux's case, her husband). Gaston Bachelard has shown how fit is the casket as a fetish object in *The Poetics of Space*.[10] In addition to these intrinsic attributes, one must take note of the circumstances in which this particular casket is placed.

The same sacral mystery that hides Madame Arnoux's sex in a penumbral darkness invests the casket Frédéric notices the first time he glimpses the Arnouxs' bedroom. When Jacques Arnoux is thanked by his wife and complimented on the casket, he leans over and kisses her, sending Frédéric into a quiet rage. This casket is indissociable in Frédéric's mind from his discovery after dinner of his only sustained vocation: to win Madame Arnoux.

Like the woman whose fetish it is, this casket is a repository of intimacy and therefore a locus of the sacred. It should stand apart from the "general community of objects," in Bachelard's phrase, just as the woman does: both should retain their mysteries. (By those curious turns of mind that often guide the adulterous, Frédéric does not think of his own appropriation of her, at least consciously, as a violation of the sacred. On the contrary, it is her rightful husband who both sequesters her from the general community of circulating objects and is viewed by Frédéric as the contaminant.) There are other significant objects than the casket, of course, and these do circulate in the course of the novel. The Dresden china chandelier from L'Art industriel, for example, wends its way from Jacques Arnoux's establishment to Rosanette's apartment. And the portrait of the Maréchal painted by Pellerin is put on display in a shopwindow to make Frédéric pay him for the work: its caption reads "Mademoiselle Rose-Annette Bron, the property of Monsieur Frédéric Moreau of Nogent" (p. 235). At times this circulation of objects takes on the coloring of farce. Flaubert describes the objects that make the rounds of the Arnoux home and Rosanette's apartment: "[A] host of small gifts . . . came and went between mistress and wife, for Arnoux, without the slightest embarrassment, often took back something he had given to one, in order to present it to the other" (p. 150). But these circulating objects, much as they smack of a betrayal of the sacred, still do not involve Madame Arnoux herself, but only Rosanette, who has put herself very much into circulation, too.

Even the apartment Frédéric elaborately prepares for Madame Arnoux, where he seduces Rosanette, is not betrayed, because Marie never comes there. Yet when he sees the casket at Rosanette's, his reaction is far different: "He felt deeply moved, and at the same time horrified, as if by sacrilege. He longed to touch it, to open it; but he was afraid of being seen, and he went away" (p. 259). His horror at encountering the casket at Rosanette's, his desire to open it, and his sense of sacrilege at the prospect are all symptomatic of his relation to Madame Arnoux as well.

But since the casket is a gift from her husband, it is therefore marked from the outset with the sign of commerce; and of course Jacques Arnoux is always the necessary condition for seeing Madame Arnoux. From the first chapter, it is Arnoux whom Frédéric sees first. When Frédéric envisions her face as she sleeps, his reverie is jarred by Arnoux's presence: "Arnoux's face appeared to him. He hurried away, to escape from this vision" (p. 86). This passage, one of the few transferred virtually verbatim from the first *L'Education*, signals Frédéric's disgust at this rival's physical proximity to Madame Arnoux. But it is not only that Arnoux is always with his wife, it is that he makes her possible as a dream. In a sense, the appearance of Jacques Arnoux in Frédéric's vision is the figuration, within that dream, of the dream's own generating possibility. It is Arnoux's money on which Madame Arnoux depends for both the leisure and the accoutrements to make herself, however unwittingly, into Frédéric's dream.

At first it is Madame Arnoux who validates the commodities, gives them the appearance of a purpose, makes Paris depend on her person and thunder around her like an orchestra. It becomes increasingly clear that, on the contrary, it is she who depends at least as much upon Paris and on its commodities for her charm. The remembrance of her image is in fact based upon the mediation of the commodities he associates with her: a reversal of the mode in which they seemed to depend upon her person. This is why Frédéric is offended when Madame Arnoux gives him a tour of the plant at Creil and points out to him a *patouillard* or drabbler: "He considered the word grotesque, and almost unseemly on her lips" (p. 198). Yet in a very true sense for Frédéric's dream, without the drabblers, no Madame Arnoux. The private ecstasy that she promises relies on the commercial traffic of the great world, of which her husband is constant and, for Frédéric, melancholy proof. Madame Arnoux's dual status, as an ultimate value outside the marketplace and as precious commodity within it, is before Frédéric from the first, in her juxtaposition with her husband and in the casket that is an ambiguous sign of their union.

It is remarkable, in fact, how long that casket retains its aura, at once intimate and exotic, for Frédéric, especially given its donor (not to mention its Renaissance origins, in light of Flaubert's views on Venetian commerce). The memory of that aura withstands even the final, inevitable indignity of reentering the circulation of commodities, of rejoining what Bachelard calls the "general community of objects" in all its secular banality. In the same way, the illusions Frédéric entertains about both Paris and Madame Arnoux are never effectively shattered. In this light, Frédéric cannot be compared, for instance, to Lucien de Rubempré of *Illusions perdues*. Other critics have rightly remarked that education is precisely what does not occur in this sentimental education. Jonathan Culler notes that Frédéric and Deslauriers have "learned nothing in this *Bildungsroman*" and "that egregious failure brings no compensating understanding."[11] If this is true, and as a whole it is, then the corollary is equally true: that Frédéric, despite the failure he cannot avoid acknowledging, does not relinquish the illusions that precipitated it. Paris remains the "one place in the whole world" where he can turn the "secret riches of his nature" to account; this despite the fact that these riches remain secret throughout the narrative, no doubt even to Frédéric himself.

Frédéric's friend Deslauriers has different views on these matters; he tries to turn his secret riches to account in ways Frédéric shrinks from doing. When Frédéric bets Deslauriers that he will not seduce the first woman they meet and Deslauriers does it, Frédéric comforts himself by thinking: "As if I hadn't a love of my own, a hundred times purer, nobler, and stronger!" (p. 85). (Incidentally, it is this train of thought that ends with the apparition of Arnoux's face.)

It would be facile, though, to conclude that Deslauriers is merely the prosaic counterpart to Frédéric's misty romanticism, as Homais is to Emma Bovary. This is insufficient, for Deslauriers, like Frédéric, has a dream, for which Paris provides the appropriate locus. That dream is in fact a public dream, a political dream. He may scorn the inflation of the erotic impulse to an ideal, but he has an ideal of his own, and it envisages Paris as Utopia.

Utopian Paris: 1848

Paris promises different things to different people. To Frédéric it holds the promise of erotic fulfillment, of an intensely personal yet transcendent love; to Deslauriers, a transcendent collective experience, but one in which his personal desires (primarily for fame and power) are realized. The homology in their roles can be seen most clearly perhaps in the first chapter of part 2, where Frédéric, after seeing Madame Arnoux in the altered surroundings of her husband's shop, meets up with Deslauriers. Both are disillusioned, the former by his love and the latter by the fortunes of his career. His compensatory dreams take a different turn from Frédéric's:

> "Ah, those were the days, when Camille Desmoulins, standing on a table over there, urged the people on to the Bastille! That was a time when people really lived, when a man could assert himself, prove his strength! Mere lawyers gave orders to generals, and ragamuffins defeated kings, whereas nowadays. . ."
>
> He fell silent, then suddenly added:
>
> "Never mind. The future is full of promise." (P. 119)

Frédéric's is the point of view through which the dominant motif of Paris is glimpsed, but the privatized eroticism desired by Frédéric is doubled by the utopian public vision that often grips Deslauriers. It is, after all, a highly subjective "dream" Paris that we get refracted through Frédéric's hopes and moods, even if that Paris is made possible through the work of the public marketplace. But the Paris of collective brotherhood, and specifically of the 1848 "brotherhood" between the middle-class professions and the workers, is also a dream Paris. This dream Paris is particularly interesting since it is, to a certain extent, the illusion of the communitarian as dreamed by people who remain, after 1848, separated from one another. The vast crowds act in unison yet each member of the crowd, after the revolution, returns to his or her private world so surely that it is a question whether that world was ever left. Benjamin describes this strange phenomenon of crowds, which he acutely views as a situation new to the nineteenth century, in the following way: "For the crowd really is a spectacle of nature—if one may apply the term to social conditions. A street, a conflagration, or a traffic accident assemble people who are not defined along class lines. They present themselves as concrete gatherings, but socially they remain abstract—namely, in their isolated private interests."[12]

For Flaubert's Paris, the crowd becomes, for perhaps a moment, a people during the Revolution of 1848. Yet it is not long before the isolated private interests of the various revolutionaries—and specifically the professionals among them, such as Deslauriers and Sénécal—once again assume the center stage.[13]

What the constant motion of the marketplace was for Frédéric the viscous fluidity of the crowd is for the utopian revolutionaries of 1848. As Benjamin describes them (and often Flaubert), they are symptomatic of the nineteenth-century urban landscape. But at the same time, they call forth the visions of a possible reversal in that landscape—and of course during 1848 they are briefly agents for what seems to be such a reversal. The crucial distinction between Frédéric's and Deslauriers's ideal is that Frédéric thinks to get beyond the marketplace of Eros by abstractly negating it in the love of one woman; he does not wish, insofar as he maintains his ideal, to realize it somehow from that marketplace. The socialist hopefuls such as Deslauriers clearly want to work with the existent crowd to realize an ideal that will change the character of the crowd—or more precisely, to give it a character. Their dream is to make the crowd a collectivity. That this dream proves incapable of realization is attributable in part to some tragic inevitability, no doubt; it is also attributable to the very specific inability of the middle-class professions, including people like Deslauriers, to ally themselves with the workers like Dussardier.

The dramatization of this failure of the communitarian ideal occurs in the same chapter as the sale of Madame Arnoux's casket and it enacts a parallel betrayal, in the establishment of the Second Empire and its miniature figuration in the shooting of Dussardier by Sénécal. Both betrayals have the inauguration of the Second Empire as a backdrop. When Sénécal shoots Dussardier, he does so in the service of a Caesarism that only parodies a genuine collectivity, but he also does it to maintain his position in the hierarchy: it is part of his job. The alliance of social classes has broken down because individual self-interest has corroded the unity and because the professional class (imaged there in Sénécal) has succumbed to its own "collective" interests as well as to its ideology of individual self-interest. The betrayal of love felt by Frédéric is here doubled by a betrayal of friendship, since Dussardier and Sénécal had once been friends.

Though they may be said to experience a common fate, the claims of love and friendship are played off against each other throughout the text. Generally speaking, it is love whose dream of transcendent personal bliss is undermined by the public marketplace, and it is friendship that crystallizes the conflict between collective dream and self-interest. Eventually it will be demonstrated that the agent of irony within each of these dream systems, undermining the personal dream by the public market and the collective dream by private interest, is finally the economic: the catalyst whereby private and public continually are forced into each other's way, often in the guise of the competing claims of love and friendship. For the moment, though, let us concentrate on the way Deslauriers and Frédéric's friendship produces a couple of parallel scenes, each of which can be said to comment on the other; each involves the disastrous attempt of one of the pair to enter the world of the other. Frédéric's disaster in particular is useful for it tells much about the communitarian dream and its failure.

On the one hand, Deslauriers's attempt to invade Frédéric's dream of love with Madame Arnoux—at first linguistic, a farcical parroting of her husband's name—becomes deadly earnest when Frédéric goes on a trip to Nogent. Deslauriers's seduction attempt is a grotesque and disastrous failure, and Flaubert is mercifully though effectively brief in presenting it. On the other hand, Frédéric's one brief attempt to attain Deslauriers's dream of power through his abortive campaign for office in chapter 1 of part 3 is more fully described and is possibly more useful for an understanding of the lineaments of the political dream, its possibilities and its failures. It is especially interesting because Frédéric's progression and the macropolitical progression of France in the unfolding of the plot comment upon one another more by their parallel lines than by their intersections. Frédéric's foray into the political wilds would seem to be the exception; but if so, then like Deslauriers's debacle with Madame Arnoux, it is the exception that confirms the rule.

When history appears onstage in 1848, Frédéric's preferred role seems to be that of audience. He walks through the revolution's carnage "as if he were watching a play" (p. 286). Still, in the wake of the revolution in which Frédéric has taken no part, he does feel that surge of solidarity, G. W. F. Hegel describes in the *Phenomenology of Mind*, that brief sense that community, pure and untrammeled by conventional constraints, is in fact possible.[14] Flaubert subtly suggests the irony of Frédéric's stance: "Frédéric, for all that he was no fighting man, felt his Gallic blood stirring. The ardour of the crowds had infected him. He greedily breathed in the stormy air, full of the smell of gunpowder; and at the same time he trembled with the consciousness of a vast love, a sublime, all-embracing tenderness, as if the heart of all mankind were beating in his breast" (p. 292).

This mixture of grandiose sentiment and bloodthirsty aggression says much that is unflattering about Frédéric, who without putting himself at risk can vicariously experience these "infectious" emotions much as a spectator does in watching a play. But it also says much about the curious situation observed in so many revolutions: that the masses of men can truly unite and exalt in their community only in the act of destruction, in negation. In *L'Education*, the process of revolution itself is often the Utopia, not the society that succeeds it.[15] This is one reason the will to revolt in 1848 savors of a desire or a compulsion to repeat the experience of the Revolution in 1789, at least as much as it does of the need to effect certain specific changes. Frédéric, however undeserving, has become for the moment a citizen of Utopia.

The one woman who dazzled and won Frédéric in the first chapter is gradually compromised in his mind by a multiplicity of women. In the same manner, the brief unitary feeling of the multitude that dazzles Frédéric at the moment of the revolution is soon compromised and almost obliterated by the bickering, fragmented multiplicity of the political contestants in the meeting selling their nostrums. But the multiplicity of women and the interchangeability of their parts presented an intrusion of the public sphere of the sexual marketplace into Frédéric's private vision of union with one woman; by contrast, the undermining of the political dream occurs when the communitarian sentiment breaks down under the pressure of private interests and careerism. All the resources of the Menippean satire are brought to bear in depicting the political meeting at which Frédéric is a candidate, where the sheer confusion of conflicting abstractions is inseparable from the babble of words, culminating in a speech that is literally in a foreign language (Spanish). Again, Frédéric is chiefly the spectator at a play, but in this one the negative implications of the theatrical metaphor are more obvious. Each speaker seems an actor who wishes all the audience for himself. Even though in the seizing of power all acted in concert, the specific proposals that follow are at best at cross purposes and at worst merely excuses to be noticed and admired. Delmar is a crucial figure at the meeting, and his self-important posturing sets the tone of much of the debate. The effectiveness of the speeches is largely illusory, except insofar as they advance the careers or the vanities of the men who make them. Frédéric is thrown out for his one offering, the obvious observation that the Spaniard's inspiring words are falling on uncomprehending ears:

> "But this is absurd. Nobody can understand a word."
> This remark infuriated the audience.
> "Throw him out! Throw him out!"
> "Who? Me?" asked Frédéric.
> "Yes, you!" said Sénécal majestically. "Get out!" (P. 307)

Frédéric attends the meeting out of private interest and self-advertisement. He does so largely at the behest of the banker Monsieur Dambreuse, a wealthy individual who is certainly no friend of the revolution, but who feels, as he puts it to Frédéric, that if in office "you might well be able to render services to your country, to us all, and to me," this last tacked on as though a modest afterthought (p. 297). (And Deslauriers early on urges Frédéric to get to know the Dambreuses, who represent vicarious fulfillment and the practical instrument of Deslauriers's ambitions: " 'You really must get into that circle. You can introduce me later on. A millionaire—just think of it' " [p. 29].) To Dambreuse's practical interest is added Frédéric's vision of himself, another stage to strut upon: in addition to the political excitement, Frédéric is "attracted by the uniform. . . . He already saw himself in a waistcoat with lapels and a tricolor sash" (p. 297). These motives, already eccentric to the purported reason for this political process, are a synecdoche for the mixed impulses motivating all of the various members of the meeting. The machinations of private economic interests, such as Monsieur Dambreuse's, combined with the desires for individual glory on the part of the participants, such as Frédéric, work quickly to make the political meeting a Babel of incomprehensible words. The clichés and conventions of the various ideologies are exchanged in a kind of vacuum. The unreality of the theater, implicit even in Frédéric's brief noncombatant solidarity with the revolution, now permeates the scene, as if the words were said and poses struck for their own sake, like scripts to be followed. The meeting degenerates into a "marketplace of ideas," in which there are few buyers and too many vendors; and this has come about by reason of the conflicting interests that have already developed in the aftermath of the revolution.[16] In the political meeting, the multiplicity of ideas keeps growing, but it leads finally only to satiation: the frequent Flaubertian comparison of mind to stomach, with emphasis on the limited ability of each to digest what it eats, is apposite here.[17]

In this proliferation of ideas and interests, the economic motives of the meeting and of the larger politics of which it is a part begin to come clear, and Frédéric himself, however unwittingly, is the clearest exemplar of this process. His innocence in being the dupe of both his own vanity and of Monsieur Dambreuse's desire for influence only underscores the sinister banality of the process. The interests of economics, both the literal kind and the barter of self and ideas, have made their way thoroughly into the revolutionary arena in the guise of altruism. Frédéric, characteristically, manages to convince himself of his own purity. He says to Rosanette: "The more public-spirited you are, the less you are appreciated; and if you hadn't your conscience to support you, the boors you have to deal with would soon make you sick of self-sacrifice" (p. 308). Like his opposite number Delmar, claiming crucifixion for his art, Frédéric sees himself as a martyr to the Republic, and it is fitting that Rosanette should make the appropriate analogy in this context: "Serve you right! That'll teach you to go playing the generous patriot. . . . She's an expensive mistress, your precious Republic. Well, go and enjoy yourself with her, my lad!" (p. 308). For all her coarseness, Rosanette has hit on one possibly damning flaw in the Revolution of 1848: it was a relatively painless revolution, with little genuine change in its wake. A republic was bought on the cheap ("vingt-cinq pour cent," as Rosanette puts it), and Frédéric's mistress of the moment, along with the feeling of solidarity that she carried in train, was easily gained and so would easily be betrayed.

Frédéric's decision to desert the Republic for his flesh-and-blood mistress does not have a successful outcome, though. He and Rosanette leave Paris and the strife of June Days for a pastoral outing. Events taking place in Paris intrude upon their idyll, which is itself much more artificial than the world they abandoned. Again, the political dream and the privatized dream undermine one another. Fontainebleau has dual connotations, symbolizing both the *ancien régime* and the forest primeval. It is from another time, standing aloof from the political struggle and the heady conflicts and commerce of the day.

When the couple is told that a battle is raging in Paris (though Flaubert's famous *style indirect libre* is as tricky here as anywhere in the text), it is most likely from Frédéric's perspective that the trees seem to bear themselves "like patriarchs or emperors" with trunks that resemble "triumphal arches" and "pillars about to fall," or that rocks begin to look like "the monstrous, unrecognizable ruins of some vanished city" (p. 323). The artifacts of nature are inevitably rendered as cultural and political artifacts, and Paris obtrudes in the metaphors themselves. Yet, owing to the setting, the potentially jarring effect of these undertones is muted, displaced to another time (perhaps to the French Revolution again, which in this situation seems almost quaint):

> Sometimes they heard the roll of drums far away in the distance. It was the call to arms being beaten in the villages for the defence of Paris.
> "Why, of course! It's the insurrection!" Frédéric would say with a disdainful pity, for all that excitement struck him as trivial in comparison with their love and eternal Nature. (P. 325)

Finally, it takes the force of friendship, once again, to point out the contradiction between the attempted serenity of Frédéric's and Rosanette's idyll in Fontainebleau and the realities of Paris and its public troubles. News comes soon of Dussardier, who has been wounded in the insurrection. Rosanette refuses to help out: "He was shocked by this selfishness, and he reproached himself for not being in Paris with the others. His indifference to the country's misfortunes had something mean and bourgeois about it. His love suddenly weighed upon his conscience like a crime" (p. 329). What had seemed trivial now assumes immense importance, and the love that had been his only interest appears to be a "crime." The political dream is not attainable, perhaps, but public reality nonetheless obtrudes upon private dreams. And Frédéric is caught up in the events of the public sphere just as surely as his politically active counterparts are caught up in the mesh of their own conflicting career goals and individual interests. But he is caught up in it in part because he wants to be, because he is drawn to people such as Dussardier and Deslauriers and to their vision, which at times he wishes to share. The line between spectators and actors, always fine, becomes nonexistent in the revolution and the aftermath Flaubert depicts, and through the closely woven pattern of Frédéric's friendships one sees why.

The mutually interfering fields of friendship and love, and of public and private dreams, do not ironize one another to the extent that the economic realm ironizes each of them (though the economic often provides the occasion for the collision of the two spheres). Unlike the rival theaters of private love and public communion, the economic is only the negation of dream, a dismantling of the theaters. It introduces the anonymity of the marketplace into the inmost recesses of private love, and it insinuates individual self-interest into a community; but the role it plays is finally destructive, as it is in *Madame Bovary*. (In both texts, this destructive function must be understood as constitutive of its enabling function and is what results when that grounding function of the economic is made manifest: in *Madame Bovary* when the debts that allow Emma's romantic dreams to flourish begin to pile up; in *L'Education* when the possessions that were an inherent part of Madame Arnoux's charm are sold off at auction, or when an essentially bourgeois revolution is revealed to have been so.)

It is ironic that the economic occasions the awareness of the competing claims of friendship and passion, as when Frédéric must decide whether to lend Deslauriers or the Arnouxs some funds at one point; but that catalyzing quality is peripheral to its chief function. The work of the economic irony in this text does not promote the claims of either the public or the private sphere but is at best an inverted parody of both and finally an enemy of dream itself. The triumph of the economic may be part of an illusion, but dream it most certainly could not aspire to be, especially unfortunate since it has enabled so many dreams to emerge. Paris becomes the marketplace of dreams, where all dreams, whether of love or of brotherhood, are discounted at *vingt-cinq pour cent.*

The fate that has befallen Paris in this novel must also contaminate the novel written to "legitimate" this Paris, for that is part of what Flaubert's novel works to do. The novel itself, and not solely on account of its subject, is as much a part of the marketplace as Paris. The same pitiless movement of the economic that threatens to reduce Paris to a commodity also threatens to reduce the text of Paris to empty, consumable clichés that can be bartered for gain.

This impasse returns us to the ironies mentioned earlier. The first irony was that even though the cultural clichés of a time and place may be fictional, this fact does not lessen their force or the felt need to maintain them. Since this fatality is so determinative for the novel's own textual practice, it would be helpful to examine a dramatization of exactly how Flaubert situates this persistence of cliché. Following good hermeneutical practice, we look to the text to explain itself. Fortunately, the last two chapters of *L'Education* provide clues to another economy for cliché, one closer to gift exchange.

Fictional Language and the Exchange of Tokens

What is denied as history is confirmed as story. This ironic "novel of education" has as its ultimate result not wisdom, which would suggest a certain teleology in the events of the preceding years, but rather remembrance: mutual recollection that retrospectively sanctifies these events through language. The process of exchange that takes place in both the first epilogue with Madame Arnoux and the second with Deslauriers is the telling of stories, of the past as a story (*histoire*). At the conclusion are two collaborative efforts: one relating a story of love, the other a story of friendship. In each case, a kind of economy is deployed; but it is characterized by a number of peculiarities.

First, the transactions are not founded on a calculative hope of gain. They are, to borrow from French theorist Jean Baudrillard, "beyond use value."[18] When Frédéric meets Madame Arnoux, the possibility of sexual fulfillment, to the extent that it even comes into question, is renounced in favor of a cigarette. When Frédéric and Deslauriers meet, it is on the ruins of their former aspirations: Neither Frédéric's dreams of love nor Deslauriers's dreams of power have been realized. The ruin of dreams is surprisingly often a good vantage point from which to reminisce on past prospects. Frédéric's world, which had suddenly "grown bigger" when he first met Madame Arnoux, has now shrunk to the point where it could be comfortably embraced in a backward glance. Unlike the narrative in "Sarrasine," then, the stories told in the last two chapters of *L'Education* are neither monetary arrangements nor quasi-monetary barters of a story told for a night of love. They are more in the nature of a gift that each party tenders the other almost for the sake of giving, for the sake of circulating it.

The second peculiarity is that the gift exchange makes each party to it the recipient of his or her own past, called forth and repeated by one with whom that past was lived. Each partner in the transaction gives the other only his or her own memory. (Frédéric asks Madame Arnoux when she first realized she loved him, and she obliges; and Frédéric and Deslauriers punctuate their anecdotes by saying to the other, "Do you remember?") Of course, like rhetoric or storytelling, the exercise is as pleasing to the speaker as it is to the listener, and the pleasure of one partner confounds itself with that of the other. When Frédéric praises Madame Arnoux's now bygone beauty, she takes the compliment as fact: "She rapturously accepted this adoration of the woman she had ceased to be. Frédéric, drunk with his own eloquence, began to believe what he was saying" (p. 414). The purpose of these transactions is not solely to give back a commonly shared past, whether fraudulently suggesting it has not ceased, like Madame Arnoux, or presenting it in a final reckoning or post mortem, like Deslauriers. The point is more to fortify a bond with the other person on the basis of a past commonly appraised or mythologized. (At least insofar as they can do this, the auctioneer has not had the last word, for this appraisal is of a different sort.) The language itself works to reconstitute this bond between the two speakers, a double repetition because it both resurrects a former time and also involves each in echoing thoughts, memories, and sentiments of the other.

The third feature of this exchange is that what is resurrected and echoed is also constructed and created; what the partners really give each other in these final sections is a fictionalized and narratized past: an *histoire.* (Frédéric recalls his own boyhood ambition to write a novel, and Deslauriers's to write a history. Their ultimate project in this final chapter is a pale imitation of either pursuit, but it is the only one open to them at this point.) This fictionalization, which involves both aesthetically motivated distortions and also the sifting and winnowing of memory's perspective, is the common project for whose sake the stories are exchanged. What each gives the other is what the other already had, in a sense, but is now transmuted from the raw material into a linguistic project, a product that confirms the sense that there was a shared past to transmute. For all the deceit this entails—and indeed as the passages from the penultimate chapter show, it is as much self-deceit as deceit of others—there is a purity to this collaborative restoration of the past that is unsullied by any immediate practical goal or urge to self-aggrandizement. The characters' lives may have been over by the time they matured, but their failure and mediocrity are ennobled in a way their scheming after love and power was not. The conversation with Madame Arnoux displays the failure of the final possibility of attaining one's dreams, which of course is the surest point from which to glimpse a place where all dreams seemed once possible of attainment: at the threshold of the Turkish woman's house.

It is worth remembering that this incident takes place in Nogent, though both the exoticism and the tawdriness of the Turkish woman's house are writ large in Paris later. Both Frédéric and Deslauriers are on the threshold of their urban pursuits as well as of a whorehouse in Nogent. And it can also be said that neither character consummates his ambitions in Paris, either. Despite this, or perhaps because of it, that story is an altogether appropriate locus for dreams, since nothing, or very little, happens in it.[19]

One measure of the difference between the two epilogues is that in the conversation with Madame Arnoux, language is used to sanctify a past in illusion but also to entomb it as a genuine possibility (certainly on the part of Frédéric); but in the conversation with Deslauriers, the language exchanged is part of the return to a place where it was still possible to believe, not so much in dreams per se, as in the possibility of realizing them.

Even though the whorehouse anecdote and Frédéric's comment on it—that that was when they had been happiest—has its outrageous aspect, it is superseded by the innocence, in more than the obvious sense, of the story: innocence pointed up in the flowers from his mother's garden that Frédéric takes with him. There is a resonant similarity of gesture in Frédéric's retreat from the Turkish woman's house and his turn of the heel when he suspects Madame Arnoux of offering herself to him. The same mixture of pleasure and fear, the same gallantry, can be read in each scene. Even though the younger Frédéric is devoid of dissimulation and the older Frédéric is all dissimulation, both are alike in that they preserve their illusions.

The very fact that Frédéric and Deslauriers, in the full flower of middle-aged cynicism, indulge in the enterprise they do is confirmation of the persistence of these governing fictions despite their fraudulence. Frédéric's capacity to retain such illusions is clear even in his choice of anecdote, which repeats the situation of its own telling, since it recounts the mutual flight of Frédéric and Deslauriers from the realization of their dreams. The whorehouse itself, not only here but throughout the novel, is the fatal contaminant of subjective illusion. Perhaps the young heroes of the anecdote see intuitively that the purchase of exotic fantasy at the Turkish woman's house will inevitably degrade the dream extended to them, just as the illusions of the East, one marketed by Venice, lost their aura through accessibility.

To recount the story of the Turkish woman's house, then, is to remain in one's fictions, both because it is a space of imagined innocence, and because, in residing there through the retelling of the story, one must ignore the corruption it prefigures. This situation is compounded by the curious fact that the incident itself became the object of legend in the town at the time: it is said to cause an immense ruckus, or *histoire.*

> They told one another the story at great length, each supplementing the other's recollections; and when they had finished:
> "That was the happiest time we ever had," said Frédéric.
> "Yes, perhaps you're right. That was the happiest time we ever had," said Deslauriers. (P. 419)

What Deslauriers and Frédéric have given each other in this exchange is not even quite their own past, but rather their own past as fictionalized by others and recounted once more by the principals. In fact, it is not altogether clear from Flaubert's context whether the two are recounting the incident itself or its form as it passed into the public domain of Nogent, which suggests the malleability of this past they are sharing.

The border between reality and its narratization, between *histoire* (history) and *histoire* (story), becomes ever hazier here; but still the tale chosen by the two men to represent the time when they were happiest, when Frédéric and Deslauriers retained their fictions, is the perfect choice because it is already a story, and indeed one that has already gained circulation with a public for whom Frédéric and Deslauriers are characters in a tale. *(Bouvard et Pécuchet* alters this motif, often playing the two principals against the townspeople's perception of them.)

Flaubertians such as Culler have remarked this affirmation of the fictional in the epilogues. Culler says that in the penultimate chapter,

Madame Arnoux and Frédéric's love is "both beautiful and very false; beautiful, not despite its falsity but because of the falsity inherent in it," and that this resort to cliché really constitutes "an affirmation that while life must be lived and while this will entail disappointment and failure, nevertheless one can, if one proceeds with care, create a purified fiction which remains disconnected from one's experience."[20] This is consistent with Culler's general argument that after his epileptic seizure at Pont l'Evêque, Flaubert turned away not so much from one life to another as from any empirical life at all to a life in language. While Culler certainly approaches the case more closely than those who hastily conclude that the closing chapters are merely grotesque or pathetic, an important dimension to this interpretation must be added.

It is true that a certain "affirmation" of the linguistically conceived life is at work in these final chapters. In both scenes, it is because the words are exchanged for their effectiveness in constructing a mutually supportive fiction—because, in effect, they are clichés—that they are productive. And it is true that the fictions built by Frédéric and his counterparts are based, both in form and in content, on implicit rejection of the experience or reality testing that might unsettle their illusions. It is even true that the use of these words as the bricks for a castle of illusion is presented, finally, as the highest act of charity these characters perform for one another; there is a strange nobility as well in insisting on these illusions despite the ever-increasing weight of bitter disillusionment. To say that a youthful outing to la Turque was the happiest time of one's life is not so much to pass judgment on the succeeding period as simply to choose to ignore it.

And yet, the fullest resonance of these epilogues is best retained if the backdrop of decisive failure and futility against which these fictions appear is kept in mind. The interview with Madame Arnoux concerns a now-dead affair that Frédéric has no interest in reviving and the conversation with Deslauriers concerns the past of two men, neither of whom, as Flaubert states, has realized his youthful dreams. What they do is, of course, analogous to what in Flaubert's conception a novelist or an artist would do: they take the clichés at hand and construct fictions out of them that will have special curative power. While this use of linguistic elements is not manipulative (it has, as shown, chiefly a gift economy, not an acquisitive or calculative one), neither does it lead beyond the closed circuit of the individuals who recount these little stories to themselves and to each other. With the gradual degradation of the historical process by the economic, action within that larger realm is neither possible nor desirable; and the same is true of the artistic project. There are several artistic "types" in the novel that suggest this, Pellerin the most persistent among them; but the author's most fatalistic conclusion about the status of narrative becomes explicit toward the end.

Written in its second and final version during the reign of Louis Napoléon, *L'Education* recounts for its readers the events of their recent past, not so much to illuminate those events as to turn these commonly held clichés into a fiction, one that does not explicate a theme or even communicate at all in the usual sense, but one that delights. At the same time, in a paradox already glimpsed from another angle, the novel must tell the story of the events that make this delight its only function. This tension suggests the horizon, the limitation, of Flaubert's vision in this regard. If the bourgeois class to whose ranks Flaubert belongs cannot make history, then all that remains to it is to make stories. But precisely since these stories rely for their status as stories of this pure kind on their lack of pretensions to referentiality (on their being overtly manipulations of cliché and not instruments for teaching or revealing a causality), the text is foreclosed from justifying its own recourse to fictionality by showing the historical situation that necessitated it. Flaubert's source of legitimacy for his textual project is such that insofar as the text itself provides justification for that project, it must do so in bad faith. The rejection of history for story has itself a history; and *L'Education* attempts to tell that story, even if its own conclusion suggests that the story can be neither true nor false.

This paradox accounts in part for Flaubert's ambiguous literary patrimony. It is true that Flaubert's realism led to many innovations by such as Zola; but another strain of his approach led also to Mallarmé and Valery. The desire to resonate in the reader at a level where semiological conventions do not reach must surely have been a part of his regular visits to his famous shouting room at Croisset, where he recited each line aloud for its effect; part as well of his concern to make a novel that, like the world itself, would be held together, would depend for its unity of impact, on the sheer internal support of its words.[21]

For the work of Flaubert to escape the realm of the economic, it is necessary that it avoid the coinage of the commonplace. Yet at the same time, it must "say something" because it is a published work of fiction that implies an audience, an addressee. Flaubert in fact fretted a great deal about the reception of his novels.[22] The satire contained within the text, because it reveals the extent of the corruptibility of all realms of human interaction by the system of exchange, also implicates the text itself in this process. If the text were to take altogether seriously the point of its own satire, it would not have been published; or at least it would stray as far as possible from the obligation to communicate which is considered central to the so-called readerly novel, as Roland Barthes terms it.[23]

The same tension that informs this thematic of Flaubert's, then, also works upon his textual practice, for much as one would like to escape the semiological marketplace where all language becomes a token, the attempt to present the conditions from which one is escaping in an intelligible way (to write, in other words, a moral history of the men of one's generation, as Flaubert has described *L'Education*) compels one nevertheless to use the symbolic arsenal of the social and literary heritage. Though one could argue that Flaubert creates, below the surface meaning, the dream Paris that can inhere in the structure of the words and sentences and that can resonate without depending on the semiological nexus, this larger didactic contradiction stubbornly remains. As poetry, *L'Education* succeeds, perhaps at instilling a sense of Paris by some osmosis without denotative content; but as the moral history of Flaubert's generation, it must rely upon Balzacian satire and its conventions (among numberless other devices) to expose the economic functioning of that same Paris.

In one sense, we are very far here from the contradictions that haunted the early Flaubert of "Les Arts et le commerce," in another very close. Whereas that early essay proposed a clean separation between the realms of practical activity, commerce, or the circulation of money and artistic activity, poetry, or language, the later text of *L'Education* displays a thoroughgoing concern with the way language itself can become a circulating commodity, part of the marketplace.[24]

Even though *L'Education* may seem to be affirming the blank refusal to communicate, or else the exchange of clichés or fictions only for their own sake, there is surely more to it than that. If the last chapters seem to turn away from the larger historical moment, this turning-away is also a pointing-toward. After all, to tell the story of the degradation of discourse by the economic realm is to deal in history, and in a determinate stance toward that history. One can be thankful that Flaubert does not rigorously pursue the legitimate options his project seems to leave him, and still ask whether the agoraphobia that attends these final chapters, their rejection both of the writing and of the living of a history, is the only appropriate response to the situation he starkly depicts.[25] To one of Flaubert's class, with the luxury of an inheritance, whose preferred epitaph was "He stayed home and wrote," it may well have appeared that way.[26] But this solution brings its own contradictions in train, and its own limitations. It emerges that for Flaubert the political economy of discourse could only be escaped through the refusal of denotative language for pure connotation and pure fiction, along with the refusal of the larger realm of circulation for a smaller realm closed to the vulgar public.

And yet he published. Perhaps this fact in itself betokened the grudging recognition that the political economy of discourse, for all the degradations of linguistic purity it seems to imply, was still a realm from which it was neither possible nor, finally, desirable to depart.

6

Phantom Publics and Imaginary Libraries:
Flaubert, Conrad, and the Institution of Literature

In *L'Education sentimentale* and the early text on the arts and commerce, the marketplace emerges as a destructive force (especially to
works of art) as much as a creative one. Furthermore, this agoraphobia
includes, or rather is made urgent by, a distaste for the bourgeoisie
whom Flaubert associates with the marketplace. At the same time, he
delighted in fame (biographer Enid Starkie relates his happy time in
Paris after the financial success of his novel *Salammbô*) and regretted that
L'Education, which highlighted the waste of a generation of Frenchmen
who would be the likeliest readership for his novel, was poorly received
by both the critical establishment and the public.[1] Nor was he above the
blandishments of representatives of the Second Empire such as Prin-
cesse Mathilde, despite his less than enthusiastic view of that regime.[2]
Throughout his career, then, Flaubert seems to have fluctuated between
the desire not to be a commodity at all, and the desire to be merely a
very high-toned one. (Jean-Paul Sartre even claims that "Princess
Mathilde was the agent through whom Napoleon III 'bought'
Flaubert."[3])

In his Flaubert biography *L'Idiot de la famille*, Sartre advances the
ingenious argument that by his very posture of disdain toward popular
acclaim, Flaubert won it.[4] With the reversal of 1848, the French bourgeoisie undergo a change in their ideology. It is still universality, for
Sartre, a legacy of the Enlightenment-style writers such as Voltaire. But
because the merchants and manufacturers reverse their position and
start forming allegiances against extending the franchise and diffusing
power, the universalism becomes negative. Sartre calls it "black humanism."[5] Even though Flaubert's goal as an artist is "to denounce the
real in favor of the imaginary," the public accepts him as a realist
"based on a misunderstanding." This misunderstanding is significant,
however, for there is "a basic truth" that unites Flaubert and his public

and that allows "equivalent meanings" for "terms superficially quite different. Misanthropy, of course, was this fundamental bond."[6] Sartre's view has the fillip that this misanthropy is a form of what Nietzsche calls *ressentiment*, though ironically here it is the outward projection of guilt by rulers, not by slaves. The bourgeoisie of the Second Empire "believed that the lower classes looked upon them with accusing hatred," and as Sartre explicator Hazel Barnes phrases it: "Unable to refute this judgment, they turned it into self-hate, subsequently projecting it outward as a hate of the entire human species."[7] Hence, black humanism.

However much truth resides in Sartre's reasons for Flaubert's public acceptance (what there was of it), it may begin, paradoxically, to explain the failure of *L'Education* to catch the approving public eye. It may have become too difficult for his bourgeois readers, confronted with such a text, to dissolve the acid historical portrait of a closely akin era and its figures into some vague distaste for eternal human nature. In any event, what is useful in Sartre's argument is the way it makes central to Flaubert's art and to his success the fact that "Flaubert was one of the first to recognize and to welcome a new phenomenon in cultural history—the divorce between the writer and his public."[8]

It may be that to extract the maximum explanatory power from his paradoxical thesis, Sartre does not acknowledge the extent to which Flaubert's own texts are realist texts, buttressed by empirical research and faithful to the narrowest historical detail. As has been shown with *L'Education*, the desire to connect with an audience, even if only to satirize it, is not buried deep within Flaubert's *impensé*, but can be read in the way that text is structured. The urge not to conclude, not to "mean" too completely, not to offer a commodity called a moral, not even, in the extreme, to communicate, is not the sole drive behind the text. There is also the urge to deliver a message, however unpleasant. These two agendas are at war with each other, not in Flaubert's unconscious so much as in the novels themselves.

As the introductory section has pointed out, the audience a writer wishes to reach and the audience likely to receive him or her are often two different things; but by Flaubert's time, the split between artist and likely public has become quite severe, for reasons already discussed. Flaubert's horror of the cliché results in the *Dictionnaire des idées reçues* from which he culled so many choice lines for *L'Education*, the famous conversation between Léon and Emma from *Madame Bovary*, and the seduction scene at the agricultural fair from the same book. This horror is not solely a belletristic or aestheticist stance, but rather a part of his profound discomfort with his readership and the values the common coinage of clichés represented.[9]

It could be argued that *Bouvard et Pécuchet*, his late, uncompleted work, is an attempt to embrace and englobe the heritage of the bourgeois Enlightenment by condensing large sections of the encyclopedic reading of the pair. By repeating many of the clichés of his time and setting them in the context of Bouvard and Pécuchet's farcical failure, Flaubert would then be parodying, putting into question, those *idées reçues* in the gesture of elaborating them.[10]

Flaubert's rejection of cliché is not merely persnickety, then, but part of a response to the values of the dominant class in the society of his time. The response is partly temperamental, partly historical, and partly institutional as well. For Flaubert stands at a point where artistic aspirations and the desire to be widely read begin to diverge. Put another way, he writes at a time when belles-lettres, or "literature," has assumed the fixity of a separate institution. The appeal to posterity—which Flaubert, for all his skepticism about the Romantics, makes like them for his own work—can be read as the appeal for inclusion in what Alvin Kernan terms the "imaginary library" of literature. One of the features of this institution is precisely its contestatory eccentricity from other institutions and their values, and so from much or most of the reading public.[11]

The master metaphor for the emptying, the "de-legitimation" of all these institutions and their communitarian substance is the marketplace. It serves, in *L'Education* and also in *Madame Bovary* in the form of Emma's vast debt to Lheureux, both as the figure of the unraveling of private and of public dream and as the mechanism for this unraveling. The process of disillusion described by Flaubert in *L'Education* leads to the making of fictions, as the epilogues to that work show. But the making of fictions is an institution as well. Flaubert's desire for *déclassement* is of course a vain urge, in more than one sense, but it furthers the formation, ironically, of the institution of literature: "Rejection of all social commitment and the refusal to write for his only real public—the bourgeois class—gradually resulted in a totally new aesthetic." This is that the literary work should be "autonomous, addressed to no one and, insofar as possible, with no reference to the personal qualities of the person who wrote it."[12] In practice, though, Flaubert's *déclassement*, the desire for which he bequeaths to modernists down to the present, works to solidify the new institution of literature: the book about nothing, written by an impassible author and addressed to no determinate audience, will create a home for itself in the imaginary library.

When Joseph Conrad takes pen in hand, he enters an institution altered by the modernist novelistic tradition inaugurated by Flaubert. Conrad's career, like Flaubert's, was one of tension between the need for public acceptance and the obligation to artistic integrity. The search for a line of filiation, a legitimate lineage, from one writer to the other is easy to establish, if perhaps not very informative. Ian Watt, for example, writes extensively of Conrad's apparent reliance on *Madame Bovary* for his first novel, *Almayer's Folly*.[13] Conrad himself has acknowledged *L'Education sentimentale* as a signal influence on his work, and Conrad biographer Frederick Karl has suggested that Flaubert was "perhaps the single most compelling literary influence on Conrad's development as a writer."[14]

The literary pedigree Conrad derives from Flaubert, then, is assured and need not be belabored anew. His enthusiasm and that of his collaborator Ford Madox Ford for Flaubert's techniques are givens in the history of literary impressionism.[15] But what other features do the two authors share? Are there any facets of Flaubert's career—aside from the albeit central feature that he founded the tradition of fiction within which Conrad wrote—that make him especially useful to Conrad as a model? Specifically, how would Flaubert's example serve to guide Conrad's response to crises of legitimation, both his own as a writer and those of his adoptive society?

Perhaps the fact that Conrad's society is adoptive in the first place establishes the most critical similarity between the two writers: both are deracinated, rootless. The main difference is that whereas Flaubert's *déclassement* is almost a project, an expression of will or aspiration, Conrad's was quite literal and complete. Poland, though Conrad remained loyal to it, cannot but have been vivid to him chiefly as the place where he buried his parents; its presence and his ambivalent response to it bedevils him all his life. Along with prompting his escape, of course, the Polish experience gave Conrad an early taste of imperial domination, a fact that is seen as contributing to his own vexed reactions to British imperialism.[16] The exilic condition of the serious writer, spiritual for Flaubert, came to be embodied quite literally in Conrad. He gave voice to this estrangement in many ways, but a letter to Edward Garnett may sum it up best: "Other writers have some starting-point. Something to catch hold of. . . . They lean on dialect or tradition—or on history—or on the prejudice or fad of the hour; they trade upon some tie or some conviction of their time—or upon the absence of these things—which they can abuse or praise. But at any rate they know something to begin with—which I don't."[17]

With nothing "to begin with," Conrad relies on his ingenuity and skill, as seen in his preface to "The Nigger of the *Narcissus*," to build the literary work out of the void.[18] He was in his way as complete a devotee of technique as Flaubert. They differed in that, for Flaubert, technique was a way of severing the work from a time, a place, or a particular audience, while, for Conrad, it served more as a means of constructing an audience for the work. To continue the marketplace metaphor, Flaubert tended to view all society as corrupted by the exchange economy and so saw the bartering of stories in the same light, whereas Conrad nursed a belief in the ability of storytelling to induce a more organic, intimate connection between author and audience that would escape the ravages of the impersonal market. In fact, the figure of the storyteller serves as a kind of patriarchal—or perhaps what Richard Sennett would call a paternalistic—emblem: a reach back to an artisanal, precapitalist time and to an oral tradition.[19] In discussing this storyteller figure, then, I will also be exploring the further ramifications of Conrad's exilic state.

Like Flaubert's, Conrad's struggle for legitimacy entailed the larger legitimative struggles of his age, which thus affected the form or rhetorical status of his work, as well as the content. Many aspects of Conrad's situation were very distinct from Flaubert's. Conrad was an outsider attempting to forge ties to a new country's readership. Imperialism was a more insistent topic for Conrad for several reasons: It had further evolved by the turn of the century; Britain's identity as a state was more completely bound up with imperialism than was France's; and Conrad's own personal background made the terrain of empire a logical one to traverse. The ambivalent treatment of the French capitalist era we have already seen in Flaubert is not altogether dissimilar from the perspective we get on the imperial venture of turn-of-the-century Britain in Conrad. Both authors are equally sensitive to the lack of legitimate authority in their societies. For Conrad, however, the question of imperialism was complicated by several factors.

His own history as the citizen of a colonized country is one such factor. This has already been alluded to, though the full implications of this history have not yet been explored.[20] One can assume its effects were profound, not only in Conrad's well-documented and self-explanatory distaste for Russians—to which *The Secret Agent* and *Under Western Eyes* attest—but also in his witness of the infelicitous effects of imperial rule. His famous essay "Autocracy and War" makes clear his belief in the link between the nineteenth-century penchant for commerce, as it enters imperialist phase, and the distinct possibilities for war: "*Il n'y a plus d'Europe*—there is only an armed and trading continent, the home of slowly maturing economical contests for life and death and of loudly proclaimed world-wide ambitions."[21] (Note especially the wedding of arms and trade in this citation.) Conrad mistrusted the imposition of rule of one people over another in whatever benevolent form—and he seems to have thought the British more benevolent than most—it presented itself.[22]

Nevertheless, Conrad himself had served in the British merchant service; and he was aware, surely, of the fact that had it not been for the empire, he would not most likely have had that career. His affection for the merchant service is evident in his novels, stories, and essays.[23] As will be discussed in the analysis of *Lord Jim*, the ideology of the merchant marine was one of which Conrad could well be disposed to be protective. He did not relinquish his loyalty to this instrument of empire, even very late.

Furthermore, Conrad was a novelist in an adopted country, writing fiction that touched upon very sensitive matters for the middle-class British reading public. A case for self-censorship would be somewhat forced, because Conrad is on record against many of the excesses of imperialism.[24] Yet as indicated in chapter 1, the process of convincing others that one belongs is primarily a process of convincing oneself that one belongs; if Conrad did engage in self-censorship on this issue, as some argue, it is at a level below the conscious.

The most critical factors in assessing Conrad's mode of representing empire are those that are least narrowly biographical: the fact that he was a European addressing other Europeans, and the fact that, to recur to this chapter's beginning, Conrad's literary project was precariously situated between the potential popularity of the romance genre and the more exalted, but less tangible or certain, acclaim of discerning posterity.

In *The Political Unconscious*, Frederic Jameson pursues this intriguing problem of the romance in Conrad from the above optics, among others. He writes, for example, of Conrad's "strategy of containment," whereby potentially subversive resonances are managed by the work on behalf both of writer and reader. He mentions especially the role in *Lord Jim* of an emphasis on the problematics of the "individual act" as a kind of decoy: "Conrad pretends to tell us the story of an individual's struggle with his own fear and courage; but he knows very well that the real issues are elsewhere, in the social example Jim cannot but set, and the demoralizing effect of Jim's discovery of Sartrean freedom on the ideological myths that allow a governing class to function and to assert its unity and legitimacy."[25] This deflection of attention is occasioned by the complicity of author and reader in the imperial system and the consequent fear of contamination by a scandal of the sort Jim's story represents. Marlow is the emblem of this complicity and this fear.

The narrative strategy of *Nostromo*, also a tale told by a European for Europeans, works as well to contain the resonances of that novel. Jameson sees the containment in more strictly temporal, rather than geographical, terms: as a repression of history.[26] He roughly locates the dilemma of Sulaco, the tiny state forming itself in *Nostromo*, when he points to the dual character of capitalism: at once an agent of "the bringing of order," it is also "not a natural growth in countries like Sulaco."[27] The critical point here, though, is that through the silver mine, capitalism presents itself as "natural" and legitimate, since it partakes of Sulaco's material properties. A fuller exposition of the silver's role will show how Conrad's text at once undermines the capitalist idealism of Gould's project and, by default, also affirms its result—the repression of history. The agent of this repression, properly diagnosed, has to do with the relation of *Nostromo* and its (primarily European) readership to the subject of economic imperialism.

Along with the structural limitations of narratives concerning empire which are addressed to citizens of those imperial governments, one must also consider the major gap Conrad as an author had to leap: that "between two distinct cultural spaces, that of 'high' culture and that of mass culture."[28] All of the Conrad novels explored here in depth—*Lord Jim, Nostromo,* and *The Secret Agent*—reveal their own entanglement in this split of cultures, in ways hidden and overt, large and small. These texts seem constantly to wish at once to preserve the kind of purity that would justify them for the imaginary library, and to develop rapport with the audience for more popular, "genre" fiction.[29] *The Secret Agent,* in many ways, is the record of a realization that mass culture's popular novels and journalism are, finally, as remote from the face-to-face rapport of storyteller and audience as high culture's Flaubertian texts.

But such assertions await the examination of these texts to be confirmed. Now that this analysis has returned to its starting point, one can see in how many respects Conrad's discomfort with his writerly role resembles Flaubert's. Let us look more thoroughly at the way Conrad's nostalgia, and that of his texts, for an emblem of earlier paternalist roles, more organicist forms of validation with an audience, gives rise to a crucial figure in some of the early works: Charlie Marlow. I propose now to consider Marlow and other instruments of narrative in Conrad in more detail, confident that in moving nearer to his texts and their elements we are approaching, and not avoiding, the larger political ideologies those texts find and fashion.

In this accounting, writing is *active,* for it acts for the reader: it proceeds not from an author but from a *public scribe*, a notary institutionally responsible not for flattering his client's tastes but rather for registering at his dictation the summary of his interests, the operations by which, within an economy of disclosure, he manages this merchandise: the narrative.—Roland Barthes, *S/Z*

You, the listener, sit opposite me. But you are silent. You don't tell me anything.—Ford Madox Ford, *The Good Soldier*

7

The Kernel and the Enveloping Haze

Many of the conflicts in Gustave Flaubert's writings stem from his uneasy relationship with his readers: put simply, his work and his life suggest an overmastering desire to lose his likeliest audience. This compulsion leads him to a phobia of the cliché so severe that it seems on occasion to provoke an artistic impasse, where the attempt to communicate at all is doomed to banality. But there are also writers whose lifelong project and whose interest reside in part in the attempt to find or to found an audience. Joseph Conrad is primarily of the latter sort. If Flaubert tried to found any audience, it is the shadowy one of posterity; in that he has succeeded. On the other hand, Conrad found his exoticism quite ready-made when he faced his British reading public; it was rapport with them that he felt constrained to fashion.

Undoubtedly, desires pulled Conrad away from his readership, too. But in the main, his works—both novels and short stories—are those of a *dépaysé*, and a part of their rootless predicament is the nostalgia for a situation in which a more immediate communion between writer and public would be possible. Like his occasional correspondent, Henry James, Conrad attempted the stage (with what would seem the most ungainly of vehicles: a dramatic adaptation of his own *The Secret Agent*); and this above all should alert us to a certain desire on the part of Conrad to transform a readership into a real audience.

The rigor with which Conrad's texts confronts matters of political import, especially the colonial question, is not surprising when we consider that his own experience as part of a colonized people, when as an *émigré*, crystallized this problem in an acute form. His desire for an audience is a part of his desire to be legitimated—to be accepted by a readership to whom he was culturally and linguistically a newcomer. Coming from a country under the control of alien powers, writing in an adopted language with which he was never psychologically comfortable and which he maintained to his sometime collaborator Ford Madox Ford was really more suited to barking than to writing[1]—through all of this Conrad came to know the eerie exile, the statelessness that has come to characterize so many serious twentieth-century writers.[2] It infects both the manner and the matter of his fiction. His outposts of progress and his merchant vessels feature either societies adrift (as in the closed community in "The Nigger of the *Narcissus*" or "The Secret Sharer") or individuals adrift from society (for instance, Heyst in *Victory*, or Razumov in *Under Western Eyes*). The more conventional European-style nation-states he deals in are either forming a precarious identity out of the surrounding chaos, like *Nostromo's* Sulaco, or seemingly peopled almost exclusively by foreigners, like Britain herself in *The Secret Agent*, or Switzerland in *Under Western Eyes*. As for his choice of forms, Conrad could not have selected a mode of writing more suited to homelessness than the novel. Georg Lukács's famous formulation applies as pointedly to Conrad as to any major novelist when he dubs the novel "the form of transcendental homelessness."[3]

The result of what for Conrad is a quite concrete as well as a metaphysical homelessness is a particularly strong yearning to return to what Lukács considers the abandoned homeland of the novel: the epic and its oral tradition. The anguish that inscribes itself in so many of Conrad's works is the wish that they were telling a story, not forming a book. What often intrigues in Conrad's fiction is the way it attempts—with varying degrees of failure—to inscribe a readership in the tale itself, but as an audience, as a group hearing a story spoken. Through "reconstructuring" a story neither spoken nor heard, Conrad's fiction also, and paradoxically, works to inscribe the impossibility of that reconstruction. Much of the famous Conradian "gloom" can be accounted for by this impossibility: a novelist cannot be a storyteller.

The storyteller, then, is a figure who haunts the interstices of Conrad's text, and that imaginary figure is a stern reproach to its creator. But it remains to define the specific contours of this storyteller: to tell its story. Walter Benjamin, the German literary critic, has come as close as anyone to telling such a story, and what follows will put into play some of Benjamin's major insights from his essay entitled "The Storyteller," and will suggest how these insights enrich Conrad's own story—and stories.

At the outset of his essay, which he wrote between the two world wars, Benjamin makes clear that the storyteller figure "has already become something remote from us and something that is getting even more distant."[4] It is quickly evident that the role Benjamin constructs for his storyteller is not confined to the telling of stories but condenses a welter of functions of which storytelling is the leading manifestation.

This figure is invested with all the nostalgia of a reluctant participant in bourgeois culture for a remote emblem of preindustrial culture. The storyteller, and those writers closest to his spirit, emerge from an artisanal world, and their work is akin to craftsmanship rather than to the industrial technology that is father to the altogether different phenomena of newspapers and novels. Since the novel, in Benjamin's view, is distinguished from story and epic in "its essential dependence on the book," its dissemination was possible "only with the invention of printing" (p. 87). Storytelling remains a part of the oral tradition, however, and so this artisanal mode meant that the life of the storyteller was as significant as the story, and traces of that life "cling to the story in the way the handprints of the potter cling to the clay vessel" (p. 92). The story's receptors are not a fragmented readership but rather "the community of listeners," where each person "listens to the tales in such a way that the gift of retelling them comes to him all by itself" (p. 91). The folk art of storytelling, for this reason, implies an active role in producing the story, not simply the passive one of consuming it. The situation with the novel is rather different: "The reader of a novel . . . is isolated, more so than any other reader" (p. 100).[5]

The decreasing "communicability of experience," as the essay calls it, means that these fictions, in addition to lacking that living interaction between artist and audience that permitted "that slow piling one on top of the other of thin, transparent layers . . . of a variety of retellings" (p. 93), also become increasingly unable to perform another traditional function of the folktale: rendering counsel. The solitary individual who writes a novel "is no longer able to express himself by giving examples of his most important concerns, is himself uncounseled, and cannot counsel others" (p. 87). The same technological force that made mass readership of the novel possible has also hastened this devaluation of communicable experience: "Was it not noticeable at the end of the [First World] War that men returned from the battlefield grown silent— not richer, but poorer in communicable experience?" (p. 84). Not surprising, as Benjamin argues, since in that war "never has experience been contradicted more thoroughly than strategic experience by tactical warfare, economic experience by inflation, bodily experience by mechanical warfare, moral experience by those in power" (p. 84). The circumstances that have emerged in modern society seem to have made individual experience less important, or at least less reliable as a guide for others to follow. There is less room for the *sensus communis* (or "sense of the community"), and so less room for stories and the moral advice they carry in their train. "Counsel woven into the fabric of real life is wisdom. The art of storytelling is reaching its end because the epic side of truth, wisdom, is dying out" (pp. 86–87).

Much of Conrad's dilemma can be understood as the result of the situation evoked in Benjamin's essay. Condemned by temperament and his time to be a novelist, Conrad inscribes in his novels—in particular *Lord Jim* and *Nostromo*—the image of a precapitalist time when storytelling and its sturdy wisdom did not yet know novel-writing and its perplexities; when an evolving discourse heard and embellished by many people had not yielded place to a finished product, produced and consumed in isolation. If the communicability of experience and the face-to-face community that allowed storyteller and audience to change roles imply each other, then Conrad and his fellow novelists have suffered a compounded loss.

One possible strategy for recuperating this loss is to construct an imaginary storyteller, a figure who should serve in place of the storyteller the author himself cannot become. Charlie Marlow is precisely such a figure for the early Conrad. Marlow—despite the text's subtle way of putting distance between the true author and the narrative voice—shares many of Conrad's characteristics and, especially in the case of *Lord Jim*, many of his preoccupations as well. Benjamin describes two types of storyteller: the one "who has come from afar," and the one "who has stayed at home," conversant with "the local tales and traditions" (p. 84). Benjamin adds that if we wish to picture each group's "archaic representatives, one is embodied in the resident tiller of the soil, and the other in the trading seaman" (pp. 84–85). Just as the community of that bygone time combined "the lore of faraway places" with "the lore of the past," so Marlow, the merchant seaman who relates his stories to other merchant seamen, also combines the exotic tale with the stay-at-home concern for a tradition commonly held with his audience.

It can be argued that for Conrad, scion of landed gentry who went to sea but always tried to recapture a lost rootedness, Marlow was one way of preserving the possibility of converting the lore of faraway places to the uses of a sustained tradition. It is clear from *Lord Jim* that Marlow sees in Jim's tale an incident with many implications for the tradition of the merchant marine and its "fixed standard of conduct," and his telling of the tale to his community of listeners involves not only another story to add to the commonly held stock of sea yarns but also an approach to the possible counsel Jim's tale might have. This counsel is especially important for the merchant marine because, lacking common background apart from the task at hand, its fellowship is established only on the basis of the practical and ethical wisdom its members share. The dual social status that bedeviled Conrad, both of landed aristocrat and peripatetic seaman at once, was for a moment reconciled in the archaic figure of Marlow: a storyteller whose task it was to "bring home" whatever moral point of counsel he could from the remote tale of Jim—or of Kurtz in "Heart of Darkness" or the crew of "Youth"—to the listeners with whom he shared a community, however precarious. Marlow was arguably for Conrad much what Jim was for Marlow: a kind of alter ego, who would serve to crystallize the socially coded desires of the beholder. If, as Benjamin says, the storyteller is truly "the figure in which the righteous man encounters himself" (p. 109), then Conrad must have encountered himself, at least in his ideal aspects, in the figure of Marlow.

The need for a personal embodiment for the storytelling function is part of the longing for the personal relations thought to characterize preindustrial culture; and this longing applies to Conrad's characters, quite often, as well as to their author. Lord Jim gathers to himself the trappings of a feudal baron; Charles Gould is called *el rey de Sulaco* and does not object; and, of course, Kurtz sees his mission in consciously priestly terms. All these characters attempt to make themselves and their power legitimate by appeal to precapitalist social vocabularies. All of the "personalized" forms of authority have their most concentrated expression in the patriarch, the father figure whose injunction compels obedience. These patriarchs take various forms in Conrad's earlier fiction, and indeed survive through *Nostromo*—though, granted, figures like Giorgio Viola, Don José Avellanos and even Gould are patriarchs that leave much to be desired. Nonetheless, the felt need to personify, and so humanize, an impersonal and pitiless process, and to retrieve patriarchal authority to justify one's power, are imperatives for the early characters in Conrad, and so a major concern of the novels themselves.

If the storyteller is one of the patriarchal figures of this earlier social vocabulary, then his tale draws its authority from his exemplary life as well as from its internal force; and that implies that the survival of his story draws some of its power from his exemplary death as well: a strong awareness of death being the condition for the transmission of the storyteller's tale and his memory, as well as the perpetual subject of the stories themselves. Benjamin points out the way the art of storytelling has declined as the consciousness of death has declined. Whereas in centuries past dying was "a public process in the life of the individual and a most exemplary one," in modern society "dying has been pushed further and further out of the perceptual world of the living" (pp. 93–94). The fact of death makes it imperative for the living to perpetuate the memory and the wisdom of the one who has died, so that they can "absorb the course of events on the one hand and, with the passing of these, make . . . peace with the power of death on the other" (p. 97). Surely this is a strong impulse behind Marlow's fascination with the story of Jim, or his self-admitted "obsession" with Kurtz in "Heart of

Darkness.''[6] Marlow, after all, is a good traditionalist, and is anxious to hand down what wisdom or memory can be preserved from his subjects, even if this wisdom is of a melancholy sort. Kurtz's ability, in his last moments, to formulate the essence of his life—"The horror!"—is admired by Marlow despite the very depravity that has made the formulation a true one.[7] Jim's last words, "Nothing can touch me," and the proud, scornful look he gives his executioners are carefully recorded by Marlow as well (even if at second hand). These climactic moments in Marlow's narratives verbally enact the drama of the deathbed. Kurtz's grim self-knowledge and Jim's superb "egotism" at the last recall a totemic scene where, in the presence of one who is dying, "suddenly in his expressions and looks the unforgettable emerges and imparts to everything that concerned him that authority which even the poorest wretch in dying possesses for the living around him" (p. 94).

The novel does preserve this memorial function of the tale, or what Benjamin terms "epic remembrance"; but it asks remembrance to perform much more heroic labors. For any given character in a typical novel, "the 'meaning' of his life is revealed only in his death. But the reader of a novel actually does look for human beings from whom he derives the 'meaning of life'" (pp. 100–101). The need to read life's meaning in the characters of a novel, or in a fate that is "graven" in the narrative's "rock" as Marlow says Jim's destiny is graven—this need is at least as crucial to the reading of Conrad as to any other novelist. Whether they involve the death of Jim or of Kurtz, of Decoud, or of Nostromo, or of the idiot boy Stevie in *The Secret Agent*, the narratives invite the reader to interpret life's riddle in the fates of the characters, as if those characters' lives, taken as a whole and memorialized, might somehow give the reader a glimpse of his or her own destiny. Benjamin concludes: "The novel is significant, therefore, not because it presents someone else's fate to us, perhaps didactically, but because this stranger's fate by virtue of the flame which consumes it yields us the warmth which we never draw from our own fate" (p. 101). Perhaps like the solitary man who receives from Marlow the letter narrating Jim's downfall, the reader of the novel nurses what Benjamin calls "the hope of warming his shivering life with a death he reads about" (p. 101).

Yet, though the reader may be warmed vampiristically by this novelistic death, he or she is ambiguously enlightened by it. The paradox is that the socially accepted modes of reading the world—those grids of meaning on which folktale could plot its counsel and high allegory could map its implied meanings—have eroded, placing more strain on one sustained narrative to yield meaning at the same time as it makes the transmissibility of that meaning more difficult. (The fact that the novelistic narrative is no longer something that the reader helps in any way directly to produce can only augment the strain.) Again, Benjamin: "The 'meaning of life' is really the center about which the novel moves. But the quest for it is no more than the initial expression of perplexity with which its reader sees himself living this written life" (p. 99). In Marlow, we see a storyteller who points to that very perplexity as he narrates the fate of Jim. As Ian Watt puts it: "The way Conrad uses Marlow is peculiarly adapted to showing the individual engaged in trying to understand what has happened to him."[8] Beyond that, one may even see in Marlow someone who occasionally hides behind perplexity in the face of some less than comfortable implications of his subject's fate. (Ironically, Marlow may become as much a buffer against meaning in this novel as he is an instrument for transmitting meaning.) Terry Eagleton takes up the point of the perplexing center that is Conrad's meaning, and says this:

> At the centre of each of Conrad's works is a resonant silence: the unfathomable enigma of Kurtz, Jim and Nostromo, the dark, brooding passivity of James Wait in *The Nigger of the Narcissus*, the stolid opacity of McWhirr in *Typhoon*, the eternal crypticness of the "Russian soul" in *Under Western Eyes*, the unseen bomb-explosion and mystical silence of the idiot Stevie in *The Secret Agent*, Heyst's nonexistent treasure in *Victory*. These absences are determinate—they demarcate the gaps and limits of the Conradian ideology, represent the "hollows" scooped out by a collision or exclusion of meanings.[9]

Leaving aside for the moment its accuracy in each detail, one can still adjudge the general characterization as accurate and intriguing. Like Kurtz's enigmatic eloquence, Conrad's texts, filled with variety and impressive in impact, often give the aftereffect of being resonantly "hollow at the core."[10] In "Heart of Darkness" the tales of Marlow are even praised for lacking a center, or counsel: "The yarns of seamen have a direct simplicity, the whole meaning of which lies within the shell of a cracked nut. But Marlow was not typical . . . and to him the meaning of an episode was not inside like a kernel but outside, enveloping the tale which brought it out only as a glow brings out a haze."[11]

What Conrad goes on to call the "spectral illumination" of that haze really results from the perplexity of both storyteller and audience at living the life they are presented; and though they pursue the meaning of that life, the futile project only illuminates a central haze. Other storytellers' yarns have morals, or kernels of wisdom. But Marlow is atypical, for along with the more down-to-earth role the storyteller must play, he has been given a further, more novelistic task: to evoke this larger meaning of life and our perplexity in the face of it. The tension between these two facets of Marlow is a powerful force behind the discontinuities of plot and theme that merit exploration in, say, *Lord Jim*. The "resonant silence" issues from the collision of a meticulously detailed narrative with its own frustration at not getting to the "point" of it all; and Marlow's (or Conrad's) struggle with this tension is an especially acute variant of what, for Benjamin, is a generic conflict within the novel in general.

It is paradoxical that the same fragmentation of social space that produces this obscurity of meaning in the novel also enforces on the novel the need to justify its narrative in ways the older folktale form did not have to consider. Because the storyteller's persona was enough to give the tale authority, the tale, which was in any event often presumed to be based on a concrete incident, needed no test of plausibility. Verisimilitude—that obsession of the realistic novel, and above all of the post-Flaubertian novel of the sort that Conrad was writing—was not the storyteller's concern. His stock-in-trade was the legend, which mixes factual chronicle thoroughly with myth. Because the spoken tale drew its power from the teller and the weight of accumulated wisdom he was thought to embody, the need for a verifiable story was unknown, or anyhow unimportant, to the storyteller's audience: an audience less concerned with inner narrative coherence or plausible psychology than the tale's usefulness as wisdom or practical counsel:

> The intelligence that came from afar—whether the spatial kind from foreign countries or the temporal kind of tradition—possessed an authority which gave it validity, even when it was not subject to verification. Information, however, lays claim to prompt verifiability. The prime requirement is that it appear "understandable in itself." Often it is no more exact than the intelligence of earlier centuries was. But while the latter was inclined to borrow from the miraculous, it is indispensable for information to sound plausible. (P. 89)

The same bourgeois readership and print technology that made the novel possible have also given rise to the newspaper, that organ of the "information" that Benjamin sees as detrimental to storytelling. As the folk legend, suspended between fact and fiction, soon splits into fact (found in newspapers) versus fiction (found, for instance, in novels), both are given a more onerous burden of plausibility to sustain. Shared cultural myth has provided a metaphorical network of assumptions insuring that the folktale was "not concerned with an accurate concatenation of definite events, but with the way these are embedded in the great inscrutable course of the world" (p. 96), as imagined by the commonly held myths of the community. The lack of a strong metaphorical grid by which to take an audience through a story means that the "concatenation of events" must alone take the reader through, by the coherence and force of its own inner necessity.[12] The novel may purport to be fiction, the newspaper, fact; but both rely on metonymic force—that is, on plausibility and causal arrangement of events—much more heavily than their common predecessor, the folk legend, ever did.

From this situation, it is not surprising that so many novelists have told us—indeed, were eager to tell us—the source of their inspiration in newspaper accounts. Conrad is no different; indeed, *Lord Jim*, *Nostromo*, and *The Secret Agent* (this last by Conrad's own insistence in his preface to that work) have their origins in accounts of the day.[13] In a way these nuggets, these kernels of information, are the most deceitful of all, since the truth is more in the glowing haze Conrad weaves around them. But it can still be said no less of Conrad than of any other novelist that his truest Muse was frequently the newspaper.

This need for authenticity works powerfully against the attempt to present emblematic characters through which the "meaning of life" can be read. *Lord Jim* promises to be an exemplum, a tale of clear moral choice with counsel for its listeners. But its own inner logic makes the outlines of that moral, and indeed of its hero, harder to perceive, until Marlow must finally admit his own perplexity. (*Finally* is perhaps a deceptive word here: Marlow admits his befuddlement all the way through.) If the story has a moral—if Jim's written life has any "meaning"—Marlow does not himself identify it. This search for the meaning of the protagonist's life is a vestige of the epic need for a moral, and Marlow's failure to deliver here is the disappointment of a clearly inscribed expectation. Jim remains, for both Marlow and the reader, "under a cloud" to the end.

Nostromo, by contrast, creates a much richer materialistic canvas—it is positively awash in verisimilitude—and splits its narrative focus among three "heroes": Charles Gould, Martin Decoud, and Nostromo himself. Furthermore, if there is a bearer of the story's "moral" in *Nostromo*, it is the legend of the *gringos* on the Azuera peninsula. But though it is introduced almost at the outset of the novel and recurs throughout thereafter, the tale remains eccentric to the unfolding narrative, a clue to its meaning perhaps, but perhaps even more an ironic counterpoint to that meaning. The *gringos* who, in searching for buried treasure in the Latin American region of Costaguana, become stranded there continue to haunt the peninsula where they disappeared. But the wise counsel of this cautionary tale is ignored by the characters who form Costaguana into the state of Sulaco—with results similar to those described in the legend. The fact that Marlow's successor as resident storyteller for Sulaco is Captain Mitchell, whose only hallmark is garrulous fatuity, confirms the marginal status of folktale in this work as opposed to *Lord Jim*. The one epic legend in *Nostromo* has wisdom but no audience prepared to receive it, while the one storyteller figure in the book has plenty of audiences but no wisdom to dispense.

By the time *The Secret Agent* is written, the folk legend, the storyteller, and the rest of the oral tradition have yielded pride of place to the newspaper. Whereas *Lord Jim* gives us a storyteller figure in full regalia and *Nostromo* offers at least a parody of the storyteller and folktale, *The Secret Agent*'s obsession is centered on the form that has largely displaced the earlier wisdom: information. Here the mode of narration has shed all the preindustrial vestiges to which the earlier novels cling. The newspaper—read silently in isolated quarters by separate readers, substituting factual data and plausibility for epic wisdom, surveying a world without heroes and stories without morals—is if anything too accurate a figure for the novel, and above all for that particular novel, where the very sources of traditional authority seem to stand bereft of legitimacy.[14]

The Secret Agent stands bereft of storytellers. We are very close here to the situation Benjamin tellingly describes: "Every morning brings us the news of the globe, and yet we are poor in noteworthy stories" (p. 89). The disappearance of stories parallels that of fathers, of patriarchs. The one "father" in the book is really a surrogate father, and that is Verloc, whose negligence kills his ward Stevie. In its bitter view of contemporary society, *The Secret Agent* is unlike the other two novels in having no compensatory nostalgia for precapitalist sources of legitimacy for that society. The possibility of finding or founding a genuine audience becomes ever more remote. Information is seldom more abundant, or experience less communicable, than in this novel.

Yet, it has been that very nostalgia for older sources of legitimacy that motivates Benjamin's vision of the storyteller. His pessimistic view of the world of his day is clear, despite disclaimers that even though the oral tradition has been dying out for some time, "nothing would be more fatuous than to want to see in [this process] merely a 'symptom of decay,' let alone a 'modern' symptom" (p. 87). Whatever the qualifiers, the storyteller is certainly a creation of Benjamin's desire, a gesture that looks toward the past to supply what the present conspicuously lacks. Benjamin admits as much at the very beginning of the essay in a startling image: "Viewed from a certain distance, the great, simple outlines which define the storyteller stand out in him [in this instance, "him" is apparently Nikolai Leskov], or rather, they become visible in him, just as in a rock a human head or an animal's body may appear to an observer at the proper distance and angle of vision" (p. 83). The simile, as is so often the case, says more than the thing it illustrates. The storyteller figure, for all the historical density given him, is also a creation of Benjamin's fancy, a chimera like that of a human head in a

rock viewed "at the proper . . . angle of vision." Thus, in addition to
the very real historical figures of Leskov, Stevenson, or Poe, the essay
has also to do with the imaginary but no less compelling figure of the
storyteller, whose marvelous incarnation comprises "not only his own
experience but no little of the experience of others" and whose devotion
to craft was such that he "could let the wick of his life be consumed
completely by the gentle flame of his story" (pp. 108–9). If the storyteller is Benjamin's fiction, then "The Storyteller" is the "meaning of
the storyteller's life," in all its complexity; and of course Benjamin is
then the storyteller's storyteller. In a sense, the storyteller is as much a
creature of imagination as is Marlow.

But if Benjamin chooses to become the storyteller of the storyteller,
Conrad chooses eventually to abandon that role, in spite of occasional
returns to it (such as Marlow's resurrection in *Chance*). In the main, it
would seem that Marlow and the artisanal world of simplicity he represents recede ever further from view. In asking why this is so, the most
convenient answer is perhaps the simplest: that the logic of the problematic Conrad's texts pursue makes the inability to resuscitate the storyteller increasingly apparent. Seen this way, the middle-period novels tell
the story of an increasing recognition, however reluctant, that the figure
of the storyteller belongs to a decisively former era, one which can be
reflected upon in melancholy nostalgia but which cannot be revived.
This well may be true, but Benjamin acknowledges the same situation
while still seeing the storyteller as the fit object of nostalgia. The gradual
disappearance of the storyteller from Conrad's text, therefore, has to do
with the impossibility of reviving him and also with the question as to
whether his world would be worth reviving in the first place.

For the legitimacy of the storyteller as a model for narration relies on
the legitimacy of the preindustrial order; Conrad is very concerned with
this order in "Heart of Darkness," *Lord Jim*, and *Nostromo*, both as
critique of the dominant capitalist model and as alibi for it. But in *The
Secret Agent*, this precapitalist order is not only contaminated by capitalism; it is, primarily, the contaminant. The ability of the ruling group to
discipline and even to annihilate a subject group—an ability that is
crystallized in the absolutist state's power of death over an individual—
is the hideous reality that is covered over (without success) in the world
of *The Secret Agent*. As with the storyteller, there is a profound cleavage
between the bourgeois approach to these realities and that of its predecessors. The ability to face death as a community, which Benjamin
celebrates in his essay, was also the ability and the willingness to view
the spectacle of public execution by the state. (In bourgeois society, as
the example of Winnie Verloc would suggest, it is read about privately
in newspapers.) As so much of the subject of *The Secret Agent* is the

plenary power of the state, the novel shows that this power antedates the rise of the bourgeoisie, even if it comes to take on a bourgeois configuration. Now not Eden but the fall therefrom, the archaic order—the *ancien régime*—has ceased largely to be the object of Conradian nostalgia, and along with it goes the storyteller whose attractiveness depends upon the moral legitimacy of that archaic time.

And that legitimacy fades, because the possibility of reviving it recedes and also because the communitarian vision it seemed to embody has been compromised at its very heart, by the absolute power of the monarch and the founding violence of the state. The kindly, patriarchal figure of the storyteller, in which "the righteous man confronts himself," has met the figure of the monarch, an authority whose power derives as much from force as from love, and whose aspect inspires not nostalgia but fear. Both are products of an earlier time who survive in altered form in industrial society; and their histories are so delicately interwoven that it is difficult to endorse the figure of the storyteller without calling forth, as his sinister double, the figure of the despot.

8

---◆---

Paragon and Enigma:
The Hero in *Lord Jim*

Charlie Marlow is a curious blend of storyteller and embryonic novelist. He combines the desire for clear moral counsel and straightforward narrative with bafflement in the face of a narrative and moral
frame that are anything but straightforward or clear. It will soon be
plain that in the case of *Lord Jim*, which of course he narrates, this
bafflement is often strategic: the story may have counsel neither
Marlow nor his audience/readership would wish to heed.

For the moment, it can be said that this odd mix of clarity and
obscurity characterizes nothing of Marlow's more aptly than his vision
of the figure of Jim. Indeed, the gap between Jim's vivid persona and
what if anything may be behind it forms a major reason for Marlow's
almost morbid preoccupation with Jim's case. In one famous passage,
for instance, Marlow relates to his colleagues his impression of Jim from
their dinner at the Malabar House, where they have their lengthy
conversation about the *Patna* incident. All that time, says Marlow, "I
had before me these blue, boyish eyes . . . this young face, these capable shoulders, the open bronzed forehead . . . this appearance appealing at sight to all my sympathies: this frank aspect, the artless smile, the
youthful seriousness. He was of the right sort; he was one of us."[1] This
description of Jim forms a vision of surface, and one which emphasizes
"appearance" in all its "frank aspect" and ingenuous simplicity. But it
is also an evocation of ineffable depths, as the following lines suggest:
"He talked soberly, with a sort of composed unreserve, and with a quiet
bearing that might have been the outcome of manly self-control, of
impudence, of callousness, of a colossal unconsciousness, of a gigantic
deception. Who can tell!" (p. 78).

The immediate appeal of Jim to "all [Marlow's] sympathies" is thus
marked by a profound ambiguity, a sense of depth sinister and beyond
reach. In fact, this fatal ambiguity may be the richest source of

Marlow's dread fascination with Jim. The way in which this ambiguity situates itself in the narrative and the means by which the ambiguity produces the resonance of Jim for Marlow and the reader both arise as issues in this vision of Jim—issues that prompt us at the outset to consider the basis of Jim's appeal to Marlow's sympathies. What can it mean to be "one of us"?

For Marlow's description inscribes a vision not only of Jim but also of a community in which he is placed. What can "one of us" refer to, though? One could read the phrase as meaning that Jim is a kind of Everyman, part of the human community or the great family of man. While this reading may not be contradicted by the narrative, it would probably be more useful to start with a more specific reading of the phrase. After all, when the reader is told that Jim has blue eyes, capable shoulders, and fair hair (also mentioned by Marlow), and that he is "of the right sort," the social and racial determinants are clear. One sees that much of Marlow's concern for Jim's case is rooted in an identification with Jim's social and professional role as a member of the British merchant marine and, more broadly, as a representative of British colonialism.[2]

Marlow's commitment to the code of the merchant marine was, incidentally, shared by his author, who as late as 1918 stoutly defended his old profession at great length against the casual remark of an obscure British M.P.[3] Marlow's desire to retain a belief in the efficacy of the merchant marine code must be understood, because it is responsible for much of the story's impact. Furthermore, the audience for most of Marlow's yarn is no anonymous gathering; they are members of the merchant service as well. Jim's "failure of nerve" must be of especially acute interest to this audience because it is invested in the code that Jim seems to represent so well out serves so poorly at the crucial point.

The contradictions of this code imply the larger question of the British Empire itself, but that problem—a problem of legitimation—is at first muted, crepuscular. Surely nobody knows better than Conrad that the smaller and the larger questions are of a piece. These connections will become clear as the narrative weaves them, but their strands will entrap Jim from the very start, despite his belief in his own isolation.

It is ironic, in a sense, that Marlow envisions this role for Jim in the first place (that of bearer of merchant marine values), since Jim considers himself totally set apart from the rest of the crew of the *Patna*, the ship to which he is assigned. Schooled in light holiday literature, Jim joins the merchant marine because he "saw himself" as "always an example of devotion to duty, and as unflinching as a hero in a book" (p. 6). In addition to this slight case of *bovarism*, Jim is isolated from the crew as well by a certain contempt and a distaste for associating with them, such as in an argument between crew members in which Jim takes no part, continuing only to smile "at the retreating horizon; his heart was full of generous impulses, and his thought was contemplating his own superiority" (p. 23). Jim is consistently presented as one who is studiedly ignorant of the conditions in which he works. He is ignorant finally on two counts: that of his own dependency on the other crew members and the necessity of working with them; and that of his complicity in the larger British commercial trading network that uses the service of the merchant marine to ship its goods.[4] Jim's ignorance is not simply incomplete understanding: it is a necessity of survival, and his self-deception, like the self-deception of Marlow, is the fate of good men attempting to keep faith with a dubious cause.

Yet, Marlow takes the very circumstances of Jim's isolation from the actual community of mariners and places him at the center of an ideal or virtual community of mariners; and this validation is based, interestingly enough, not on what Jim actually does, but rather on his aspect or image. The appeal is always to Jim's physical appearance, as though this in itself provided the evidence of superiority. Jim sees himself in splendid isolation, whereas Marlow places Jim in the center of the mariners' tradition. However contradictory of each other, both visions are equally deluded, at least on the evidence of the *Patna* incident itself. At the crucial moment, Jim joins the crew whose membership he sought to shun (and who are not at all eager to have him, either). Since he was paralyzed by his disdain for his crew and his unavoidable complicity with them, "he had preserved through it all a strange illusion of passiveness, as though he had not acted but had suffered himself to be handled by the infernal powers" (p. 108). It is Jim's inability to recognize his own complicity with the other crew members—even after his jump—that renders him incapable in turn of understanding his action as an action. He experiences it—or at least speaks of it to Marlow—as something thrust upon him. "I had jumped . . . it seems" (p. 111).

The question thrown into the starkest relief by Jim's actions involves the bedrock of values that the merchant marine code of conduct is supposed to be. Marlow speaks of "those struggles of an individual trying to save from the fire his idea of what his moral identity should be, this precious notion of a convention, only one of the rules of the game, nothing more, but all the same so terribly effective by its assumption of unlimited power over natural instincts" (p. 81). If Jim, who represents for Marlow the highest aspirations of that virtual community of the merchant marine, can join the actual community of the *Patna* crew who desert their ship, then what of any attempt to see the marine as based on codes of conduct deeper than expedience or pecuniary motive? The fact that the merchant marine derives its functions from the larger pursuit of empire does not suffice to justify its existence; it only increases the ambiguity of its status. It is worth noting that the above citation can refer equally to Jim and to the narrator Marlow; for if Jim fails to perform according to the code of conduct, who is to say that this failure might not be contagious?

The code of conduct assumes for Marlow's narrative a kind of talismanic function, as a way of fending off the contamination of moral failure or paralysis of will. The character in the early part of the novel who serves as the cautionary figure for Marlow and his listeners in this respect is Montague Brierly, of whom Marlow says: "He had never in his life made a mistake, never had an accident, never a mishap, never a check in his steady rise, and he seemed to be one of those lucky fellows who know nothing of indecision, much less of self-mistrust" (p. 57). The implacable Brierly is compared to a rock whom the sting of life would only scratch like a pin, and his "self-satisfaction [at the inquiry into the *Patna* incident] presented to me and to the world a surface as hard as granite." (Marlow adds laconically, "he committed suicide very soon after" [p. 58].)

As he proceeds to discuss Brierly, Marlow presents the contamination more explicitly by saying that, while he was examining Jim, "he was probably holding silent inquiry into his own case," and that he must have found himself guilty because "he took the secret of the evidence with him in that leap into the sea" (p. 58). When Brierly, during the trial, denounces the publicity and asks Marlow "Why are we tormenting that young chap?" and "Why eat all that dirt?" the latter surmises that "at bottom poor Brierly must have been thinking of himself" (p. 66).

In Brierly's view, it is all a question of professional trust and confidence:

> "We are trusted. Do you understand?—trusted! Frankly, I don't care a snap for all the pilgrims that ever came out of Asia, but a decent man would not have behaved like this to a full cargo of old rags in bales. We aren't an organized body of men, and the only thing that holds us together is just the name for that kind of decency. Such an affair destroys one's confidence." (P. 68)

Even in the course of defending his "decency," Brierly reveals much of the reason why it fared so poorly on the *Patna*: the merchant marine and the traders it serves make little distinction between the people they transport and a cargo of "old rags in bales." Brierly's hope is to give Jim two hundred rupees to clear out of town; in proposing this, though, he reveals his own susceptibility to the cowardice Jim has shown in jumping ship in the first place. Clearly, he has reason to fear for his confidence.

Brierly's suicide enacts a sinister inverted parody of Jim's abandon-

ment of the *Patna*; only his peculiar retreat is from internal guilt rather
than external circumstance. His mate recalls that "four iron belaying-
pins were missing round the mainmast. Put them in his pockets to help
him down, I suppose. . . . Maybe his confidence was just shook a bit at
the last" (p. 61). The small narrative of Brierly and his demise is a
warning exemplum, presenting the danger of contamination that Jim's
story contains. This danger, unspoken by Marlow, haunts his narrative
nonetheless. For if the man whose role is that of exemplary model for
gentlemen seamen deserts his ship and the code of the sea, surely this
suggests a vacuum into which more and more seamen will be drawn,
like the "everlasting deep hole" Jim falls into when he jumps—a vacuum the more fearful because it seems to figure an inner emptiness (p.
111). Whether Marlow's narrative is a remedy for the disease or itself a
poison depends in part on whether Jim's failure of nerve is unique to
himself, susceptible of explanation only in metaphysical or psychological terms, or whether his story is synecdochic for an already existent, if
latent, epidemic. Marlow's own obsession with Jim's case suggests the
latter explanation; yet the rhetoric of Marlow's tale suggests the former.
The dissonance between these two views of Jim will persist as we pro-
ceed, for this tension is crucial to the narrative. What seems to implicate
Marlow's audience in Jim's behavior is constantly changed into inscrutable fate or caprice of individual temperament. But could Jim's fate be
inscribed in the conflicts of his position in the social and material world
of his seaman's trade? If that is the case, his story indeed becomes a
cautionary tale to Marlow's mariner audience.

The code of conduct to which Marlow and Jim both have recourse is
essentially aristocratic in origin; the seamanship invoked implies a military model that is preindustrial. Yet the function of the merchant marine at this time was very much a part of industrial society: to ship men
and goods from port to port. The pilgrims on the *Patna* are human cargo
to the British crew; the notion of "stewardship" and the solidarity of
crew with vessel it invokes are inappropriate for these conditions. The
split between the pilgrims and their stewards is also racially coded, and
this racial connotation to the incident deepens the conflict and the
subsequent shame of Jim's actions in joining the crew. Albert Guerard
focuses this problematic in treating the "Malay helmsman" Conrad
fleetingly alludes to in the course of the *Patna* narrative:

> "The two Malays had meantime remained holding to the wheel"—
> only thoughtless, immobile figures, not even part of our moral universe.
> . . . [But our attention is directed by the information that the ship didn't
> sink.]
> We then move away from the *Patna* to the inquiry, where the two

helmsmen were questioned, as for relief. . . . The first helmsman, when asked what he thought of matters at the time, says he thought nothing. The second "explained that he had a knowledge of some evil befalling the ship, but there had been no order; . . . why should he leave the helm?"

Marlow refers to the helmsman rightly as an "extraordinary and damning witness."[5]

Guerard is correct to stress the significance of these Malay helmsmen in the drama of the *Patna*, not only because their heroism throws Jim's protestations of heroism into unpleasant contrast but also because their race emphasizes the cultural identity of those who abandoned the *Patna*, as opposed to those abandoned. It is their dual function, as victims of the *Patna* incident and as the sole adherents to the code of the sea, which redoubles the indictment of Jim and the crew and contributes mightily to Jim's shame.

This failure of stewardship and the accompanying shame set in motion the search for rehabilitation. The result is the second major story of the text, involving the island of Patusan. Patusan becomes for Jim the place of atonement, the arena where high intentions can be transmuted into action rather than, as in the *Patna* case, alibis for action. In that connection, it is worthwhile to note that the "artistic necessity" of the Patusan episode is a part of its thematic interest for this question of good intentions. If, as some have contended, *Lord Jim* is a short story that overstayed its welcome, then that claim rests in some measure on the belief that the second major narrative development—Jim's attempt to establish a separate community in Patusan—says nothing new, that it is simply a matter of Jim's trying and failing once again. To deal with that objection, it is well to examine the thematic connotations of the Patusan section and to suggest ways in which it complicates and enriches those of the *Patna* section.

That there is a relationship between the merchant marine and the larger economic thrust of empire is clear; yet this relationship is not immediately germane to the incidents related in that first story but subsists only as a haze around the narrative's glow (to borrow Marlow's famous metaphor in "Heart of Darkness" yet again). One can argue many of the implications of the *Patna* incident without engaging those matters, and critics have generally done so. This becomes more difficult in the Patusan chapters, as the resonances widen in concentric fashion to embrace the larger complex of the British project of empire and the "white man's burden" ideology of stewardship for which Jim is such a splendid figure. For at issue in *Lord Jim* is the legitimation of empire: not legitimacy, which is more in the nature of a *donné*, or established fact, but legitimation, which is the process of establishing that fact. The Patusan narrative makes explicit the problems of legitimation that were only implicit in the *Patna* affair; for now the matter of governance is foregrounded in the logic of the narrative itself, in the second chance Jim is offered.

It is part of Jim's desire to do right by the indigenous people as a compensation for his failure of stewardship. This opportunity is granted him when Stein, a merchant friend of Marlow's, assigns him to his trading post in Patusan; it seems at the time a way of gaining back the honor lost on the *Patna*. At the same time, of course, Jim does go into Patusan as heedless of the nature of the colonial project that engages him as he was on the deck of the *Patna*.

No doubt the Jim of the Patusan chapters is a more active soul than the Jim of the *Patna*, but the illusory relation of actor to deed still operates—arguably, to even more deadly effect. Jim still views his deeds as self-generated, uncontaminated by an outside. Just as the absolute split of inner and outer allowed Jim to treat his jump as if he really had nothing finally to do with it, so it now allows him to attribute his temporary success in Patusan to his own high-minded activity, and that alone. More than once, Marlow notes the obverse side of this coin in the form of Jim's unwitting reliance on the community of Patusan for his own validation. He points out that "all these things that made him master had made him a captive, too. He looked with an owner's eye at the peace of the evening, at the river, at the houses, at the everlasting life of the forests, at the life of the old mankind, at the secrets of the land, at the pride of his own heart: but it was they that possessed him" (pp. 247–48). The very way in which the pride of Jim's own heart is catalogued here on the same footing with the particulars of Patusan's history and geography demonstrates how thoroughly Patusan becomes for Jim a specular space, whose image entraps him as Narcissus was entrapped in his own reflection. It is not only the land itself that possesses Jim in this remark of Marlow's, it is also the pride of Jim's own heart.

But his reliance on this space for his self-definition is not a relation he has consciously appropriated. Perhaps this is at the base of the paradoxical "contemptuous tenderness" that Marlow sees in Jim's entire attitude toward Patusan. The contempt is Jim's response to the local people, who needed an outside force to bring order into their chaos; the tenderness an unacknowledged but firm dependence on Patusan as the reflection of his own handiwork—indeed, of his very soul. When Dain Waris is described, this bond of specularity is again evoked: "If Jim took the lead, the other [Dain Waris] had captivated his leader. In fact, Jim the leader was a captive in every sense. The land, the people, the friendship, the love, were like the jealous guardians of his body. Every day added a link to the fetters of that strange freedom" (p. 262). That

Dain Waris's "function" has been filled by Jim as his double and that this situation further fetters Jim becomes obvious by the conclusion of the novel.

Unlike the situation on board the *Patna*, it is evident that here Jim's obsession with self has by no means paralyzed him to act. To the contrary, in subduing Tunku Allang and in keeping him at bay, Jim displays much courage. It is not in action or inaction per se, but rather in the fantasized relation of self to action that the ideological moment resides; and this relation continues to hold sway, even though Jim seems at first to do quite a bit of good in Patusan. The lack of a conscious grasp of the social conditions of his actions in Patusan leads Jim to seek isolated realms where his powers can be fully realized and reflected in the arena of action, with no external contaminants. Royal Roussel has put the matter this way:

> Patusan is a world where Jim's "word was the one truth of every passing day" . . . and associated as it is with his voice, Jim's control suggests the absolute power the consciousness of the artist exercises over the world he has brought into existence. Yet because this power results from the fact that this world . . . is self-contained, a world apart from the life of men, the creation of such a world inevitably involves the limitation of the consciousness of the artist. His power is only good in this fixed area.[6]

In addition, Jim's failure fully to realize his power in the fixed setting of Patusan arises less from his imprisonment in his own handiwork than it does from his inability to accept that Patusan never was his handiwork in the first place; it was already "contaminated" by an outside, just as Jim's actions are in turn already contaminated by the imperial apparatus that calls them into existence.

This contamination of Jim's world, or rather this preexistent situation that only seems a contaminant, goes to the heart of the legitimation question. Avrom Fleishman has argued in *Conrad's Politics* that Conrad was in most essentials the inheritor of a nineteenth-century English organicist tradition of political thought, in which the indigenous state is "the ultimate political norm and is conceived . . . as a *nation*, the community of people bound together by organic ties derived from their historical tradition and sense of place, their continuity in time and space."[7] The terms of the organicist model tend to meld together familial and political modes, so that political legitimacy comes to resemble (sometimes more than metaphorically) that of a son to a father. In his reign at Patusan, then, Jim is caught between two lines of filiation, from both of which he attempts to draw legitimacy.

In the first place, he partakes of a line of merchant-traders which extends back from the Portuguese Cornelius, through the Bavarian Stein, to the Scotsman M'Neil. It is Cornelius whom Jim at once displaces and represents in the Patusan trading post. In the second place, he rules Patusan as the displacing representative of Dain Waris, who is the blood-son of Doramin. Jim is therefore caught between two systems of authority: the Patusan system, which is based on a straight-forward blood tie, and the European system, which is based on a chance concatenation of interests (and nationalities) and which only parodies an organic line of filiation. Jim's uneasy position, lodged as it is be-tween these two loyalties, prepares the way for his fall.

To clarify what the first line of filiation really signifies one must also ask what these landless European interests are. The fact that Jim is described as building a fort with the labor of ex-slaves, planning his coffee plantation, and obtaining a monopoly on the gunpowder in Patu-san indicates it clearly enough. These are commercial interests. Con-rad's exposition of the connection between colonial expansion and pe-cuniary motive is consistent, running from "Heart of Darkness" through *Nostromo* to *Victory*. This commercial skein is also woven in *Lord Jim*, but in a peculiar way: as something to be defined, ignored, willed out of existence. This tale is Marlow's to tell, and his tendency (as much as Jim's) is to find reasons for empire which are noble and good. Just as the audience for Marlow's after-dinner story was significant for the narrative, so the addressee for the bundle of letters which tells the last part of the story provides a clue to its implications. Marlow writes to this man:

> You said . . . that "giving your life up to them" (*them* meaning all of mankind with skins brown, yellow, or black in colour) "was like selling your soul to a brute." You contended that "that kind of thing" was only endurable and enduring when based on a firm conviction in the truth of ideas racially our own, in whose name are established the order, the morality of an ethical progress. (P. 339)

To Marlow's correspondent, it is not love of gain but contact with the savages that makes colonialism shameful; still, Marlow agrees with his essential contention that the so-called British idea could redeem the imperial adventure from taint of whatever type. The notion of trusted stewardship and altruism is part of Marlow's creed—and perhaps proof to him of racial superiority as well. This belief in the British idea ("racially our own") informs Marlow's mode of description in evoking his last vision of Jim on the island of Patusan. As his ship departs,

> two half-naked fishermen had arisen as soon as I had gone; they were no doubt pouring the plaint of their trifling, miserable, oppressed lives into the ears of the white lord, and no doubt he was listening to it. . . . Their dark-skinned bodies vanished on the dark background long before I had lost sight of their protector. He was white from head to foot, and re-mained persistently visible with the stronghold of the night at his back.

. . . That white figure in the stillness of coast and sea seemed to stand at the heart of a vast enigma. The twilight was ebbing fast from the sky above his head, the strip of sand had sunk already under his feet, he himself appeared no bigger than a child—then only a speck, a tiny white speck, that seemed to catch all the light in a darkened world. (P. 336)

This passage, the conclusion of Marlow's first tale and an account of his last glimpse of the protagonist, is nothing if not chiaroscuro, where this "white speck" in a "darkened world" is the white lord and protector of the "dark-skinned bodies" around him. Like the code of the sea, this language of patronage also has recourse to the preindustrial codes of lord and vassal (especially ironic since Jim has earlier abolished formal feudalism in Patusan). This stewardship of the sovereign, imaged in Marlow's final glimpse of Tuan Jim, hearkens back to the vision of a personal social order: an order that appeals both to Jim and to Marlow, and whose strong cultural symbolism is used both to neutralize the racial collision brought about by imperialism (as Jim listens patiently to the fishermen's complaints) and also, paradoxically, to suggest the innate superiority of the race whose exemplar Jim is (as he alone captures all the light in a darkened world). White "from head to foot," in contrast to the scarcely dressed fishermen who blur into the wilderness background, Jim is the helpmeet of these "trifling, miserable, oppressed" peoples because he saves them from themselves. There are undercurrents of doubt even here. If Jim stands at "the heart of a vast enigma," is that enigma Patusan, or is it Jim's existence and motives? In other words, is he, like Kurtz in "Heart of Darkness," himself the enigma at whose heart he stands? Despite these darker shadings, and despite the odd detail that Jim increasingly resembles a child as he grows distant, it is nonetheless accurate that Jim is here cast in imagery far removed from the cloudiness Marlow so often bestows on him. Whether he is clearly seen in Marlow's last rendering, he is without question brightly seen; the blinding light he radiates here demonstrates just how much the narrator shares in Jim's own fantasies of nobility.

Given the symbolic freight that this vision of Jim carries, where by synecdoche his project comes to stand for the process of colonization itself, a character like Chester, for instance, who wants to put Jim to work for him, inspires the most profound shock and revulsion in Marlow. It is the British idea itself, in all its altruism, which Chester threatens to contaminate. A "West Australian," Chester "had discovered—so he said—a guano island somewhere," which he considers as "good as a gold-mine" (p. 161). He argues that Jim's conduct before the board of inquiry proves he is the man for his operation, because "he can't be much good" (p. 166). He states that "I'm going to dump forty coolies [on the guano island]—if I've got to steal 'em. Somebody must work the stuff. . . . Let him take charge. Make him supreme boss over the coolies. . . . Surely he wouldn't be afraid of anything forty coolies could do—with two six-shooters and he the only armed man, too! It's much better than it looks. I want you to help me to talk him over"(pp. 166–67). Marlow indignantly refuses. What startles in Chester's scenario is how closely it resembles Jim's subsequent position in Patusan as "supreme boss" over the indigenous population, gathering to himself as much gunpowder as possible. Chester's scenario for a man he sees as "no earthly good" is a strangely inverted version of the role Jim actually assumes—though he assumes with it the altruism that is supposed to make all the difference between a "supreme boss of the coolies" and the white lord and protector Jim has become for Marlow in his closing glimpse.

The potential for Chester to infect the hero is contained because Marlow himself puts a stop to it, and Jim is not asked to enlist his services in the pursuit of his schemes. Yet, Chester is not the only figure in *Lord Jim* who personifies greed in search of opportunity. Gentleman Brown, eventually an agent of Jim's downfall, is himself the fullest image of the crass materialism prefigured by Chester.

Brown is a more formidable contaminant than Chester because, whereas Chester must get Jim's active acknowledgement and help in order to succeed, Brown needs only his acquiescence or paralysis. Chester's plan requires Jim's certitude that the two of them are in some way alike; Brown only needs Jim's uncertainty as to whether the two are so very different. In any event, Brown's appearance—unannounced and unthinkable—proves a fatal contaminant to Jim in his new role of feudal patron in Patusan.

Critics have argued endlessly over what it is that causes Jim to cave in to Brown. Some emphasize racial factors, others Brown's status as a kind of double for Jim.[8] These are finally not contradictory reasons for Jim's paralysis; in fact, they feed on each other rather well when the psychological leverage needed (and obtained) to produce the paralysis and uncertainty Brown uses to advantage is considered in more detail.

Brown at least is motivated by clear, if unsavory, purpose; his project is, if anything, too painfully apparent, and its goals are simple. The fuzziness that so frequently accompanies idealistic motivation is not his problem: "I came here for food. D'ye hear?—food to fill our bellies. And what did *you* come for?" (p. 382). Jim's ambiguity of motive is what most handicaps him against Brown. After all, there is a strength, an integrity, in Brown's opportunism which Jim's high-mindedness lacks. Brown seems cognizant of his position in the social and material network of self-interest much more than Jim does. Similar as Jim and

Brown may be in their complicity in the exploitation of others, Jim does not really acknowledge this complicity—to himself above all. Brown, on the other hand, accepts this fact of life and glories in it. As a result, Brown knows with firmer resolve who his friends (or accomplices) really are: "This is as good a jumping-off place for me as another. I am sick of my infernal luck. But it would be too easy. There are my men in the same boat—and, by God, I am not the sort to jump out of trouble and leave them in the d——d lurch" (pp. 382–83). This could, of course, be just more of Brown's talk, but its power derives from the fact that Brown credits his identity with and reliance upon the other members of his crew; the contrast with the Jim of the *Patna* is sharp, to say the least. The scabrous integrity of Brown draws its strength from his firm knowledge of his own entrapment in imperialism's commercial motor. Both men are trapped, in a sense; but Brown understands the contours of that confinement, while Jim can only apparently guess at them.

As the narrative unfolds, one sees that despite his search, Jim never really found who "his people" were. For better or for worse, Brown knows who his people are, and he is stuck with them. But that very weakness is the psychological strength that bests his antagonist, whose supposed freedom from mere self-interest in turn becomes a prison of self-deception. Roussel says that "Jim, like the artist, who creates such an enclosed work, finds that he has become the prisoner of his own creation. He finds, in the words of Marlow, that he is 'imprisoned within the very freedom of his power.'"[9] This is a fair statement of the case, with the proviso that Jim is not finally the prisoner of his own autotelic creation so much as of an island and the preexisting human community on whom he still relies for his validation.

Chester and Brown are thus figures of contamination, not to mention that all-pervasive source of contamination, Cornelius, Jim's abject and constantly lurking sidekick. These contaminants are all heavily invested with the thematic of raw capital accumulation and greed, and they all threaten Jim either because they recognize a similarity in Jim's position to their own (as with Chester or Brown) or because they "go with the territory" as a part of Jim's role (as with Cornelius). Yet these figures, though dangerous to Jim's "integrity," are straightforwardly so. The merchant Stein is a more insidious contaminant, perhaps the most fateful one, in large part because his motives are good. Stein's place is therefore the locus of some of the most telling structural ambiguities of this tale.

If Jim seems to evince the delusion that he can separate his individual heroics from the material social structure that makes them possible, then Stein's must be to think that effective idealism can be promoted and sustained by imperialism's cash nexus. In line with this delusion, Stein sends Jim to Patusan in the first instance, seeing it as the "practical" thing he can do as a favor to Jim, to give him an "opportunity." In a famous passage, Stein says to Marlow:

> A man that is born falls into a dream like a man who falls into the sea. If he tries to climb out into the air as inexperienced people endeavour to do, he drowns—*nicht wahr?* . . . No! I tell you! The way is to the destructive element submit yourself, and with the exertions of your hands and feet in the water make the deep, deep sea keep you up. (P. 214)

This admonition can be read as Stein's formula for a romanticism that comes to be tempered by its very contamination. By trying to fulfill his ideals—by "following the dream," as Stein goes on to suggest—Jim will learn to endure the reality that will confront him in his attempts. It is a neat formula, though flawed in some signal respects. Even Marlow has his doubts: "The whisper of his conviction seemed to open before me a vast and uncertain expanse, as of a crepuscular horizon on a plain at dawn—or was it, perchance, at the coming of the night? One had not the courage to decide; but it was a charming and deceptive light" (p. 215).

Like Chester, Brown, and Cornelius, Stein's primary motivation in coming to Asia was capital accumulation. The mentality that accompanies the merchant instinct is surely not alien to him, though neither is political activity as Marlow relates. But the naked greed whose aura clings to the others does not attach to Stein. For one thing, he is presented as more interesting psychologically than the others. For another, there is a temporal displacement at work, since Stein's active exertions on behalf of wealth are long since finished. He has, so to speak, made his pile, and it is only atop that pile that Stein can convince otherwise sensible critics that he is some sort of *raisonneur* in the *Lord Jim* drama.[10] It should be clear, though, that in addition to commenting upon the action, Stein is himself an agent in the drama. Some sense of his role can be gleaned from an unlikely source: his butterfly collection.

The famous butterflies Stein collects have admittedly been subject to innumerable symbolic readings, but one irresistibly suggests itself to the reader mindful of his past career. Pursued by Stein and pinned to his board, they are part of the process by which he has pursued wealth in all its varieties. Indeed, they are analogous to those living, breathing men whose labor Stein has taken and converted into storable capital. In concert with the larger colonial structure, Stein can take the activity of men, transform that activity into a fixed object, and store it; and the pinning down of the butterflies enacts, as in a sacrificial ritual, the way Stein converts this labor into money. When, at the close of the major sacrificial ritual in the book, Jim's death, Stein is described as sadly waving to his butterflies, how, in the light of the above interpretation of those butterflies, is that gesture best read?

I dwell upon the death of Jim because it brings to a head the contradictions in the ideology of sacrifice that grounds imperialism as a legitimate form of rule. Everyone, Marlow, Brierly, Jim, and even Marlow's anonymous correspondent—who decries it—takes it for granted that the British mission of empire is profoundly altruistic. Many readers of the novel, taking similar assumptions for granted, choose to read Jim's acquiescence in his execution as his fullest moment of recognition and a voluntary sacrifice of self before the community of Patusan. Thus, Conrad commentator Avrom Fleishman states:

> In the final analysis, colonization is a viable—the only viable—form of imperialism, not so much because it ameliorates the worst conditions of native life but because the commitment to social progress allows the individual to discover himself in the community formed and improved by his efforts. He can then egoistically surrender himself to the community, wearing, as Jim does, "a proud and unflinching glance."[11]

Leaving aside the larger question of colonialism as viable governance, one notes that Jim's decision to have Doramin put him to death is less an admission of personal guilt than a concession to local custom; this suggests that the egoism Fleishman remarks is not in the surrender to a community that reflects Jim's handiwork, but rather in fatal alienation from that community. He shows no remorse and in fact repeats again his frequent statement "Nothing can touch me"—fitting words for a man incapable of admitting any contamination, much as he formally accepts his guilt. His gesture of sacrifice—performed, as usual, by another "priest" than himself—contains within it the recognition that, in the view of his adopted community, he has done wrong; it also serves to show the community and himself that he can, the *Patna* incident to the contrary, overcome the fear of death. But atonement for felt guilt, as the "proud, unflinching glance" attests, is not at issue for Jim. What seems at first glance to be the act of profoundest altruism, the sacrifice, is really the moment of greatest egotism. In this respect, the climactic scene recalls a paradox that bedeviled Marlow when Jim took his medicine and testified at the *Patna* hearings: it soon became clear in that instance that he did so less out of eagerness to admit his mistakes than out of stubborn refusal to see them as mistakes. Furthermore, as Roussel points out, this willingness to die represents a reneging on his commitment to Jewel never to leave her—Jewel, who is his surest claim to legitimacy in the Patusan native line—and in that sense, his decision is, if anything, the opposite of altruism.[12]

It is nonetheless accurate for Ian Watt to state that "Jim does something which no other hero of a great twentieth-century novel has done: he dies for his honour."[13] He has, finally, little choice but to be true to what Marlow calls the "shadowy ideal of conduct." And despite its narcissistic overtones, Jim's death is still a sacrifice of a sort: a sacrifice on the altar of Stein's good intentions. The "opportunity which, like an Eastern bride, had come veiled to his side" is, in this inverted wedding imagery, not Jewel but death itself, and the bride is unwittingly given away by Stein (p. 416). His plans for Jim are to be ways of uniting the mix for a time, becoming at once proprietor of a thriving trading post and enlightened leader of the Patusan people. But the presence of Cornelius is at once the emblem for the impossibility of this alliance and a crucial factor in bringing about the death of Dain Waris, a direct cause of Jim's ultimate downfall. This structural ambiguity within Jim's position makes a quandary of the sort occasioned by Brown almost inevitable.[14] For all his talk of the "destructive element," Stein does not acknowledge the dissonant lineages built into Jim's position as the adoptive heir of both Doramin and Stein: dissonant claims that Jim must live up to as the representative for both Dain Waris and Cornelius at once. The sea of Patusan is supposed to bear Jim up, but somehow he only drowns in it.

Jim's failure to act in this second part of the narrative is a failure of legitimation for this adoptive son in a way the *Patna* incident was not. His position is one of direct governance here; the reader and Jim himself both see the people whose lives are affected by what Jim does, whereas in the early chapters the pilgrims are on the periphery of vision. More importantly, Jim's conflict in the first section involved whether to admit he was a spiritual member of his crew. In the Patusan crisis, his loyalty, however furtive or unacknowledged, to one class of people is in active opposition to his loyalty to another class. Like his indecision on the *Patna*, his indecisiveness in Patusan only makes matters worse, and the inevitable split in loyalty destroys him. He comes to resemble one of Stein's butterflies in his very victimization by the situation Stein has presented him. We recall here one very potent symbol of the fragile union of opposites entailed in Jim's position: the silver ring of Doramin's that Stein confers upon Jim as his first introduction to Doramin, and which rolls against Jim's foot as Doramin rises to shoot him. Watt points out the silver ring's curious status as talisman of the brittle marriage of interests between colonizer and colonized; he even notes how the ring seems to be "an ironic variation on the folk-tale motif of the poisoned gift."[15] Watt does not elaborate upon how this ironic gift motif, if accurate, could be presumed to reflect on the giver; but then perhaps elaboration is not needed. The "poisoned gift" may speak for itself.

Jim is not completely victim, however. Although a clash between the indigenous peoples and other interests was sooner or later likely, Jim's inaction makes him a collaborator in his own destruction beyond the requirements of the situation, as if to display, despite himself, his a priori contamination by what he thought could never touch him. For like the ideology he takes with him, Jim was always already contaminated by the larger colonial structure that he sought at once to justify and to deny. Indeed, when Marlow describes him as a "disembodied spirit astray amongst the passions of this earth, ready to surrender himself faithfully to the claim of his own world of shades," we are tempted to read it as a definitive sign that Jim is an embodiment of ideology itself—an insubstantial mirage existing uncomfortably among brute material and social facts.

What Marlow has in mind, though, is something much more metaphysical, and—usually the case with Marlow—more mysterious. Jim's sickness, as Marlow represents it, is ontological rather than historical; and the language Marlow uses when he reflects upon Jim's malaise consistently seeks the high ground of opaque subjectivity. In fact, the logic of the narrative as sketched here is systematically elided by Marlow, who at crucial points takes refuge in two realms: the inscrutable workings of fate and the murkiness of individual motive. When Marlow reflects, the thematic accent is on ambiguity; at times everything seems, like Jim, to be "inscrutable at heart," "under a cloud." Marlow's despairing remark "I am fated never to see him clearly" can be said to reflect upon the viewer as well as the object viewed.

In the first section of the story, concerning the *Patna*, the obsession with subjective motive predominates. Marlow's evocation of mood in going to dine with Jim sets the tone for the revelations: "The views he let me have of himself were like those glimpses through the shifting rents in a thick fog—bits of vivid and vanishing detail, giving no connected idea of the general aspect of a country. . . . Upon the whole he was misleading" (p. 76). As the novel progresses and Jim becomes further dogged by the consequences of the *Patna* incident, the emphasis becomes less "existential" and shifts rather toward the unfolding of ineluctable fate: "A clean slate, did he say? As if the initial word of each our destiny were not graven in imperishable characters upon the face of a rock" (p. 186). And when Jim makes the crucial decision to allow Brown passage, Marlow says: "There's no doubt his mind was made up that Brown should have his way clear back to the sea. His fate, revolted, was forcing his hand" (p. 391). Indeed, this stress laid upon fate has led many critics to argue, however incorrectly, that the novel has a tragic overtone, or that Jim himself is a tragic hero.[16]

To a large extent, then, the reading of *Lord Jim* pursued here, prompted though it is by the narrative logic, is denied systematically by the narrative voice, as if Marlow (or his author) were trying to halt the synecdochic logic of the narrative terms and put them in "quarantine" to stop the contamination; as if (perhaps in the wake of Brierly's example) something must be done to stop the expanding concentric circles that widen from the plot incidents to implicate Marlow himself and his reader.

Like any novel, *Lord Jim* is not so much a document recording a world as it is a way of construing values to itself and to its culture. In that signifying role, *Lord Jim*'s rhetorical function is to present a possibly devastating threat to specific assumptions of Conrad's audience—assumptions Conrad seems to have shared, at least in part—and to resolve the resultant contradictions in such a way as to reaffirm those values. For those purposes, it is not enough that Jim be a romantic idealist; his romantic idealism, as I have indicated, must be of a sort consistent with the British idea. It is his status as the carrier of British public-school values and colonial ideology which makes him a source of identification and interest for Marlow and for the virtual audience of the narrative. yet the results of Jim's attempts to realize the British idea prove too damaging to be resolved on their own terms without breaking too many ideological constraints. To retain its implicit "pact with its audience," to reaffirm the endangered values, the text occludes the historical generalizations about imperialism and its mission which are suggested by the very terms used to make the readership concerned with the story in the first place; instead, the narrative moves to a thematic level that pointedly drops the implications of the narrative for its larger historical moment, at those instances where the narrator reflects upon the events.

The gap between the narrative logic and the thematic metaphysics is the rhetorical space that Marlow creates and from which he speaks: it measures the extent to which the "white man's burden" ideology has become, by the time of *Lord Jim*, very fragile indeed. As a further step in the fathering contamination, Jim's final tragedy in Patusan becomes for Marlow what the *Patna* incident was for Brierly: a danger to be warded off. Marlow must make Jim's fate into either the totally individual drama of an isolated man or else the ritual emblem for the human condition, rather than admit his own more immediate entanglement in the larger whole of which Jim was a part. By making Jim's story a pure emblem—and an emblem of mystery at that—Marlow has erected a talisman of metaphor which should be proof against the spreading contagion of the narrative's more direct causal (or metonymic) implications. The metaphysics of doom and fate here have the paradoxical effect of helping to rescue the British idea from the taint of Jim's failure.

On the ashes of the narrative's own logic, Marlow attempts to reconstruct a community of identification for Jim. One should recall

Marlow's initial meeting with Jim in the Malabar House in reading his farewell lines:

> He is one of us—and have I not stood up once, like an evoked ghost, to answer for his eternal constancy? Was I so very wrong after all? Now he is no more, there are days when the reality of his existence comes to me with an immense, with an overwhelming force; and yet upon my honour there are moments, too, when he passes from my eyes like a disembodied spirit astray amongst the passions of this earth, ready to surrender himself faithfully to the claim of his own world of shades. (P. 416)

He sums Jim up in a characteristically ineffable line: "Who knows? He is gone, inscrutable at heart" (p. 416).

The community of "us" in which Marlow places Jim, the "us" from whose shifting locus Marlow speaks, has a much different resonance from that first community Marlow evokes when describing Jim in the Malabar House. That Jim in the Malabar House is above all "of the right sort": he has a mission, is exemplary of a particular nation and class, and embodies public-school ideals. It is in this narrower sense that this specific Jim can be called "one of us." In the closing evocation Jim retains his typicality—but of what has he become typical? Of everyone and, in a sense, of no one; and he is typical primarily by virtue of his inscrutability. Even the times when Marlow professes to see Jim clearly, as the closing remarks suggest, it is the force of his existence, some kind of mythic quantum, which is felt—and not any generalizable notions derived therefrom. Even when Jim shines brightly, he is obscure. The more specific freight of symbolism he starts out with—public school, the British idea, and so forth—are stripped from him at crucial moments in the narrative, and only his murkiness is allowed, finally, to remain.

Again, it is not so much that this shift in Jim's allegorical weight is somehow wrong or intrinsically absurd; the rhetorical point would be that, strategically, the shift is just right. It is symptomatic because it is an elision of the text's own narrative logic. One is initially drawn to Jim's story by the assumption that it may have something to reveal about the legitimacy of the merchant marine and the British project of empire, and that the story would provide clues to the viability and fate of that larger project. Yet, as the story reaches its conclusion, those specific historical dimensions are ignored in Marlow's reflections in favor of the abstractly metaphysical and the unknowable. But this turning-away is a pointing-toward, symptomatic of a profound unease with the imperialist project which gains increasing currency with both authors and audiences in Britain, as witness later, more full-blown "thesis novels" on the British in Asia, such as E. M. Forster's *A Passage to India*.

Marlow's oscillation between his own narrative's logic and thematic ambiguity is an indication of the way Conrad has fashioned a narrative by taking over the prevailing ideology of the "white man's burden" and transforming it. This ideology has been pushed close to its limit by the narrative, and that ideology's failure inscribed in the consequences of Jim's very actions. That Marlow must then have recourse to the metaphysics of ambiguity in reflecting upon that failure is only a measure of the extent to which *Lord Jim* has exposed the limitations of the historically based values that were its raw material. To read the attempt to retrieve the British idea from the consequences of its own failure is to measure the gap between narrative logic and thematic reflection. It is this gap that is Marlow's space of enunciation, and this doomed effort that he speaks. Or which speaks him.

9

Lost in Azuera:
The Fate of Sulaco and Conrad's *Nostromo*

Marlow and his perplexities, as well as the emphasis on storytelling that he figures, are not a feature of the two subsequent novels of Conrad now under consideration. It seems that as the author leaves the East Indies behind, he leaves his narrator behind as well.

This gradual disappearance of the storyteller in middle-period Conrad results from more than a mere change of scene: it results also from a change, or rather an extension in implication, of the thematics he has already been pursuing. These thematics, and what they mean for the narrative itself, continue to concern the related matters of rhetorical and political legitimation, as they have in *Lord Jim*. But in *Nostromo* they are complicated by the more overt role played in the novel by economic forces (what a main character, Charles Gould, calls "material interests"). Although the problem of legitimation is still in some measure an imperial one, the economic dimension in this text as in *L'Education sentimentale* pursues a tortuous itinerary: one that is apparently even daunting for the author himself, who compares his completion of *Nostromo* to the conclusion of a long, exhausting trip. On his return from the writing of the book, Conrad reported "I found (speaking somewhat in the style of Captain Gulliver) my family all well, my wife heartily glad to learn that the fuss was over, and our small boy considerably grown during my absence."[1]

Aside from the specific resonances of the comparison to Gulliver, the metaphor of voyage is suggestive of many aspects of Conrad's project. For in writing *Nostromo*, Conrad is indeed journeying to Latin America, that region "famed for its hospitality" (p. 11), and like that of many a *gringo* in the lower hemisphere, his journey has not been only for pleasure but also, and perhaps primarily, for business. Conrad is engaged in the process of fetching something back from what he calls his sojourn in Sulaco, and what he is fetching back–what he is exporting from the lands he has visited—is a certain reconstruction of the land itself and a certain meaning that he has drawn from it.

It is, finally, the land of Latin America itself which has been exported as the raw material of artistic creation.[2] Or, more precisely, the already written histories and remembered images of Latin America—the text or, in Roland Barthes's sense, the "myth" of Latin America—are the raw materials Conrad uses in writing *Nostromo*.[3] To turn these materials to profit, though—to "sell," as it were, what he has exported—it is incumbent on the author to transform the raw material into a finished product that will interest his market, his readership. It is not surprising, then, that *Nostromo* becomes a kind of cautionary tale from a European viewpoint, since it is this viewpoint Conrad and his readers share. From the very beginning, in fact, the landscape of Costaguana is textualized; it is made to yield a treasure of meaning for the European market, and it does this by presenting a salutary lesson.

Most of the opening chapter of *Nostromo* is devoted to a detailed description of the natural setting of the town of Sulaco. It is true, of course, that any descriptions of a landscape, by encompassing through discourse what is described (or more correctly, what is created), will by definition "textualize" what it describes (or creates) and so transform it. But it is the specific way the Sulaco setting is textualized and the way in which that textualizing process is foregrounded that is crucial here. Along with the surrounding mountains, the Isabels and the Golfo Placido, the region is also said to be inhabited by ghosts, whose tale is melded into an otherwise largely naturalistic rendering of landscape.

The part of the landscape that produces a narrative in this way is the Azuera peninsula; it is the scene for the legend of the two adventurers from far away, "*gringos* of some sort for certain," who once searched for the "heaps of shining gold" that "lie in the gloom of the deep precipices cleaving the stony levels of Azuera" (p. 18). The *gringos* gave one sign of their whereabouts, "an upright signal of smoke," and "were never seen again." Their legends, their stories, have seamlessly passed into the landscape itself, as have, according to legend, their shades:

> The two *gringos*, spectral and alive, are believed to be dwelling to this day amongst the rocks, under the fatal spell of their success. Their souls cannot tear themselves away from their bodies mounting guard over the discovered treasure. They are now rich and hungry and thirsty—a strange theory of tenacious *gringo* ghosts suffering in their starved and parched flesh of defiant heretics, where a Christian would have renounced and been released. (P. 18)

The living fate of the two adventuring *gringos* is prophetic; it prefigures the fate of Charles Gould, for instance. It is also repeatedly referred to throughout the rest of the narrative, and gradually takes on the force of a cautionary legend. The narrator is careful to put some distance between the larger story and this superstitious tale. Yet, for all that, he does not fail to extract an implicit lesson from this legend put forth by the local natives. Already the Sulacan region has been made to yield a treasure of meaning, and a meaning particularly applicable to Europeans. In the very gesture of presenting this cautionary tale, the narrator repeats the process that entangled the *gringos* in the Azuera peninsula. That is to say, he enters land surrounding Sulaco and works to extract from it a certain lesson, just as the *gringos* worked to extract the gold. The thematics of deadly success and its "fatal spell" are signal for the rest of the novel, but paradoxically the representing of this fatal spell of success runs risks very similar, perhaps identical in structure, to the situation represented.

This modest fable, dropped amongst the geographical particulars of this first chapter, can serve as a synecdoche for a larger movement within the text of *Nostromo*, since it is part of the text's project to construct an imaginative terrain that uses elements of the Latin American setting and that disposes them to furnish a lesson. Like the Azuera legend itself, these elements are as much cultural and political as they are natural. The topology of Costaguana is made to yield a tópos. This process of limned, perhaps hyperbolically, by Edward Said when he says that "*Nostromo* is a novel about political history that is reduced, over the course of several hundred pages, to a condition of mind, an inner state. It is like a trompe-l'oeil painting of a city that upon closer inspection turns out to be an anatomical drawing of the brain."[4] Without quibbling over the extreme subjectivism this view seems to imply, one can agree that there does appear to be in the course of *Nostromo* a certain emptying of the locale that is at first constructed with such thorough detail. And if Costaguana is gradually hollowed out by the narrative, this result may derive from thematic strands such as the Azuera legend and from the narrative strategies that accompany them.

There is a sense in which *Nostromo* can be read as a story with a moral; and in fact, that moral is not far from the one presented in fabular form in the first chapter. Yet it is the sad fate of the narrative, as will become evident, that to elaborate its lesson fully, it must itself become contaminated by the failure it dramatizes. Like the *gringos* and their treasure, *Nostromo* will succeed as a cautionary tale insofar as it fails; for the textualizing or mythologizing of Latin America constitutes a kind of imperialism, and its fatality is homologous to that of the *gringos*. That Conrad must export a treasure of meaning from his sojourn in Costaguana, and that the conversion of Latin America into a mythic text must ignore the warning lesson of the very tale which results from this conversion, is an irony that persists throughout *Nostromo* and becomes ever more insistent as the text proceeds. The Azuera legend serves to locate the irony, but it remains to map the contours of that irony, or at least the space it creates, which is the space of Sulaco.

Sulaco is in one respect the clearest arena of dispute over state legitimacy that Conrad presents in his middle novels. Whereas works such as *Lord Jim* and "Heart of Darkness" locate the problem of legitimation in the confrontation of two distinct cultures, the situation of Sulaco is distinct from and, in one crucial particular, more complex than such clear oppositions. In the depiction of Sulaco, one sees a political entity whose very formation and reformation, whose ontological status itself, is dependent on this process of legitimation. As it suffers the various changes of government within the larger state of Costaguana, from Guzman Bento's dictatorship to Ribiera's parliamentarism and Montero's revolt, the region gradually constitutes itself as a legal entity, a state. In *Nostromo*, the legitimation process is starkly dramatized as a struggle for legitimation, a struggle that generates political space. This political space is also a narrative space, since the story depends for its own "legitimacy" on the reader's (libidinal if not financial) investment in Sulaco's future, not merely for its own sake but also because it in turn should legitimate the Europeans'—and so indirectly the reader's—point of view.

If Conrad first exports and transforms the raw material of Latin American history so that it yields a legitimating moral for the narrative, then the "text" of Latin America yields another text in Conrad's reading of it, and this first text grounds, or justifies, the second.[5] The curious thing about *Nostromo* is that within the plot of the narrative itself the opposite process is described: the "text" of other cultures—precisely European cultures—is imported into the Latin American terrain of Costaguana to impose some validity on the confused emergent society. Like the text of Latin America Conrad uses in the novel itself, the texts that would provide authority in Costaguana must inevitably be transformed by importation to that scene. Furthermore, although they may appear to ground the political events of Costaguana, they must in large part be created after the fact. And the state of Sulaco that is eventually wrenched from the chaos of events is, of course, formed by the Europeans on European models. Here, as elsewhere, it is a question of legitimation, not legitimacy; the grounding text results from the exigencies of the political moment, much as the actors engaged in that moment may wish to present themselves as the heirs of a genealogical line leading back to some originary principle.

Nineteenth-century Europe is constantly pressed into service both as a model for what otherwise is refractory to the intellectual and practical mastery of the Europeans and as a guide to making the politics of their adoptive country conform to their expectations. The parliamanetarism of the *blancos* and the Constitution of the Occidental Republic of Sulaco drafted by Decoud are European "texts" imported, though transformed, into the Latin American landscape. Even Pedrito Montero hearkens back to the reign of Louis Bonaparte (not without reason) in elaborating his vision of political power. In talking with Charles Gould, he emphasizes his devotion to the cause of Caesarism: "The imperial rule based upon the direct popular vote. . . . Look at what the Second Empire had done for France. . . . The Second Empire fell, but that was because its chief was devoid of that military genius which had raised General Montero to the pinnacle of fame and glory" (p. 335). Like the other European "texts" imported into Costaguana, the text of the Second Empire is revised and edited. Only what Montero perceives as the favorable portions of that text are retained; the fall of Louis Napoléon is elided.

Like so many of Conrad's locales, Costaguana and its rebellious province are lands of exiles, states of the stateless. Many of the central figures in its history are from Europe, such as Gian' Battista, the Viola family, and Emilia Gould from Italy, and Captain Mitchell from England. Others are natives in name but have firmer ties across the Atlantic. Such are the Paris boulevardier Martin Decoud, "seldom exposed to the Costaguana sun under which he was born" (p. 134), and Charles Gould, who, even though the Goulds have been "established in Costaguana for three generations," still looks English. With his "flaming moustache, a neat chin, clear blue eyes, auburn hair, and a thin, fresh, red face," he is easily mistakable for a "new arrival from over the sea," and in fact is called by the natives "the Englishman of Sulaco" (pp. 50–51).

For these native aliens and deracinated Europeans, it becomes important to ground the play of events in Costaguana, and to do that the text of Europe must be constructed anew and achieved; its meaning must be taken, not merely accepted as a given. At the same time, however, this seizure must appear to be simply a reading of the originary meaning; the violence that inevitably accrues to this appropriation of meaning must be suppressed, and the result must appear natural, not contrived. Once the events have been legitimated by means of this imported model, the importation itself must be legitimated as the essential tendency of the events—a formidable task. Small wonder that Giorgio Viola, for instance, chooses to affirm his European ideal by enacting it behind the shuttered windows of the Albergo d'Italia Una.

The Europeans in *Nostromo* figure Conrad's dilemma as well as their own. Jacques Derrida has expressed this dilemma succinctly in terms of the literary text wherein if it "always gives itself a certain representation of its own roots, those roots live only by the representation, by never touching the soil, so to speak. Which undoubtedly destroys their *radical essence*, but not the necessity of their *racinating function*."[6] For the Europeans of birth and breeding who dominate the point of view in *Nostromo*, the representation they provide of Sulaco's historical roots legitimates the flow of events by never touching that soil in the first place. And yet the Europeans must construe the text of Europe as touching these events (and in a more profound way than simply by their own fiat) for the "racinating function" to obtain. If the Europeans' need to make sense of Costaguana causes them to import these understandings and to act on them, it is their need to justify their role to the Costaguaneros and to themselves that moves them to efface the traces of this imported representation, and that impels them to insist (as to Mitchell, Holroyd, and Sir John) on its rootedness in the inherent destiny of the land and its people. Gould, who upbraids his wife for forgetting that he "was born here" (p. 53), wishes to be considered a Costaguanero—and is, by birth. The tragic paradox is that the natives who see him as an Englishman are finally closer to the truth.

Captain Mitchell's comic attempts in his monologues to fit all the events of Sulaco into a grand scheme of "history," at whose center one invariably finds Mitchell himself, may be emblematic of the European dilemma. But Gould's attempts to legitimate his power in a way that would transcend appeals to the text of European political history—his urge to prove, in his own words, that the Concession "has struck such deep roots in this country . . . that nothing but dynamite shall be allowed to dislodge it from there" (p. 177)—will create a much greater, and somewhat less comic, dilemma. What is urgent from the outset, though, is the hope that somehow the *tópos* of Europe will ultimately create a political topology for Sulaco, a "common place" within which Sulacans, whether native or Europeans, could stand. The constant Costaguanan faith in pronunciamentos is disdained by Gould and indeed, it seems, at times by the narrator. Pedrito is described at one point as giving the people a speech as if in lieu of "some sort of visible largesse" (p. 322). The point of the satire is surely not altogether lost if one realizes also that in the end these pronunciamentos are perhaps the only largesse capable of establishing that common place for Sulaco. And the success of the Europeans in importing their own text to establish Sulaco in their own way not only mirrors Conrad's own exportation of the Latin American myth to Europe but also constitutes the central concern of the narrative Conrad exports.

The fates inscribed for the three major characters—Martin Decoud, Nostromo, and Charles Gould—should yield the *topoi* by means of which Sulaco's own fate can be mapped. After all, the Costaguanan landscape, like the Sulacan Republic to which it gives birth, is not only inhabited but also in large part created by these three figures. Beyond that, their fates are also intrinsic components of the very history of the republic. Like the Sulacan state, the paths they take to validation are projects embarked upon, not homecomings to a pregiven source of legitimacy, although the embarkation may be the simulacrum of a homecoming. The effigies of authority must be constructed, but they must be taken also as totems found rather than made. Decoud's love for Antonia Avellanos produces a desire in him to legitimate his project (both for her and for his republic) by appealing to her father and his godfather, Don José Avellanos, making him thus a kind of mentor. Similarly, Nostromo's betrothal to Giorgio Viola's daughter Linda makes him a potential son-in-law who appeals to Giorgio as a validation of his own activities. In neither case is the father figure a direct lineal patriarch or functioning authority whose word is law—quite the contrary. Their authority is the effect of the necessity to have a validation of the (sexual and political) desires of their respective ''sons.''

The third major actor on the stage of Sulaco's history, Charles Gould, has no discernible father figure other than his own actual father; his authority derives by direct descent from his father, and its material base partakes directly of the Sulacan landscape, a repository of wealth. (His popular title, *el rey de Sulaco*, indicates a genealogical line of succession, although it casts a certain doubt on the republican nature of the Occidental Republic.) Gould and his mine, however, are the major sources of contamination in Sulaco, and his legitimacy—which he bases on "material interests," a source of value he perceives as beyond the play of rhetoric and opinion—is really a parody of legitimacy, just as his stance of detachment from politics only parodies the apolitical. The source of his legitimacy is only another tyranny.

Though each major character takes his paternal authority from a different source, each father or father figure pronounces a kind of warning, as the Azuera legend serves as a warning to the Europeans; and just as the Europeans (and the novel) ignore their warning, so the three major characters in the novel ignore theirs—in neither instance with impunity.

Both Decoud and Gian' Battista have dreams of political power and influence within the geographical space of Sulaco, but to bring about these dreams each must create a space, rhetorical or theatrical, for himself. If Sulacan politics can become a stage for them, the community must approve the parts they play. The difference is, of course, that whereas it is Decoud's active use of persuasive language that garners the approval he requires, Nostromo must rely upon his deeds and the conversion of those deeds into widespread legends and stories, to gain his reputation. (Decoud addresses an audience, whereas Nostromo performs for spectators.) The choice of father figures also follows this pattern. Nostromo's mentor, Giorgio Viola, who was a silent but storied Garibaldino, and Decoud's mentor, Don José, who participated in political activity by molding opinion as well as by action itself, describe an economy where being well-spoken, in Decoud's case, or being well-spoken-of, in Nostromo's, is convertible into credit within the Sulacan community—credit here meant in both senses. The currency of *doxa*—the interplay of opinion, polemics, or hearsay reputation—is part of a political economy as well as a rhetorical space. (Since Nostromo, of course, cannot directly appropriate this rhetorical space, he needs Captain Mitchell, for example, to give his deeds currency. In return, the latter gets the vicarious satisfaction, through his "Capataz de Cargadores," of feeling close to the center of things, "in the thick of history" [p. 121].)

Discourse is Decoud's currency as well, but unlike Nostromo, he is able to generate his own. His validation rests less on the recognition by others of his deeds than on his active persuasion of others by his words. He is not as beholden to a recorder of history such as Captain Mitchell, for in making history he promulgates his own interpretation of it. It is fitting that his godfather and would-be father-in-law is Don José, whose *Fifty Years of Misrule* is a polemical weapon as well as a historical record.

Decoud's interest in the politics of Sulaco is chiefly a function of his desire to gain rhetorical power over the future Sulacans. His initial decision to return to Costaguana was prompted by his position as a correspondent for the *Parisian Review*. The fact that the Constitution of the new Occidental Republic is written by Decoud is evidence that his main mode of action is, finally, indistinguishable from his rhetoric. He starts out in the narrative as a keeper of records, and his letters to his sister parallel and provide counterpoint to Captain Mitchell's absurdly inflated chronicles.[7] But the essentially passive relation to language that the notion of record keeping implies is always in play with a more active relation to language, figured in the manipulation of rhetoric and political polemics; even Don José's book is at once a history of the period up to his own day and an attempt to affect that history. It is ironic that Decoud's attitude toward the usefulness of words, and toward his own facility with them, seems to be one of contempt, but as he himself confesses, his political rhetoric springs from other sources. He remarks of one of his speeches that he "poured out an impassioned appeal to [the audience's] courage and manliness, with all the passion of [his] love for Antonia" (p. 200). As with Nostromo, Decoud's political ambition is doubled by an erotic design. But the sad fact is that Decoud's rhetoric is not enough to gain him either political or romantic advantage, since in dying he loses both.

But this means neither that the political rhetoric was merely the sublimation or superscription of personal passions, nor that this rhetoric has no subsequent effect on the life of Sulaco. In fact, Decoud's plan is adopted, ironically enough, by the new Occidental Republic founded after his death, and Captain Mitchell is the first to tell us that "his plan [was] a glorious success. . . . And there's no doubt, sir, that it is. It is a success" (p. 402). In the Sulacan space where rhetoric is such a central force, it is unfortunate that Decoud, like Nostromo, must ultimately entrust to Captain Mitchell the task of telling his story.

Both Decoud and Nostromo, then, rest their hopes for validation on the vagaries of *doxa*, on the shifting bases of rhetoric, persuasive power, opinion, and personal reputation in the community. For the role of the aristocrat who purports to mold that rhetorical space, Don José is appropriate, and for the "man of the people" (as Conrad christens Nostromo) whose best hope is to occupy a privileged station in the rhetorical space created by others, the Garibaldino Giorgio Viola is the logical choice. For both figures, the search for erotic fulfillment parallels the search for some form of legitimation in the community as a whole, and this befits what is (or in the Conradian scheme, should be) an organic society. But each figure transgresses the paternal injunction (in the name of fidelity to it) and reaps dire consequences, just as the moral of the Azuera story is used by the text to breach its implied injunction (though breached in the name of providing a further illustration of it).

Consider Nostromo. It is not surprising that he takes as his model this Garibaldino and republican for his distinguished past if not his inglorious present. Yet, he breaches his covenant with his model by gradually taking up the thievery that Giorgio despised. In the same stroke, Nostromo also decides to reject Giorgio's daughter Linda, whose marriage to Nostromo Giorgio had encouraged and who provided an additional bond between the two men, choosing instead to pursue by stealth his other daughter Giselle, whom Giorgio wishes to stay with him. Whereas before the erotic urge had followed the same course as the desire for recognition by the community, now the greed for silver and the covert longing for Giselle conspire to effect a turning away from the gaze of Giorgio, as well as from the gaze of the community as a whole. Indeed, for Nostromo, Giselle and the treasure are closely connected, and although he sees the treasure as a means to Giselle, in practice the twin goals meld into one:

> With Giorgio established on the Great Isabel, there would be no need of concealment. He would be able to go openly, in daylight, to see his daughters—one of his daughters—and stay late talking to the old

Garibaldino. . . . In the dark . . . night after night . . . he would dare to
grow rich quicker now. He yearned to clasp, embrace, absorb, subjugate
in unquestioned possession this treasure, whose tyranny had weighed
upon his mind, his actions, his very sleep. (P. 433)

This passage refers no doubt to the "treasure" that Nostromo has been
gradually appropriating from the Great Isabel. But the knowledge the
narrative has already given us about Nostromo's secret plans for Giselle
(not to mention the sexualized language in which Nostromo's obsession
is rendered) suggests that the "treasure" may be read as Giselle. To the
end, Giorgio is sublimely ignorant of both goals.

Ironically, Nostromo is encouraged to embark upon his theft of the
silver by a statement Giorgio himself has made. As Nostromo fumes
over his betrayal by the Europeans, he recalls an offhand remark of his
mentor's: "'There is no mistake. They keep us and encourage us as if
we were dogs to fight and hunt for them. The *vecchio* is right,' he said,
slowly and scathingly. He remembered old Giorgio taking his pipe out
of his mouth to throw these words over his shoulder at the café. . . . This
image fixed his wavering purpose" (p. 345). The words uttered by
Giorgio himself are misread and used to justify a course of conduct that
Giorgio himself would reject without question. Nostromo's "wavering
purpose" is fixed upon becoming a thief, precisely the form of revenge
for injustice his authority figure most despises. (Giorgio is contemptuous of the motives of the Sulacan revolts in general, regardless of faction, and thinks of the rebels as "not a people striving for justice, but
thieves" [p. 30].) To compound the irony further, it is as much the
vision of Giorgio himself in all his patriarchal eminence as the force of
his words that fixes Nostromo's purpose. But Giorgio is none the wiser,
and he is unable to reassert his authority, even at the conclusion. One
could interpret the ending of the Nostromo story as a kind of reprisal for
offense along the lines of Doramin's shooting of Jim at the end of *Lord
Jim*. But the fact that it owes to an accident wherein Nostromo is
mistaken by Giorgio for another person confirms for us that it is more
useful to observe the contrast between the two incidents, and to read
Giorgio's shooting of Nostromo as a structural parody of the former
incident. In his action Doramin dramatized the reestablishment of patriarchal dominance, whereas Giorgio's act represents only the uninten-
tional evidence of debility and myopia. That he kills Nostromo but
proclaims that he has "shot Ramirez" (p. 453) provides the final cruel
measure of Giorgio's true irrelevance to the political and moral landscape of the novel.

It is not only Giorgio who shows signs of debility. Decoud's mentor
Don José suffers from a similar weakness. Don José is in no fitter
circumstance to assert his power than is Giorgio. In fact, as Decoud

notes without much pity, he is moribund. His decline coincides appropriately with that of the text that embodies his injunctions. As the Monterist revolt gathers force, Decoud writes in a letter to his sister:

> Whatever happens, he will not survive. The deception is too great for a man of his age; and hasn't he seen the sheets of *Fifty Years of Misrule*, which we have been printing on the presses of the *Porvenir* [Decoud's newspaper] littering the Plaza, floating in the gutters, fired out as wads for trabucos loaded with handfuls of type, blown in the wind, trampled in the mud? I have seen pages floating upon the very waters of the harbour. It would be unreasonable to expect him to survive. It would be cruel. (P. 200)

For one whose political efficacy was so closely bound up with the success of his rhetoric, those stray pages are a bad omen. Whether or not to expect him to survive is cruel, it does prove unrealistic. He dies during the revolution.

The classic text of European republicanism, as embodied in the heroism of Giorgio or the parliamentary eloquence of Don José, is lost as a grounding possibility; it is converted into a dead letter. Both men and what they stand for are equally irrelevant to the future of the Occidental Republic of Sulaco. (It is of course another question whether European republicanism, imported as it is to Costaguana, was ever relevant to events there.) In any event, both authority figures are also warning figures. Their fates signal the fates of the protégés in the political arena. Nostromo will die and his influence on Sulacan affairs will thus be lost; Decoud will survive but only, oddly enough, through the constitution that is his text. It is important to note this distinction, though, that the characters follow in their mentors' footsteps and repeat their mentors' fates in large part because they ignore the paternal injunction.

Whereas Nostromo goes against his mentor's wishes by justifying himself in his mentor's words, Decoud acknowledges that he is at odds with Don José—but only, he argues, to ultimately further Don José's truest ideals. In opposite terms, both figures display an ambivalence toward their sources of authority: an ambivalence whose resonances, since these men are guides of a sort to Sulaco's political topology, encompass Sulaco's ambivalence toward a tradition within which it tries to achieve legitimacy.

Decoud's plan of separation is a clear break with Don José's federalism, which always held that Sulaco should remain a province of Costaguana and not become an autonomous state. Rejecting this belief, Decoud argues that a new conception is crucial. But as he presents the matter, even though it is contrary to Antonia's and her father's express vision, separatism will be necessary to realize what remains of that vision in the final analysis: "Oh, yes, I know it's contrary to the doctrine laid down in the *History of Fifty Years' Misrule*. I am only trying to be sensible. . . . It may yet be the means of saving some of your convictions" (p. 160). Decoud even fancies, perhaps for his own peace of mind, that Don José has approved his constitution on his deathbed: "God knows whether the old statesman had understood it; he was unable to speak, but he had certainly lifted his arm off the coverlet; his hand had moved as if to make the sign of the cross in the air, a gesture of blessing, of consent" (p. 233). Despite this questionable reconciliation, Decoud's schemes go directly against the paternal injunction.

In crucial instances, then, these sources of validation are radically misconstrued, and disaster ensues as a result. In both cases, the traditional authority figure (or as close to such as these *dépaysés* Europeans can devise) are misread or ignored, but in favor of what? Nostromo's greed for the silver is what initially causes him to go against his mentor's wishes; and Decoud's separatism soon entangles him in the silver as well, for he knows its safe possession is crucial to the independence of the new state. Silver is the agent of this transgression for both men. By extension, the purely economic validation of the silver will soon contaminate and displace forms of legitimation based upon the rhetorical ability to compel the respect of the community in the state of Sulaco as a whole.

What are the implications of this contamination by the silver, and what are its results for the respective characters and for the state they both form and figure? To answer this, I take up the third major actor on Sulaco's stage. He claims a native heritage, survives where Decoud and Nostromo perish, seems to derive his power from a realm beyond both politics and rhetoric, and has his own father for a father figure. Charles Gould would seem to possess an organic form of legitimacy which the others cannot claim, and his fate may thus reveal more about the fate of Sulaco.

Unlike either Nostromo or Decoud, Gould has no desire to be validated by political rhetoric and the good opinion of his community. Indeed, it is his desire to reside as far as possible from the realm of language itself. His distaste for parliamentary institutions is part and parcel of his distrust of the language that is the life's blood of parliamentary polemics. When Don Juste proposes to Gould that he lend his prestige to the assembly that is to govern the region, Gould reflects on the "pity" he feels "for those men, putting all their trust into words of some sort" (p. 305). For Gould, on the other hand, "taciturnity was his refuge" (p. 305). It is a refuge that Gould can, quite literally, afford, since his wealth from the silver mine allows him to spare his words, giving each one more weight; his "impenetrability" is backed up by the weight of the San Tomé mine: "The King of Sulaco had words enough to give him all the mysterious weight of a taciturn force. His silences, backed by the power of speech, had as many shades of significance as uttered words in the way of assent, of doubt, of negation—even of simple comment . . . since behind it all there was the great San Tomé mine" (p. 175). It is the silver of the mine and his status as the administrator of that silver which allow Gould to forswear speech and to put his trust in the silent validation of the mine. After all, his father, who "could be eloquent, too" (p. 80), was unsuccessful in his project of making the Gould Concession operational. Indeed, when Charles Gould first gets the news of his father's death, his reaction is: "It has killed him!" (p. 62). ("It" here, of course, is the Gould Concession.)

Considered alongside Decoud's and Nostromo's authority figures, the case of Gould's father is particularly interesting, since in this instance the father figure's fate in itself constitutes a warning along with his words—but again, both the warning and the injunction are ignored. Nostromo applied the words of Giorgio in such a way that he is eventually killed by Giorgio, and Decoud's separatism is a studied heresy against Don José's political ideals. In each case, the transgression is justified as furthering the larger spirit of what is transgressed: the deviation is really a form of obedience. The same rationale occurs in Gould's case, when he explicitly rejects his father's pleas not to take over the San Tomé mine upon his death, but rejects them in the name of somehow justifying the father's memory and suffering. Gould puts his criterion for justification quite squarely to his fiancée Emilia:

> "Anyone can declaim about these things, but I pin my faith to material interests. Only let the material interests once get a firm footing, and they are bound to impose the conditions on which alone they can continue to exist. That's how your money-making is justified here in the face of lawlessness and disorder. It is justified because the security which it demands must be shared with an oppressed people. A better justice will come afterwards. That's your ray of hope. . . . And who knows whether in that sense even the San Tomé mine may not become that little rift in the darkness poor Father despaired of ever seeing?"
> [To which Emilia replies:] "Charley . . . you are splendidly disobedient."
> (P. 81)

The words themselves are ominous in Gould's speech, describing the material interests as imposing the conditions on which they can "continue to exist." And Emilia's reply puts the issue into perspective: if Gould's disobedience is to be justified, it must be a splendid disobedience. Gould is more ready to believe it is such and to feel that the mine, taken over by him in violation of his father's wishes, is sure to become the means of reaffirming his father's values: "A vague idea of rehabilitation had entered the plan of their life. That it was so vague as to elude the support of argument made it only the stronger" (p. 73). Emilia, too, is anxious to justify her husband's decision, as much if not more than he is: "The dead man of whom she thought with tenderness (because he was Charley's father), and with some impatience (because he had been weak), must be put completely in the wrong" (p. 73).

But the text notes elsewhere how the "wealth of the mine" is the sort of weapon that always seems "ready to turn awkwardly in the hand" (p. 303). One may say that Gould's father is proven both wrong and right in the end: wrong when he insists the Concession cannot be made profitable, right when he claims that the mine will enslave and master anyone who attempts to run it. Gould does not die in the mine's service, but he lives in death. He is a victim of the mine's success as much as his father is the victim of its failure.

Gould's desire is to be a gray eminence, apart from the give and take of the Sulacan Parliament and its polemics; his favored model (as *el rey de Sulaco*) is a monarchical one. (Even the "equestrian statue of Charles IV" in the central section of Sulaco parodies Gould's English "style of horsemanship," described in the same passage [p. 52].) Nevertheless, Gould does not desire to transcend his silver mine. Like Stein in *Lord Jim*, Gould believes that the success of his ideals is necessarily the result of the success of his "material interests." It is Antonia who calls his attention to his own sterling reputation when she tells him "It is your character that is the inexhaustible treasure which may save us all yet; your character, Carlos, not your wealth" (p. 300). But this sterling character, like his few words, would not achieve this solid weight were it not for his wealth, and Gould knows it. It is paradoxically the corrupt and corrupting silver mine that makes Gould's word (his utterances and his character) as good as gold.

Like Stein, Gould hopes that what appears to be the instrument of self-interest will prove to be the means of realizing ideals as well. But in the course of realizing these ideals, Gould is forced to engage in the bribery and corruption characteristic of the region. These contradictions are so glaring that even he is compelled on occasion to notice them, for instance when he must strike a deal with the powerful bandit Hernandez and he senses how similar he and outlaw really are: "They were equals before the lawlessness of the land. It was impossible to disentangle one's activity from its debasing contacts. A close-meshed net of crime and corruption lay upon the whole country" (p. 300). It is, incidentally, at the point where Gould makes his deal that Don José is glimpsed "hardly breathing, by the side of the erect Antonia, vanquished in a life-long struggle with the powers of moral darkness" (p. 301). The triumph of the king of Sulaco is in this way symbolically (even melodramatically) ransomed by the death of its republican spirit, and it is especially ironic that Antonia's praise of Gould's character also occurs in this chapter. But the contamination of the country that is said to "infect" the mine is able to do so, finally, only because the mine is already a part of that contamination, and beyond that, actively promotes the corruption that it finds.

There are words Gould especially seeks to abjure: "Liberty, democracy, patriotism, government" have a "nightmarish meaning" in Sulaco, "a flavour of folly and murder" (p. 337). If he recoils from too many words, it is arguably because Gould has seen the harm that the language he has heard can do. Yet, the very wealth that allows Gould to measure his words as he does—that which gives his discourse its validity and weight—is itself a product of bribery and exploitation. (The confrontation with Hernandez only confirms this.) But more importantly, this wealth only becomes active insofar as it is expropriated so that it can return as credit from foreign banks such as Holroyd's in San Francisco. In other words, the wealth that backs up Gould's character is also a means of depleting that character, just as the silver itself, once circulated, depletes and hollows out the San Tomé mine from which it springs.

The enslavement to the silver is a recurring theme in *Nostromo*. The title character himself is described time and again as the "slave of the silver," and (in perhaps an altogether too heavily symbolic moment) Decoud drowns himself in the Golfo Placido by using bars of silver for weight. The king of Sulaco himself does not escape subjection to the mine; he is as much a slave to the mine as is any of its workers. In her vision of Gould's fate, his wife sees the mine "possessing, consuming, burning up the life of the last of the Costaguana Goulds; mastering the energetic spirit of the son as it had mastered the lamentable weakness of the father" (p. 428). It is unquestionably a "terrible success for the last of the Goulds" (p. 428). Just as the father is killed by the failure of the mine, so the son lives a death in the mine's service: service that drains him of energy and idealism as it draws resources from the lode itself.

The fact that Gould is the last of his line suggests a further consequence of his contact with the mine: the gradual impoverishment of erotic life. Gould's fierce loyalty to the mine is part of "that subtle conjugal infidelity through which his wife was no longer the sole mistress of his thoughts" (p. 303). Just as Nostromo loses Giselle and Decoud loses Antonia, so Gould comes to lose, for all intents and purposes, his wife Emilia. For all three men the weapon of the silver turns awkwardly in the hand. Gould's fate, though less dramatic than the death and suicide of the other two, is in some ways more interesting. Unlike them, he gains the success he wishes, marries the woman he desires, and retains his life. But the silver mine makes his success indistinguishable from slavery, alienates him from the woman he has married, and makes his life seem a kind of death. Like the silver mine itself, the man who embodies its power in the narrative is slowly hollowed out; and the more powerful he grows, the more hollow he becomes.

If Gould is hollow, it is in part because, unlike the political and parliamentary pronunciamentoes that function as promissory notes against future assets for the other Sulacan leaders, his currency (both in wealth and in character) is drawn against reserves. The king of Sulaco, like any king, must validate both the political and the economic currency, and he does both by means of the silver. It is not surprising, given the fate of their other legitimating texts, that the Europeans of Sulaco turn to the silver as a source of value. But the pursuit of this legitimating silver causes the three major characters to turn against their precursors, their community, and their love objects. The silver is thus a destroyer of tradition and an agent of solitude. Decoud is stranded on the Great Isabel in the course of saving it and Nostromo is reduced to stealth in order to acquire more and more of it. The silver is also a kind of solvent which dissolves each person's source of validation. The suicide of Decoud is brought about by his inability to use or to hear the words on which his reputation has been based: "The cord of silence could never snap on the island. It must let him fall and sink into the sea, he thought" (p. 410). To Nostromo, who exists most vividly when he is seen and admired by others, the silver which is to be his means of recognition proves to be the bringer of darkness, "the only secret spot of his life; that life whose very essence, value, reality, consisted in its reflection from the admiring eyes of men" (p. 430).

The place of silver is always one of silence and solitude, though it seems to make possible the legitimacy, peace, and prosperity of the social order and enables the country to obtain outside credit from the Americans and Europeans abroad. Decoud's constitution is a success, as Captain Mitchell characterizes it, because it has the mine to back it up. Yet, like the Indians who guard the silver mine itself, the Europeans make the silver into an object of worship, a fetish to be sought. Curiously, despite the fact that everyone seems to place great faith in the silver, it means something rather different to everyone, because its use as a means varies in each person's plans for it.

The stability of this legitimator is undermined in part precisely because everybody wants it and because its only genuine use is in circulation. It seems to be merely "an incorruptible metal that can be trusted to keep its value for ever" (p. 251), as Nostromo says at one point. But it is finally a neutral substance in itself, owing nothing to Sulaco other than its origins. It can only redound to the region's credit as a result of export: "Let it come down [says Decoud] so that it may go north and return to us in the shape of credit" (p. 190). The "legitimacy" in the outside world that is bought by this silver and the resultant prosperity cost more than the silver alone. Their price is the total stifling of political activity and, finally, of history. The ironic peace of the Occidental Republic combines the absence of political discourse with the crushing power of the mine, under whose impact the Sulacan sense of community and its *doxa* gradually dissolve. This fact is underscored by Captain Mitchell's benign narrative, the most appropriate form in which to give the reader a hint of the tedious latter years of Sulaco. The lack of dynamism in the Republic under Gould is imaged in the endlessly repeated tour Captain Mitchell gives to his visitors: a tour that always comes full circle to end where it began.[8]

In previous narratives, Conrad has presented us with a storyteller figure who shared the values of a well-defined group. The figure of Charlie Marlow is the most famous. Here, the audience for Captain Mitchell's narrative is the occasional "privileged passenger," less an audience than a "more or less willing victim" (p. 402). Lacking the commonality of values and concerns that attended Marlow's narratives, Captain Mitchell's stories also lack their urgency and imagination. Neither storyteller nor audience here is a native Sulacan. Both, in a sense, are just visiting. Audience and storyteller exist in a realm where cultural and therefore narrative origins are quite difficult, at times, to discern.

The disruption of cultural continuity in the region of Costaguana has occurred so long ago that there is no way in the novel to determine whether anyone is legitimate, at least according to any genealogical measure. This chaos of cultures presents itself in the narrative as a chaos of detail, event, and character. Like Giorgio, whose "gaze could not take in all its details at once" (p. 35), one reads the confused identity of the region through the shifts of perspective, the welter of character and plot. Much of the panoramic quality of *Nostromo* derives from this confusion of national identity, as do the larger lineaments of the narrative action.

Insofar as the region has any guarantor of identity, it is the silver. While the Golfo Placido and the Higuerota Mountains exclude Sulaco from the rest of Costaguana, only the silver offers a true possibility of independence or sovereignty. But this "independence" is founded at the price of dependence on silver, which results in two things: first, the silver as source of economic value becomes the corruptor of other values; second, it subjects Sulaco to even greater dominance by foreign masters. (It is ironic that Nostromo's rebellion against his masters takes the form of enslavement to their silver.) The process by which this guarantor of legitimacy becomes a contaminant for Sulaco is homologous to the way this process has worked upon the three major characters. What was to be a means for each became his end, in both senses. This weapon also turns just as awkwardly against the larger community—its capacity for purposeful action, its political discourse, and its material interests themselves.

The silver is always a means to an end, or is so perceived; but it is a circuitous means. The silver shipment whose fate occupies so much of the novel never reaches its destination, and in similar fashion the larger destinations of the silver are never reached, or are reached only ironically. Its excess, which eventually contaminates the republic of Sulaco itself, is seen by Gould as a circuitous means of returning to the republic a security and an independence that will compensate the region for its loss of both its resources themselves and its traditional memory. Decoud sees the silver as essential to his republican ambitions as well, but he understands that it is only by means of a circuitous route that the silver can have effect as "credit" to the region. A native resource is to be dispersed to distant Americans such as Holroyd with the supposed result that it will return to the general population in the form of security and eventual prosperity. Dr. Monygham, who despite his prescience is devoted to the mine and to Mrs. Gould, realizes that "the time approaches when all that the Gould Concession stands for shall weigh as heavily upon the people as the barbarism, cruelty, and misrule of a few years back" (p. 419). As the narrative progresses, Dr. Monygham, though a pariah, becomes a central figure in the town, as part of the increased focus on solitude that occurs as the mine gains hegemony over the region.

The Gould Concession manages to monopolize the polemical discourse of Sulacan politics as well as the material means at hand, since it is ironically Gould's kingship that founds the purely formal republican government. The feeble stirrings of parliamentary debate—compared repeatedly to the insensate "buzzing" of insects (pp. 305, 322, 410)— are not proof against the greater weight of the San Tomé mine. Despite this despotism, Gould sees the reign of silver as benevolent. Whence his misunderstanding?

The silver, like its proprietor, is mute. But like the natural surroundings of Sulaco, it is already textualized, already put into the service of various positions and ideologies. (Decoud, for example, gives nature itself a voice when, in addressing Antonia, he declares that the very mountains of Sulaco cry "Separate!") This textualization, discussed at the outset, involves not only the level of plot where the region qua region is the object of a political dispute but also a "formal" level, because the novel itself uses naturalistic effects to produce its impact. Even the Golfo Placido, said by generations of critics to represent the silence of nature, must be figured in human discourse: it must speak its muteness. This anthropomorphizing tendency is, of course, intrinsic to rhetoric, but it is the link between the use of nature as raw material for rhetoric and Gould's mining of the silver to produce value that must detain us here. Both are riskier enterprises than they first appear.

The geography that Gould appropriates is clearly not the indifferent other of the Golfo Placido, in whose immensity Decoud allows himself to be "swallowed up" (p. 412). It is a function more semiological than allegorical that Gould gives his silver as a measure and embodiment of human value. Now human value, naturally, is a fluctuating phenomenon given only false solidity in "incorruptible" silver. Since neither indigenous culture nor geographic necessity validates the nation-state of Sulaco, its only validation lies in this silver, and then, strictly speaking, only as productive of credit and thus as valuable to outsiders. Because these outsiders will confer validation on the silver only after it has been extracted and exported, this value is a parasitic one that thrives inevitably on the depletion of its source. In the absence of a father to whom the judgment of the community can be referred—i.e., in the absence of a clear genealogical line or quasi-tribal organic tradition—the only father to emerge is Gould, and his grounding text is the price of silver on foreign exchange markets.

That he emerges in this way is attributable to a twofold illusion regarding the nature of this fetishized source of value: first, that the silver is a repository of value unmediated by interpretation, a kind of value incarnate; second, that because the silver is a part of the geographical region of Sulaco its use will inevitably benefit the community as a whole. Each prong of the illusion rests upon a "pseudo-physis" that presents the silver as simply natural, beyond the play of history and political passion: the material is intrinsically worthwhile apart from the cultural process of assigning value and that worth will simply accrue to the region from which it comes, without sequestration by any smaller group within the region. Both illusions are of course undermined by events in the narrative.

The narrative itself, however, is undermined by the same token. After all, as the novel progresses the silver assumes greater importance. The heading of each major section refers either directly or indirectly to the metal, and each major figure revolves in various ways around it. Yet as the silver is focused upon with more intensity, the dense social and materialistic structure of the first section is progressively hollowed out.[9] The last section, involving the death of Decoud and the domestic tragedy of the title character, moves further into interior drama, with stark backdrops such as the lighthouse on the Great Isabel, and away from the complexity of Sulaco itself. That the public stage of Sulacan politics is left for the fatuous Captain Mitchell to describe is indicative of its impoverishment at this point. With the triumph of material interests the narrative seems not to have much else to say. Though Conrad says it was only after Nostromo's death that "there was nothing more for me to do in Sulaco" (p. 14), one cannot help feeling that he may have overstayed his welcome at that. The silencing of Sulaco's political rhetoric tends to impoverish the novel's rhetoric, too. Do the events themselves, as the novel sets them in motion, warrant this impoverishment?

The dismantling of Sulaco's *theatrum mundi* is dictated not so much by cynicism about the value of any political endeavor as by the fact that the text is written from a determinate perspective. Owing both to Conrad's sources and to his own situation, this is a European perspective; because the moral of *Nostromo* is intended for European consumption, a kind of horizon obtrudes on the narrative, a state of affairs that cannot be seen beyond. This state of affairs coincides with the triumph of the Gould Concession.

Gareth Jenkins argues that despite the narrative's ironic view of Captain Mitchell, "Mitchell's Sulaco is in the end endorsed."[10] By subjecting Nostromo, the one character in the novel capable of revolutionary activity, to the corruption of the silver, the text is able to "twist the historical logic into a demonstration in favour of the society and culture produced by one of the ruling groups [of Sulaco]."[11] Because Nostromo is presented as a prey of these influences, Jenkins argues, the text short-circuits the true possibility of political revolt and implicitly sanctions Gould's kingship as inevitable, if unedifying:

> By enslaving Nostromo to one element of the production process whereby the oligarchy maintains its power, Conrad has forbidden workers the opportunity of breaking with oligarchic-imperialist society. . . . Since the future can now *only* be one governed by material interests then necessarily Conrad's apologia for capitalist society is a tragic one.[12]

Jenkins overstates the case for Nostromo as a viable alternative to Gould's status quo, but it is still likely that the text's turning away, conscious or not, from the next logical stage of political conflict (that between Gould's European interests and the indigenous Costaguaneros) is strategic. The turning away here is also a pointing toward, and what it points to is the horizon of the text; its perspectival limit. The

Europeans in Sulaco would no doubt play a part in any future political contestation, but it would not be likely to be either a heroic or a victorious part. The tragic situation of Sulaco in book 3 must be presented as somehow inevitable, if only because the conflict that could overturn it must remain unthought. It is not history itself, but a particular aspect of it, that *Nostromo* chooses to disavow.

The absence of that history is felt acutely in the last sections of the novel; the reader feels quickly that most of the resonance of Costaguana has already been "exported." Just as the silver that gives Sulaco value is hollowed out of the mine, so the exportation of meaning to the reader from the text of Sulaco hollows out that text and impoverishes it. This is true in two senses. First, as was shown with the Azuera *gringos'* tale, Sulaco is appropriated only insofar as its events provide a fable for Europeans. Second, the monetary "value" that becomes the focus of concern gradually eclipses other values that could unite a readership and a narrator, thus hollowing out the resonances even for a European audience.

The impoverishment thus works both ways, and, in this distorted economy, Sulaco's loss is the reader's as well. The crucial difference is that whereas the population of Sulaco is corrupted and drained of meaning through an external agency, the Europeans in the novel—and those reading the novel—are willing accomplices to this emptying of meaning. At the furthest limit, the readers of *Nostromo* become the consumers of Latin America as a cautionary tale for Europeans, unaware perhaps that fable and reader alike fall prey to the fate described in the fable itself. What seems to be a plenitude of meaning is again the agent of impoverishment.

The tale of the *gringos* has its prophetic powers within the narrative, and the tale of Gould certainly reveals this. But the novel must be to Gould what the fable of Azuera is to the *gringos*. The result and, to an extent, the contributing cause of this situation is the disappearance of the storyteller's figure itself from *Nostromo*. In *Lord Jim*, for instance, Marlow contained the damage of Jim's ultimate failure, from which Marlow could draw lessons that were at least comforting if not inspiring. Jim's fall, through Marlow's intervention, could be interpreted as tragic and heroic in character, and the imperialist project itself, though undermined, could be preserved as a possibility.

Nostromo is another matter, however, both because it is explicitly a story of European economic influence in foreign politics and because it has a minimal narrative voice (who apparently is that of a *gringo* in the region on business). On the level of content, one could argue that it is Stein's story rather than Jim's. Gould shares Stein's delusion that the instruments of empire can be legitimated by serving an interest broader than those of their wielders. On the formal level, there is no first-person narrator who shares the reader's assumptions and who can deflect the contamination when Gould's practical success in gaining power over Sulaco proves the course of his moral failure. There is no event to overturn the deathly reign of material interests and the mine, because the European point of view cannot see past them; neither is there a Marlow to philosophize away the failure of this regime and to preserve a resonance for the text. The economism that has driven the narrative has made the European point of view as barren of positive inspiration as it is constricted. (That Captain Mitchell is the only figure in the book who embodies a Marlow-like storytelling function only underscores this myopia and this sterility; Captain Mitchell's pompous disquisitions are a pale variant of Marlow's yarns whether or not they are a deliberate parody of them.)

The disappearance of the storyteller, along with his audience, is a symptom of this failure-in-success of European values. As a survival of the attenuated European tribal memory, the storyteller figure must also stand aside for the forces of modernization, just as the sources of paternal wisdom in Sulaco must be swept aside, regardless of consequence, for the sake of "progress." There is neither a narrative personality nor an inscribed audience in *Nostromo*, and the bleak terrain left by material interests and the austere silver leaves few bonds between storyteller and audience. In the wake of Gould's failure-in-success, isolated readers, with neither narrator nor audience to give them a common place of warmth, can scarcely fail to be chilled by the silver's touch.

In the next novel, *The Secret Agent*, the readers' isolation is also a characteristic of many of the characters—and the storyteller does not exist even in parodic form. The only narrative form for which there is any use in this realm seems to be the newspaper, organ not of a community (there is little community in *The Secret Agent*) but of something very different: public opinion. Further, if there is an ancient memory in the London described by Conrad, it is certainly not of an organicist community but rather of absolute state power, and its ability to condemn without appeal. There is a shift in the concern with what makes power legitimate in this novel as opposed to the previous ones, not only because the subject matter is closer to home, but also because that change in focus also alters perspective on the assumptions implicit in the prior ways Conrad has formed the problem of legitimacy. In *Lord Jim* and *Nostromo*, there remains some nostalgia for precapitalist forms of legitimacy and a collateral sense that a source of legitimacy—usually tribal, patriarchal, and organicist—is being lost. In *The Secret Agent*, the present regime, brutal as it is, is not played off against a golden past age; rather it contains the guilty origins of state power and adds subtler rationales

10

The Structure of Suspicion in *The Secret Agent*: The Panoptical City

Given the relentless scrutiny of the wilderness of eyes portrayed in *The Secret Agent*, it is curious that the event that stands at its heart is glanced over. The death of Verloc's young charge Stevie is, though "the central event of the novel . . . never directly described. Stevie's end is hinted at, imagined, and approached by various people, but remains hidden, a blank space in the center of the narrative."[1] This strange absence and the fact that it is indirectly caused by the helpmeets of order (such as the Ambassador Vladimir and the spy Verloc) rather than of anarchy, point to two aspects of this novel where the question of political legitimation is most forcefully engaged. The world here is preeminently one of surveillance, yet the most crucial matters are left unsurveyed; and those who attempt to identify themselves with forces of order in fact are more effective at perpetrating violence than the declared opponents of order. Not only the effectiveness but also the legitimacy of the forces of order are questioned deeply in *The Secret Agent*, and it is the mode by which they are questioned that concerns us here.

The chain of events that inadvertently leads to Stevie's death is initiated not by the anarchists but by Vladimir; and his intended project, the blowing up of the Greenwich Observatory, is the parody of anarchist revolt, not the real thing. Vladimir's collaboration with the Professor by way of Verloc makes the interweaving of authority and violence hard to ignore: an interweaving that has as its expression the arbitrary ability to impose death. Surveillance on the part of any authority, to be effective, must be shorn up by the capacity to punish, which has its origins in the brute power (not necessarily the vaguer "authority") of the state. But, beyond that, even the surveillance is doomed, apparently, to failure for reasons that have to do with the increased need for surveillance itself. One crucial reason for the proliferation of suspicion in Conrad's world is the effacement of the border between public and private realms. Verloc himself, as untrue in his private identity as Stevie's caretaker and Winnie's husband as he is in his political "anarchist" persona, is a sympton of this phenomenon; but as will be shown, its occurrence and its implications both extend beyond the Verloc household, as well. Those implications have a way of ironizing—in this very ironic novel—both the pragmatic and the moral rationales of the system of surveillance and punishment sketched by Conrad in *The Secret Agent.*

Perhaps the writer who has best sketched the process by which this system emerged in the nineteenth century is Michel Foucault, who shows in his book *Discipline and Punish* that the earlier, more direct revenge structure of torture and death was increasingly supplanted by indirect methods of surveillance and threat, as the growth of police in the nineteenth century attests. The threat of punishment and the insistent fact of observation work to intensify and internalize the repressive violence that was once a direct instrument of vengeance. Fear of punishment becomes gradually more important as the fact of punishment becomes occulted, and the act of God that founded the sovereign order is refashioned and experienced by the citizenry as the ever vigilant eye of God.

This movement is expressed and discussed in *Discipline and Punish* as the movement of panopticism, taking its name from Jeremy Bentham's influential notion of the Panopticon.[2] This slim central tower, from which can be seen all of the surrounding segmented prison cells and their occupants but whose occupants themselves cannot be seen in turn by the prisoners, was the pinnacle of the art of surveillance and its emblem, in accordance with the principle that "power should be visible and unverifiable. Visible: the inmate will constantly have before his eyes the tall outline of the central tower from which he is spied upon. Unverifiable: the inmate must never know whether he is being looked at at any one moment; but he must be sure that he may always be so."[3]

But since the new order is alleged to be founded on rational principles of justice and moderation, as well as on the ultimate concern for the good of all men, and even, at least in rhetoric, for the good of the criminal—the panoptical vision of this eye of God is benevolent. Thus, the "maternal vigilance" of Winnie as she glances towards her brother transforms itself in the succeeding chapter into the benign and protective gaze of Adolf Verloc upon Hyde Park as he walks to Knightsbridge and his embassy:

> It was unusually early for him . . . and even his heavy-lidded eyes, refreshed by a night of peaceful slumber, sent out glances of comparative alertness. Through the park railings these glances beheld men and women riding in the Row, couples cantering past harmoniously, others

advancing sedately at a walk. . . . And a peculiarly London sun—against which nothing could be said except that it looked bloodshot—glorified all this by its stare. It hung at a moderate elevation above Hyde Park Corner with a [*sic*] air of punctual and benign vigilance.[4]

The "bloodshot" sun that stares at the scene with a vigilance both "punctual and benign" is a kind of all-seeing eye—an eye that, like God's, glorifies what it beholds. What is presented in this way, as J. Hillis Miller says, is really "a reflection of the pervasive light which makes things visible."[5] The sun, that source of light that is the medium of the visible, is also a double of Verloc's own stare, which reflects the sun's rays and its benignity as well:

He surveyed through the park railings the evidence of the town's opulence with an approving eye. All these people had to be protected. Protection is the first necessity of opulence and luxury. They had to be protected; and their horses, carriages, houses, servants had to be protected; and the source of their wealth had to be protected in the heart of the city and the heart of the country; the whole social order favourable to their hygienic idleness had to be protected against the shallow enviousness of unhygienic labour. (P. 24)

Verloc's "approving eye" looks upon the opulence before it as something to be protected and preserved.

His protective glance is an ironic repetition of his wife's maternal vigilance, though, since its object of solicitude is not a defenseless child but a social order more than capable of defending itself. It is further undercut by the fact that Verloc's eye, which he uses in defending the social order he so approves of, is that of the secret agent: the eye of suspicion rather than of benevolence, in a double vision to which we shall recur. Finally, of course, the protective glance of Verloc—like the Hyde Park sun itself a figure for the benign intent of authority—immediately precedes his visit to the embassy, where he learns that his assignment is precisely to destroy one of the mainstays of this social order, the Greenwich Observatory. The way this news deflates him is evident by the rude contrast of his trip to the embassy with his trip back home: "Mr. Verloc retraced the path of his morning's pilgrimage as if in a dream—an angry dream. This detachment from the material world was so complete that, though the mortal envelope of Mr. Verloc had not hastened unduly along the streets, that part of him to which it would be unwarrantedly rude to refuse immortality, found itself at the shop door all at once" (p. 43). The path that Verloc had traced in a benign, somatic oneness with his surroundings is now retraced in total detachment from his surroundings; his walk home reverses his walk to Knightsbridge in more than the literal sense.

Yet, despite the way it unnerves Verloc, Vladimir's choice of targets is instructive and quite clever, if not too clever. Astronomy, besides being an embodiment of the fetish of science, is also the more powerful symbol for the "punctual and benign vigilance" that should characterize the eye of God. Surveying the entire solar system, it partakes of the reliability and predictability of the sun, and it symbolizes the overseership of the sun as well. It embodies—in fact, it operates—a desire for universal knowledge, for the most thorough appraisal of time and space alike: it charts the movement of bodies and so uses this information to regulate time. No other branch of science crystallizes so well the abstract search for truth as astronomy; as Vladimir points out, "no material interests" are "openly at stake" (p. 40) in the case of astronomy. It is the closest thing to pure mathematics which presents itself as a target. The Greenwich Observatory is the form of overseership itself, an omniscient presence that takes in the universe by its gaze. It is the man-made equivalent of the eye of God. It is benign, and if it is not punctual that is only because it provides the possibility of punctuality itself.

The eye of benign vigilance is still an instrument of social control, just as the sun is not only the "observer" of its planets but in part the regulator of their movements and patterns also. The first meridian is a political function, if only because it brings unprecedented precision to a valuable political component: time. Avrom Fleishman has shown the extent to which time and its measurement permeate *The Secret Agent*, and he demonstrates how often the text cites exact times and durations. He suggests as well that time is "a political weapon, for men would become slaves of the person who could confer time—life itself—upon them. Above all, the shortness of life and the frailty of man are seen against the magnitude of the universe's time, eternity."[6] The all-seeing eye of the Greenwich Observatory is, in one sense, the ultimate political institution, insofar as it grounds and gives form to time; as the creator of time, the Observatory itself can be said to occupy a kind of eternity.

Beyond that, the drive toward omniscience that is embodied in the Observatory (the impulse toward panopticism) has its counterpoint in the activities of the authorities as the text presents them. The executive arms of imperial authority to which one is introduced in the book, such as Chief Inspector Heat and the Assistant Commissioner, are primarily concerned with tracking down information and tracing movements. The bodies whose motions they watch are, of course, those of enemies of the state, and Verloc is a part of this arsenal of information. Just as Verloc's eye of benevolence is doubled by an eye of suspicion, so the magisterial, grand eye of the Greenwich Observatory—a triumph of seemingly disinterested bourgeois science—is doubled by the ever-present eye of suspicion. Needless to say, the entire plot of *The Secret*

Agent concerns the modes of surveillance and the uncovering of secrets: knowledge here is power. In addition, as the scene with the Professor previously cited indicates, they are very much troubled to be sure that the people being watched know it. "When I want you," Heat warns the Professor in their incongruous confrontation, "I shall know where to find you" (p. 86). Heat's position, is, in fact, dependent on his ability to monitor the activities of suspicious characters. He tells a "high official" a few days before the Greenwich attempt that he knows "what each of [the anarchists] is doing hour by hour" (p. 79). Yet, the narrator goes on to qualify the Chief Inspector's hopeful assertion by pointing out that "in the close-woven stuff of relations between conspirator and police there occur . . . sudden holes in space and time." Despite constant surveillance, "a moment always comes when somehow all sight and touch of [a given culprit] are lost for a few hours, during which something (generally an explosion) more or less deplorable does happen" (p. 80). Much of the irony in this very ironic tale of Conrad's is generated by the misinformation of the information-gathering authorities; it is evident, for one thing, that the "hour by hour" charting of movements which Heat portrays to his superior does nothing to prevent either the initial explosion or its aftermath. Furthermore, Heat is mistakenly convinced for a time that the "ticket-of-leave apostle," Michaelis, is in some way in on the bombing, whereas the Professor, whose talents are responsible for the bomb that is used, is never caught. Panopticism is in place and at work, but still it does not seem to do its job.

Part of the reason for this is the way the supporters of the social order work at cross-purposes to one another. In addition to gathering information about enemies of the state, the authorities, at crucial moments, are intent on keeping certain information from one another. Thus, the Chief Inspector advises Verloc to "clear out" of the country when he realizes Verloc was the perpetrator of the bombing. His reasoning is characteristic of the strange logic prevalent in his line of work:

> The turn this affair was taking meant the disclosure of many things—the laying waste of fields of knowledge, which, cultivated by a capable man, had a distinct value for the individual and for the society. It was sorry, sorry meddling. It would leave Michaelis unscathed; it would drag to light the Professor's home industry; disorganize the whole system of supervision; make no end of a row in the papers. (P. 176)

If Verloc is apprehended, vital sources of information might be jeopardized (as well as Heat's reputation for competence). His interest in calling on Verloc is precisely the opposite of his supervisor's, which is why the narrator lays such stress on Heat's "private capacity" when he pays his visit. He is zealous in getting to the bottom of the affair of Stevie, but only because he is worried about what will happen if the Assistant Commissioner gets to the bottom first; and when he finally does dislodge the information, he is more than willing to conceal the results from the other authorities.

At the same time, the Assistant Commissioner is eager for truth in the same way Heat is. Again, though, his motives have little in common with the workings of justice but smack rather of the desire to remain well regarded by his wife. Since Heat's suspicions, as they are voiced to the Assistant Commissioner, focus upon Michaelis, the former is rightly worried that the arrest of Michaelis would put him in the position of having to superintend the arraignment of a darling of his wife's social set. This prospect is his chief impetus to act: "As soon as he was left alone he looked for his hat impulsively, and put it on his head. Having done that, he sat down again to reconsider the whole matter. But as his mind was already made up, this did not take long" (p. 117).

As he proceeds to Brett Street, the Assistant Commissioner stealthily pursues his way, so stealthily that he hides at one point from an officer on the beat, "as though he were a member of the criminal classes" (p. 130). Like Heat and Vladimir before him, the Assistant Commissioner betrays at critical times a curious affinity for the "criminal classes" he supposedly works against. This slippage of law enforcement into illegality is one of the principal narrative motors of *The Secret Agent*. Foucault says of the Panopticon that it can provide "an apparatus for supervising its own mechanisms. In this central tower, the director may spy on all the employees that he has under his orders. . . . He will be able to judge them continuously . . . and it will even be possible to observe the director himself."[7] Though the authorities in this text strive for the panoptical principle, in this crucial particular and hence in many others that principle remains an elusive one. (One is reminded of one of the items which prompted Conrad to produce his book: Sir Harcourt's remark to a junior official that "your idea of secrecy . . . seems to consist of keeping the Home Secretary in the dark"[p. 10].)

This failure of authority to police itself is symptomatic of the circumstances that give rise to panopticism rather than of panopticism in itself. After all, Foucault begins his discussion of panopticism with the description of seventeenth-century measures that were traditionally undertaken to deal with a town that was stricken by plague. The strict partitioning of space in quarantine, the constant surveillance and routine questioning of all families in a plague-town, the recording of all movements—these techniques were the habitual response to a condition of plague. The nineteenth century's panopticism incorporates all of these techniques and, in a way, represents their apotheosis. But this

increasing application of the methods of the plague-town to the every-
day life of the community presupposes a situation in which the plague
can spread to anyone. The question as to what the plague consists in—
whether actual disease, or criminality, or insanity—is less relevant than
the fact that this condition is increasingly viewed as the one to be
assumed. Whether this assumption characterizes European society of
the last century is too large a question to answer (though undoubtedly
Foucault would tend to reply in the affirmative). What is more demon-
strable is that the world Conrad constructs in *The Secret Agent* is one in
which the very anonymity of the citizenry, the lack of interaction among
them, increases the mutual distrust among men. The fear that fuels the
society's urge to total surveillance is based not only on the understood
possibility that others may spread the plague, but also on the recognition that everyone is susceptible to contamination, that the boundaries
between the healthy and the diseased member of the social body cannot
be easily drawn. The upholder of the social order exhibits most disturb-
ing tendencies at times, just as the fiercest opponents of that order often
mirror, in authoritarian zeal, the panoptical desire itself. One recalls
Ossipon's strange vision of the Professor's "black-rimmed spectacles
progressing along the streets on the top of an omnibus, their self-
confident glitter falling here and there on the walls of houses or lowered
upon the heads of the unconscious stream of people on the pavements"
(p. 63). The Professor becomes in this passage truly a one-man
Panopticon.

This paranoid situation, where one's inner doubts increase the
doubts about one's fellows and where anyone is a contaminant because
all are contaminated, is deepened by the segmentation of the city where
anonymity breeds uncertainty. It may not be accidental that a text that
so fully delineates the perils of panopticism also contains a pointed
meditation on anonymity. It is the Assistant Commissioner, a Briton
more at home in the tropics than in Britain, through whose perspective
the meditation on displaced personhood is rendered. As he is on the way
to Brett Street to ensnare Adolf Verloc, he stops in an Italian restaurant.

The restaurant has an "atmosphere of fraudulent cookery mocking
an abject mankind in the most pressing of its miserable necessities" (p.
128). The Assistant Commissioner seems to "lose some more of his
identity" in what is called an "immoral atmosphere"; but with this loss
of identity goes a sense of "evil freedom. It was rather pleasant." In
relinquishing his characteristic role, he gains by compensation a freedom to do as he likes, in this case to exceed his delegated authority in
hunting down Verloc. As he regards himself in the mirror, he is "struck
by his foreign appearance." The vastness of the city allows him to
become another person, rendering him alien to himself as a result. (He

becomes somewhat alien to the reader by this stroke, too, since, for one thing, he is only known to the reader as the "Assistant Commissioner.") The Assistant Commissioner cannot read his own appearance; and it is not so much that he looks a different nationality as that he simply looks foreign, displaced.

As he pays his bill, his eyes begin to take in the surrounding area, all "baited with a perspective of mirrors." His sense of his own displacement now expands to embrace the clientele of the restaurant as a whole, and he finds that "the patrons of the place had lost in the frequentation of fraudulent cookery all their national and private characteristics" (p. 128), which is especially ironic because what should give nourishment only consumes, or drains, those who frequent it. It is in this milieu of loss of national and private identity that the Italian restaurant becomes for the Assistant Commissioner a "peculiarly British institution," a place of crepuscular exile. Like the dishes they consume, the patrons have a kind of "unstamped respectability," which is without identity "professionally, socially, or racially"; the Assistant Commissioner cannot "place them anywhere outside those special establishments." Neither their occupation nor their places of residence are readable to the eye. Their identity seems consumed by their momentary role within the institution (a peculiarly British one) that nominally serves them. They seem, to the eye of the foreigner, to have been "created for" the Italian restaurant, inseparable from the furniture of the place they inhabit. The perplexity of the Assistant Commissioner arises from the the tension between his temptation to see the patrons in this light, and his knowledge that they, like he, must have aspects of their existence that cannot be subsumed under their role in the restaurant. This double vision rebounds finally on the Assistant Commissioner himself, as he reflects that his own identity must be as unreadable to the other patrons as it is foreign to his own eyes: "And he himself had become unplaced. It would have been impossible for anybody to guess his occupation." Despite the freedom the Assistant Commissioner initially feels, however, he is more than happy to leave this establishment: "A pleasurable feeling of independence possessed him when he heard the glass doors swing to behind his back with a sort of imperfect baffled thud" (p. 129). The little restaurant that grants anonymity to its patrons by suppressing their characteristics is also a kind of imprisonment; "long and narrow," and "baited with . . . mirrors" like a specular Minotaur's den, it gives the impression that its customers, in some strange inversion, are its servants or its captives. The promise of freedom becomes rather a symptom of slavery, and the enigmatic identities of the customers as much a token of queasy conformity, of "unstamped respectability," as of freedom from the judgment of others.

This loss of identity is not so much an existential as a social phenomenon. The Assistant Commissioner's identity is lost not to himself but to his imagined audience, whose first member is himself. He is the mystery to the other people at the restaurant that they in turn are to him, but it is not strictly speaking an alienation from self. (After all, the self-mistrust that increases mistrust of others may in fact come of knowing oneself too well.) The social dimensions of this eerie restaurant scene are limned concisely by Richard Sennett in *The Fall of Public Man*, in which he argues that the nineteenth-century urban landscape in Western Europe, combining an influx of disparate groups with a decline in the public codes through which people could express themselves, produced a situation in which outward appearance—clothing, for instance—becomes increasingly a means of concealment rather than of signification. Whereas previously appearance was the straightforward inscription of one's occupation, class, and social group, the nineteenth-century approach takes the outer garment more as a palimpsest, as an overt message through which the practiced eye may read another, truer inscription. According to Sennett, the people of this time "took each other's appearances in the street immensely seriously; they believed they could fathom the character of those they saw, but what they saw were people dressed in clothes increasingly more homogeneous and monochromatic."[8]

The attempt on the part of the patrons to remain anonymous is the logical extension of a world where people's dress is viewed with suspicion and scrutiny as a set of involuntary clues to private behavior. The line of demarcation between public and private becomes hazier, and this haziness contributes both to the surveillance and the attempt to remain anonymous. The notion that one's actions in public were clues to one's personality

> destroyed the public by making people fearful of betraying their emotions to others involuntarily. The result was more and more an attempt to withdraw from contact with others, to be shielded by silence, even to attempt to stop feeling in order for the feelings not to show. The public thus was emptied of people who wanted to be expressive in it, as the terms of expression moved from the presentation of a mask to the revelation of one's personality, of one's face, in the mask one wore in the world.[9]

The concealment of oneself from others, at first the condition of a kind of spurious freedom, becomes enslavement to the narrow perimeter of public gesture and decorum which is maintained to avert the gaze of others. It is less the "fraudulent cookery" of the restaurant than its atmosphere—which partakes of the increasingly barren public space of Britain—that is finally the enslaver of its customers, the agent that makes the patrons seem somehow to have been "created for the restaurant" rather than the other way around. Since their anonymity is founded on reticence, the patrons—including the Assistant Commissioner—become paradoxical captives of the restaurant, its mute victims. The shell of anonymity calcifies around each one, and the public space of the restaurant—that place of unplacing—solidifies into a prison.

The monochromatic attire of the Victorian period, which encourages people to look for involuntary disclosures of private traits, has the same structure as this unplacing, because this fact leads to a more extreme effort to place people. If Stevie has committed one sin for which punishment could be exacted in the curious world Conrad creates here, it is his inability to remember his own name and address. The London of *The Secret Agent* is above all an exile's London, a realm of displaced persons. The "slimy aquarium" of London contains many "queer foreign fish" that become ad hoc assimilated through fraudulent cookery or otherwise to the "genius of the [British] locality" (p. 127). The Assistant Commissioner's knack for seeming foreign recalls Vladimir's "amazingly genuine English accent" (p. 42) and Verloc's dual status as a natural-born British subject and the son of a Frenchman. (If the locality of Conrad's London has a genius, it is one that confuses both national and private characteristics.) The Assistant Commissioner becomes another of the queer foreign fish, just as the supposed foreigners who frequent the fraudulent restaurant become indistinguishable from Britishers. But, as the restaurant scene dramatizes, the exile is in many ways more at the mercy of his temporary abode, more its prisoner, than at first seems the case. One has only to think of Ossipon's anxiety to leave Britain with Winnie, where the "insular nature of Great Britain obtruded itself upon his notice in an odious form. 'Might just as well be put under lock and key every night,' he thought irritably" (p. 231).

The imprisonment of the characters in this novel (it is appropriate that the Panopticon model was used first in prisons) extends from Michaelis's literal imprisonment and splendid figurative captivity in London high society to the Professor's imprisonment to his twenty-second lag in detonation time. For the imprisonment is not only true spatially but also temporally; one returns to the political function that lurks behind the Greenwich Observatory's disinterested eye of benevolence. (Ossipon is trapped not only by the insular nature of Britain but also by the train timetable.) In a milieu where anyone can be a criminal (or an informer) and the public space is primarily a place of concealment, the need to fix people in both space and time—the need for what Foucault calls "docile bodies"—increases in inverse proportion to the mystery people try to cultivate.

The maze-like quality of Conrad's London itself, with its "Squares, Places, Ovals, Commons" and "monotonous streets with unknown names" (p. 245), "its maze of streets and its mass of lights . . . sunk in a hopeless night," the inhabitant of "a black abyss" (p. 222) and its diabolical numbering system that gets the best of Verloc in chapter 2— this unreadable city is an extension of the inscrutability of the persons who move about it. The characters in this text do not walk around London so much as they make their way through it. It is very much the Victorian London that Sennett describes by way of Thackeray: "People who lived so that they would avoid detection on the street, sought . . . to 'deny to probing eyes a knowledge that should come to none indiscriminately in the city.' Theirs was a world of shaded lamps, hooded bonnets, rides in closed carriages."[10] This is a world very much with us in this text's evocation of London, which the aquarium image captures so well: a clear glass for surveillance, but a murky medium that renders this surveillance next to impossible. This image, like the physical landscape it describes, allegorizes a condition of social epistemology, and, it appears, a relatively recent condition. The bright sun that beams benevolently on Hyde Park is an anomaly; the London of *The Secret Agent* is no sunlit world.

The restaurant scene suggests that this suspicion engendered by the increasing anonymity of people is not restricted to the official servants of power, but is, of course, a suspicion by all citizens of all citizens. The few citizens lacking in suspicion, such as Stevie, fare very poorly.

These suspicions return to the realm of intimacy in a particularly sinister fashion. To consider Winnie and Ossipon, one recalls that Ossipon's theorist Lombroso believes in the precise correlation of physical characteristics to criminal pathology: a *reductio ad absurdum* of the many theories of the involuntary disclosure of character developed in the nineteenth century and discussed by Sennett. Yet, this absurdity crystallizes Ossipon's distrust of Winnie as they are at the point of fleeing London: "He gazed at her, and invoked Lombroso, as an Italian peasant recommends himself to his favourite saint. He gazed scientifically. He gazed at her cheeks, at her nose, at her eyes, at her ears. . . . Bad! . . . Fatal! . . . Not a doubt remained . . . a murdering type" (p. 242). This moment of scientific, or pseudoscientific, revelation is an ironic reversal of Ossipon's initial attraction to Winnie. All the features that at first interested him then only disturb him now; this fear contaminates his interest in women as a whole, because he sees now a trap in all intimacy. The collapse of the public / private distinction—here as in the Verloc household itself—only serves to infect intimacy with suspicion, not to bring intimate warmth to the public sphere.

Ossipon, then, serves as an ironic figure of tendencies in the social structure he purports to attack; even his utopian vision of the good society, which the Professor rightly characterizes as "the idea of a world planned out like an immense and nice hospital" (p. 246), is very close to the panoptical institutional ideal. But he is also a victim, at least in metaphor, of the operations of the Panopticon. After he escapes from the train bearing Winnie out of London, he walks back to his home through the streets of nighttime London. He is seen as he walks, not by men, according to the text, but by the objects of London, and by the streetlights:

> He crossed the bridge. Later on the towers of the Abbey saw in their massive immobility the yellow bush of his hair passing under the lamps. The lights of Victoria saw him, too, and Sloane Square, and the railings of the park. . . . His robust form was seen that night in distant parts of the enormous town slumbering monstrously on a carpet of mud under a veil of raw mist. It was seen crossing the streets without life and sound, or diminishing in the interminable straight perspectives of shadowy houses bordering empty roadways lined by strings of gas-lamps. (Pp. 244-45)

The lamps become the agents of panopticism, as well as the correlatives for Ossipon's own guilt. Picking out his form from the maze of London, the lamps are the visibility and the unverifiability of surveillance; and Ossipon's room becomes a cell where he sits with his knees drawn up, "clasping his legs." He stays awake immobile in his room all night, "sitting still for hours without stirring a limb or an eyelid" (p. 245). Ossipon's sense of isolation, his fear, and his uncomfortable conscience make his night a sleepless one, like the prisoner who spends his life in "a sequestered and observed solitude" before the central tower of the Panopticon.[11] The benevolent sun that finally sends its dawn rays into Ossipon's cell—banishing the night and with it, paradoxically, his sleeplessness—is the antidote to Ossipon's internalized eye of suspicion: "Comrade Ossipon slept in the sunlight" (p. 245).

This antidote is only temporary, though, as the book's conclusion demonstrates. That internalized eye has driven in too deep; the plague has progressed too far and Ossipon has become too susceptible to it. The plague, of which Winnie was a carrier, is not only criminality but also madness (though a man of Ossipon's convictions is sure to identify the two). "He was becoming scientifically afraid of insanity" (p. 249)—not of Winnie's insanity or of Stevie's, but of his own.

The agent of this insanity is the newspaper account of Winnie's suicide in the English Channel, obliquely imaged in Ossipon's walk as he stares into the river, "a sinister marvel of still shadows and flowing gleams," and thinks of the "wild night in the Channel" (p. 244). This suicide is emblematized in one sentence of the story, a sentence that pursues Ossipon as surely as the street lamps of London: "'*An impenetra-*

ble mystery seems destined to hang for ever over this act of madness and despair.'
. . . He knew every word by heart" (p. 249). The words are "an obsession, a torture" to Ossipon and they paralyze his will with the women he once sought. The impersonal voice of the newspaper, not quite public opinion and not quite the locus of authority, speaks from a curious space indeed, and it partakes of the power of the institutional hierarchy and the power of the undifferentiated public at the same time. But this very lack of definition which makes its pronouncements seem to be the voice of God also loosens it from any definitive ground. The discourse in the newspaper is not the incitement to specific action nor the addressing of a defined audience; its intended readership is everyone and no one, and it is consumed in anonymous seclusion, one reader at a time. Its "public" is only the statistical aggregation of private readers. One may say that it is the mysterious tendency of social epistemology and the collapse of distinctions between public and private realms with the increasing surveillance thus engendered in both, which give rise to the anxiety of Ossipon. This fear of displacement by anxiety, of insanity, finds its corollary in the "unplaced" discourse of the newspaper.

Insanity for Ossipon is a plague and it can be caught from anyone, because all motives, all human personalities, are a source of "impenetrable mystery," veiled like Winnie to both her husband and Ossipon. The scolding newspaper article is one way the fear of the surveying gaze is internalized as remorse of conscience; but it is also a symptom of the fragmentation and unreadability of public discourse that prompted the urge for surveillance.

Yet it is this public discourse—called "public opinion"—that is the virtual target of so much of the activity in the book. Vladimir hopes that the Observatory bombing will rouse public opinion, which mirrors (like so much else about Vladimir) the Professor's concern to shake up public opinion with "madness and despair," his "lever to move the world." The public opinion these people aim for, as well as the public opinion Heat constantly fears, is always elsewhere. It is, by definition, the opinion of others, of a public of which one is never oneself a member when one considers or speaks of it. The "public" addressed by both Vladimir and the Professor, like the readership of the newspaper, is not palpably concerned or affected in any way by any of the incidents in this text. The worry that momentarily haunts the Professor ("What if nothing could move them?") seems in large part justified.

But if the newspaper story of Winnie's death does not move the public at large, it has an undeniable effect on Ossipon as an individual. Furthermore, what is true of Ossipon is, in one sense, equally true of the woman he abandons. Winnie is also pursued by a newspaper article, but its content is slightly different from that of Ossipon's nemesis.

Winnie thinks, after murdering her husband, of all the newspaper accounts of hangings she has read: "The impossibility of imagining the details of such quiet execution added something maddening to her abstract terror. The newspapers never gave any details except one, but that one with some affectation was always there at the end of a meagre report. Mrs. Verloc remembered its nature. It came with a cruel burning pain into her head, as if the words 'The drop given was fourteen feet' had been scratched on her brain with a hot needle" (p. 220).

That sentence—"The drop given was fourteen feet"—becomes the survival of the origin of punishment in the world of panopticism. The judgment of the newspapers is enough to dog Ossipon for his act of faithlessness but it does not prevent it; even more so, the newspaper reports of hangings are enough to frighten Winnie, but they do not prevent the deed. Because of the loss of public space of discourse—discourse that the anonymous paper only simulates—the private selves of the citizenry become more and more public business; but the loss of a clearly defined social space increases the alienation of the citizenry one from another, and so increases the plague of crime. The atomization that gives rise to panopticism also breeds the conditions for crime to flourish, and this is why the surveillance of the nineteenth century is not enough; its guilty origin in the state's power of punishment must be preserved in the minds of the citizens. If the words that pursue Ossipon emblematize the atomization in Conrad's London, then the words that torture Winnie are the embodiment of the sovereign retribution the state may still exact. For while the newspaper's voice of God pronounces judgment on Ossipon without knowing it, that same voice, again without knowing it, pronounces sentence on Winnie.

But this "act of God" is not a spectacle. None of the deaths in the novel—not even the most crucial and the most meaningless death, that of Stevie—is public. One is in the world of *The Secret Agent*, about as far from the spectacle—whether of punishment or of anything else—as one is likely to get. The theater of this spectacle is Winnie's own consciousness, and the rehearsal for it is provided by hangings that are not publicly held, only reported after the fact by newspapers without editorial comment. There are public spectacles in *The Secret Agent* but they are all imagined, like Vladimir's Greenwich bombing or the restaurant explosion envisioned by Ossipon. None of them are ever realized in the novel. Yet Winnie's interior spectacle, where the one imagining sees herself in the place of the victim, is carefully preserved as a possibility by the institutional apparatus of her rulers. The fact that the state can exact the ultimate retribution from the condemned is no longer celebrated as the flexing of sovereign power; but the fear that it could happen is deliberately maintained in the guilty minds of (actual or potential) enemies of the state, all possible carriers of the plague.

The public executions of the eighteenth century took place in the open *theatrum mundi*; but with the emptying out of that space, these latter executions have a different backdrop entirely. Punishment in *The Secret Agent* is no longer enacted on the stage of public life as a spectacle, but is rather rehearsed in the mind of each private citizen as a possibility. A gallows—the counterpart of the Panopticon's central tower and likewise a locus of visible and unverifiable power—is erected on the stage of Winnie's interior theater, as she reads her newspaper; and a similar gallows has been set up in the mind of each of her fellow readers.

The reading of a novel is not, after all, far different from the reading of a newspaper. The voice of the author, particularly when the author is Conrad, is not as unplaced as the voice of the newspaper, but its "public" is still as much a mere statistical collection of private people as the paper's public. Although Conrad subsequently arranged for the staging of *The Secret Agent* as a play, it is clear that the novel's situation of the mass society of its time is mimed in the experience of the newspaper; addressed, like the novel, to anyone and to no one, consumed, like the novel, in isolation by anonymous readers. Whether Conrad thought that his text could inscribe itself on the minds of its public like "a hot needle" is a matter of mystery, though the ironical style in which the narrative is presented suggests a certain doubt. In the face of such a fragmented public, a storyteller must have experienced some of the uncertainty of the Professor. He must often have wondered whether anything could move his very private "public," and perhaps more disturbingly, whether he could ever know they had been moved. He must have known that the public for Conrad's novel would be situated in much the same space as the public within the novel: that is, elsewhere.

Conclusion

We have encountered in these pages two novelists in profound tension with their readerships, if for divergent reasons, and both were aware of that tension. We have also encountered similar movements within the novels we have explored: all of them contain some aspect of their structure that mimes or dramatizes their vexed relation to the phantom audience.

L'Education sentimentale, in its depiction of a vast bourse where everything is bought and sold and in its use of economic metaphor for art, suggests its own dual status: as art (individual expression) and as vendable commodity (public commonplace). It is for this reason the exemplary Flaubert text, not because it is the most autobiographical of the mature works. It is exemplary because it sets forth with appropriate clarity and complexity the skewed thematics of the artist in the emerging society of the late nineteenth century, and specifically of his relation to the increasingly insistent commercial traffic. We saw how the neat polarities of Flaubert's early essay on the arts and commerce are undone in the later work. Art is an explicit element in *L'Education,* along with the text's reliance, despite itself, on the common coinage of cliché for its pathos. In the economy Flaubert limns, there is no way out of the cliché network, other than to exchange it as gifts with friends, rather than anonymously on the market. Hence, the model of fiction in the epilogues of *L'Education* looks remarkably similar to that in Conrad's nostalgic storyteller figures. In preparing for this facet of Conrad, in focusing the problem of political legitimacy for the Second Republic and the Second Empire, and in dramatizing the corrosive action of the marketplace in undermining both the public sphere and the (seemingly) sacred private realm of art—in all these ways, *L'Education* provides an appropriate framework of motifs within which to look at Conrad's middle novels. Under the circumstances, it has made sense to give this Flaubert text a scrutiny at least approaching those of Conrad's.

It has also made sense because the situation set forth in that novel has impact as well on the novel's own telling: on its rhetorical status, and on the contours of its virtual, or phantom, audience. This "boomerang effect" is also a feature of the Conrad novels selected for study. In each case, the ideological condition dramatized in the novels turns back, in some fashion, upon those novels themselves. Unlike Flaubert, Conrad does not much thematize the question of art or of fiction in these three works; yet, the boomerang effect is still felt in subtler ways.

With *Lord Jim,* imperial ideology is engaged at a moment of scandal when it is in great peril.[1] If one sticks with the narrative logic of this text, it becomes very hard to see the story as anything other than a profound register of disquiet with the pretensions to honor that made the merchant marine and the empire as a whole seem nobler than perhaps they were. Yet, because of the choice of narrator—Charlie Marlow guides the tale through all but the first few chapters—most critics apparently read it chiefly as "a tale of courage and cowardice, a moral story, and an object-lesson in the difficulties of constructing an existential hero"—even though, as Fredric Jameson points out correctly, this superficial version of *Lord Jim* "is no more to be taken at face value than is the dreamer's immediate waking sense of what the dream was about."[2] The chief reason for this deflection of emphasis is Marlow, who turns aside from the ideological ramifications of Jim's story when these become uncomfortable for him. Though it is as a representative of what is best—and what is flawed in what is best—in the empire that Jim rivets Marlow and the putative readership, the implications for that empire of Jim's *dénouement* are not dilated on, and instead mystical imponderables such as fate and individual character are invoked. The contradictions within the British imperial stance clearly turn back upon this text, eventually causing a mutual interference between narrative logic and thematic reflection.

If the boomerang causes seemingly limited damage to *Lord Jim,* this is because Marlow's narrative voice serves admirably not only as a model of the storyteller but also as a foil. In extremity, one can suggest that the inconsistencies that speak Marlow are only a part of his "unreliable narrator" baggage. By the time of *Nostromo,* however, there is less use of storytellers, and the de-legitimating rot spreads further. Here, the economic, which was a muted element in *Lord Jim,* becomes the central agency of corruption in the form of the Gould Concession; at the same time, the emerging state of Sulaco is much more foregrounded, more fully realized, than Patusan. As this vital land is slowly divested of its resources to benefit Europeans' "material interests," it becomes evident that a similar grim economy operates Conrad's narrative. The text, like the gold-hunting *gringos* soon lost on the peninsula, takes a region's history and culture to transform it into its own property. It fashions that history and culture into a cautionary tale, and markets it to a European audience—from whose point of view the novel is presented, even when the egregious Captain Mitchell tells the story of Sulaco toward the conclusion. The competing values of embryonic Costaguana are soon reduced to exchange value, to that which can be exported; in depicting the process, *Nostromo* makes the reader sense that the novel is performing the same function—not by virtue of depicting such a process (to narrate a crime is not to commit one) but because its rhetorical and political space is so similar to that of the Europeans in Sulaco. Thus, one has the paradoxical situation that as the novel bears down ever harder on its theme of the silver's corruption, *Nostromo* seems to lose its reason for being. Insofar as the corrosive effects of the economic have de-legitimated the activities of *Nostromo*'s exporting Europeans, the novel's own attempts to use Latin America to extract a salutary lesson for Europeans falls under a like stricture. This boomerang is severer than that affecting *Lord Jim* because there is no storyteller to deflect the contamination and because it is less devastating for a story to have a lesson it ignores than it is for a story's lesson to question the moral legitimacy of the story itself.

The Secret Agent, the last of Conrad's middle-period novels before *Under Western Eyes,* emerges in the aftermath of *Nostromo* and its problematical resolution. The remnants of oral culture have largely disappeared, along with imperial themes and content: Conrad has "come home," but it is hardly a homelike London he portrays. To be sure, the spy genre works against the homelike; but this world of Conrad's is anomic with a vengeance. The public sphere is an absolutely alienated realm, ruled on no consensus other than fear of the gallows, or in a milder form, public opinion. All intimacies, such as those between the Verlocs, are equally false, partaking of the larger social fraudulence and duplicity. The narrative voice is cool, ironic, and third person. The one unambiguously moral character in the text is an idiot boy who is killed while carrying someone else's bomb. The clearest way to see how this social etiolation turns back on the rhetorical status of the work itself is to look at the role of newspapers in *The Secret Agent:* as parodies of the revelatory, bardic role of the poet. These mass-produced, vendable objects have no audience, merely a circulation, and their relation to their readership ("public opinion") is generally indifferent, at best aggressive. (Winnie Verloc, for instance, is psychically invaded by the news story of an execution, and Ossipon is obviously going slowly mad to-

ward the end by revolving the account of Winnie's suicide in his head.)
Once again, the de-legitimating process has implicated the narrative
itself. The state has no claim to authority other than some founding
violence, just as a novelist's only claim to popular legitimacy in an age
of anonymous publics is the sheer strength of sensation or brute rhetorical force. The educative or pedagogical possibilities of art are assumed
illusory from the start, are given over.[3]

This rebound seems the most radical of all. Whereas *Lord Jim*'s
narrative undermines the position only of its narrator and *Nostromo*'s
moral lesson undermines only itself, *The Secret Agent*'s bleak scenario
undercuts the viability of literature as an institution. After all, if there is
no legitimate ruling order, no cohesive audience, and no moral authority in this world—and for this text to be successful, that world must be
convincing—then there is not much of a role for literature as an institution to play. At such a juncture, the legitimation of literature becomes
purely aesthetic, a question of style. Candidacy for the imaginary library replaces the educative, even paternalistic role of an author confronting and contributing to a culture. The curious bifurcation seen in
Flaubert, where style is the only redemptive medium and thematic
content is declared void, begins to install itself here. Rather than con-
verging, the desired audience and the probable readership also drift
farther apart than ever.

All of the novels examined here, then, exhibit the boomerang effect:
in various keys, but all of them working to undermine and to question a
stable rhetorical status and sense of audience for themselves. The parameters of the questions raised are largely set, as previously shown, by
Flaubert, not incidentally referred to now and then as the "founder of
modernism"; the middle-period Conrad novels are a fuller elaboration,
in a slightly different historical register, of these questions.

In this connection, a number of other questions come naturally to
mind. Are these self-undermining moments peculiar to Flaubert and
Conrad? If not, why pick these authors in particular? If so, why focus
on these moments as especially significant? How can we as readers
know that these self-undermining moments are "really there," and not
merely inferred for no reason? Similarly, how do these questionings
arise in a text? Are they assimilable to the meaning structure of a text?
Or, conversely, do they englobe and reflect that meaning structure in a
kind of self-aware irony?

To begin with, the opening chapter is devoted largely to demonstrat-
ing the universal need for legitimation that inscribes itself in all utterance, whether written or spoken. In positing itself, before any specific
content, as utterance, discourse by that same act calls into being a
justification, reason, or lineage for itself, and so immediately installs

itself within a relation to previous discourse. To speak or to write is to usurp silence and to call for recognition; but to be recognized must mean resembling, or drawing validity from, what has been said and written before. (That is the original root of the word, "re-cognize.") That which posits itself—any speech or writing act—must posit itself as something, and in so doing must establish its legitimacy with respect to a prior model, or at least one posited as prior.[4] From the inception, before considering human subjects, agents, or any other elements, the act of utterance sets this process in motion, whether or not it is willed by a speaker or writer, whether or not any author or audience is even aware of it.

At the highest level of abstraction, this is what happens; and if that were all there was to it, there would not be much point in moving beyond this level. But as can readily be imagined, this abstract scheme is only the beginning of the story—or the end. The urge to legitimation takes forms more or less explicit and is more or less successful, according to the occasion of utterance. No persuasive move is ever an assured success—that is true even insofar as the self is object of the persuasion. And to say that this is true is only to say that any speech or writing act has a history and is part of a history.

More narrowly, every speech or writing act is installed in a definite social, cultural circumstance. The forms by which the recognition of any act of discursive positing is gained—whether a cry for food, a letter, or a constitution—will be provided, if not determined, by the time and place of that act. Even moves to alter some aspect of the existing order are usually couched in terms of that order. This means that the legitimative strategies of a discourse are somewhat easier to elicit if one knows the general historical moment impinging upon it and the specific constraints imposed by the traditions of that genre of discourse.[5] Thus, the theoretical power politics suggested in the structure of usurpation and later justification that molds all discursive practice comes into contact with the legitimative problems of what is more commonly called politics rather quickly.

Given this historical dimension, it follows that there are certain periods, societies, and circumstances where the need for legitimation is especially obvious, is somehow thematized. Jürgen Habermas has called these moments of heightening urgency "legitimation crises." To the extent such a crisis can be identified, it can disclose with special clarity both the enduring insistence of this feature of all communication and also the particular contradictions of a certain era and culture. To further narrow the focus, the era of the bourgeois nation-state—emerging roughly at the conclusion of the eighteenth century and, in mutated form, still largely with us—has exhibited special strains as it labors to acquire legitimacy for its tenure. Its frequent recourse to precapitalist images of authority for its cachet, images Richard Sennett calls "paternalist," can serve as a symptom of this condition. (This state may be too ongoing to be called a crisis, but it is still too acute to be called, for instance, a malaise.) Selected in part for this reason, the novels in this study present some of the most troublesome facets of this condition: the frustrating search for a social validation of the activities of the market-place is a recurrent motif, for example. That the authors are bourgeois writers addressing a bourgeois readership does not weaken their usefulness for this analysis, but rather confirms it. Any text that operates as rigorously as these against the backdrop of this crisis will rework and elaborate—but never fully escape—its toils: a fact that can be demonstrated by observing the movement of argument of a major theoretician of writing who at one point seems to suggest that it can be escaped.

The young Roland Barthes in *Writing Degree Zero* states that a given language is "a horizon, which implies both a boundary and a perspective; in short, it is the comforting area of an ordered space. The writer literally takes nothing from it; a language is for him rather a frontier."[6] This fiercely optimistic stance, characteristic of early, "revolutionary" Barthes, is gradually tempered and qualified out of existence. The frontier, by paragraph's end, is a less dynamic limit—"the geometrical *locus* of all that he [a writer] could not say without, like Orpheus looking back, losing the stable meaning of his enterprise and his essential gesture as a social being."[7] For Barthes's "language" one could substitute Iser's narrower "expectation norms," for essential "gesture of social being," "legitimation," and have a fair depiction of the dilemma facing any novelistic text, especially in a society where narratives bear heavily on the values of dominant elements in the society (or to put it more plainly, where many people read serious fiction).

Like that for political legitimacy, the desire for rhetorical legitimacy causes a search backward, for precursors, models, fathers: "It is under the pressure of History and Tradition that the possible modes of writing for a given writer are established; there is a History of Writing. But this History is dual: at the very moment when general History proposes—or imposes—new problematics of the literary language, writing still remains full of the recollection of previous usage, for language is never innocent."[8] Even rebellions against the prior state of a genre or a linguistic practice are often cut with, or even posed in terms of, legitimating forms and commonplaces.

Such, then, are the broader enabling historical constraints that illuminate, and are illuminated by, the novelists I consider; and the more specific generic constraints of the novel as a form have also been situated within this perspective. At the point where literature comes into play, though, an obvious problem with this scheme can be raised. After all, since a work of literature—to the extent it is literature—is definable as "autotelic," as creating its own world, without reference to the uses and purposes of the outside society, or even to questions of truth and falsehood, by what means can such a problematic be applied to fiction?

First of all, the belief in a literature removed from the world's uses may be relatively recent: construction on the "imaginary library" was probably begun in earnest only in the mid-nineteenth century, with Flaubert, ironically, as one of the architects. The act of publication sullies this notion, introducing as it does questions (usually answered in the negative) of fame, money, love, and other unliterary matters. Nevertheless, even were it granted that "pure" literature, or the purely aesthetic, was a viable ideal, still the work of art, insofar as it is written, is a linguistic activity whose goal must reside in something communicated: delight, say, or awe and pity, or emotion recollected in tranquillity. This requires the acceptance, at least, or the active assent, at best, of the reader. Evidently true of published work, this need for reader validation is even—perhaps especially—urgent in the case of those who allege to write only for themselves. Writers can scarcely be the same persons in reading their works as they are in writing them.

As soon as the work of art is admitted to have even this purpose—that of gaining credence–these legitimate matters become clearly relevant. The phantom reader from whom credence is sought is no more than the concatenation of cultural codes that have institutionalized a set of past expectations and prohibitions; and in trying to "say something new," writers necessarily have appeal to those anterior codes even as they fashion a new readership from the old. Terry Eagleton demonstrates the political component of this readership: "Any particular act of reading is conducted within a general set of assumptions as to the ideological signification of reading itself within a social formation—assumptions which . . . belong . . . to the general 'ideology of culture.'"[9] What is true for an act of reading is true as well for an act of writing, which is a project proceeding and drawing its force from the previous writing that has inscribed itself on a readership. Eagleton's general "ideology of culture" is a construct that both enables and constrains any work, without the need for a theory of intentionality. In order to function, a work of art like any other piece of language must situate itself to be taken in a certain way by its audience, which means situating itself with respect to previous literature. In theory, a work has virtually infinite reference to other works; but a strong sense for how a work is situated in a specific historical moment vis-à-vis particular audiences can provide the most fruitful frame of reference.

Eagleton's point is, then, by way of suggesting that although there are specific parameters to the act of reading fiction, that act is also part of a larger, socially determined horizon of expectations—with all the ideological baggage attendant upon that status. This realization may not account for what has come unhappily to be called the "literariness" of literature. But there is an increasing sense among textual theorists that the division between fictional or poetic textuality and textuality or language *simpliciter* is not so clear-cut as was once assumed.[10]

In fact, the social validation literature seeks is if anything harder to achieve than that of other discourses that have a secure niche within a culture and its institutions. Much is made of the advantage of literature in being marginal to other of society's discourses; and this surely accords it greater critical insight and freedom. Along with this freedom and insight, though, goes a desire for greater persuasive force and even for respectability. (The urge to respectability is, indeed, often greatest on the margins.) The intensity and the object of this urge—the shape of the desired audience—changes with writer and period; however, the constant tug-of-war between the poles of eccentricity and respectability is a necessary feature of what fiction is. The "expectation norms" a text sets up can be stretched, even flouted, but not erased. Indeed, the more interesting the text, the more ingenious is likely to be its mode of treating the built-in expectations of its phantom audience.

This phantom becomes ever more elusive, as shown in the discussion of the novel as a form. A fictional narrative's legitimacy is probably somewhat harder to secure in this modern age than previously. Lacking a utilitarian rationale but still claiming for itself a value as a kind of wisdom, serious fiction turned increasingly for recognition to coteries, to the perfection of technique (perhaps hoping that artistic and scientific progress were analogous), to the religion of art, even to posterity— surely a last resort in more than one sense. The increasing fragmentation of the literate public and the concomitant weakening of the traditional identity of artistic forms are often seen as positive and liberating (always a term of benediction). There is no question that modernism did "make it new," exploring the possibilities of narrative voice, frame, descriptive nuance, and point of view. At the same time, it is clear that modernism was a constant search for validating forms, often theological or mythological, and for a stable, usable literary tradition that (in T. S. Eliot's case, for instance) was closely associated with a lost religious tradition. For fiction in particular, these experiments with descriptive fidelity to raw life, with point of view and with narrative voice, were ways of trying to account for the fragmentation of values and assumptions in the readership, and still tell a story.[11] As the allegorical fabric continued to fray, appeals to verisimilitude—or the equivalent contrary move, assertions of the free play of imagination—became ever more insistent. What the advanced techniques and new perspectives adopted by the modernists may well have worked to do, perversely enough, was in fact to further fragment, or to diminish, their likely audience.

One ironic result of this loss of a public for serious fiction has been, at least among professional critics, a compensatory overvaluation of the "literariness" of the work of art: both assume that the object of one's study is autotelic, a serene pause from the sordid, messy jumble of merely ordinary discursive or pragmatic language. That this appears so to so many people is precisely the result of the institutional processes that have set aside literature as the "sacred" (for reasons, no doubt, as much of quarantine as of reverence).[12]

Even the special status of a literary text, then—what might be called its "biblicality"—is produced by institutional structures not altogether unlike others in a society, alterable as societies change; and it is addressed to an audience which, if not as determinate as, say, the intended recipient of a letter, is typically less diffuse than all present and future readers of English or humanity in general. The assumption that a work of art partakes of and addresses its own time and place, and that this feature is critical to fathoming its meaning, has guided this study.

The attempt here has been to observe some of the contours of the emerging modernist work's relation to its audience by examining closely the works of two writers who rigorously mapped, within their narratives, the large-scale political patterns of their respective historical moments, and whose works bear the imprint of a new entanglement with the middle-class reading public. The question that often arises at this point is whether these texts—in which the thematic tensions worked through the narrative rebound on the telling and situation of those narratives—are truly "self-reflexive," aware ironically of their own fatal intrication in the ideological ruptures they dramatize. Does Flaubert fully realize that the encroachments of the marketplace delegitimate his own published work as well as Frédéric's vendable dreams? Is Conrad truly apprised of the way his text's own narrative stance in *Nostromo* depends upon a relation to the part of the world, the European, which his text is demystifying?

Such questions invite citations from biography and letters. But note that even if biographical evidence of Flaubert's or Conrad's awareness of their own artistic projects were produced in the abundance they possess, the question is still unanswered, and one suspects unanswerable. Ultimately, it would be hard to imagine either author—or their texts—being completely cognizant of the contradictions brought to light here, because if they were, they would either have somehow worked around them, and in so doing no doubt produced other contradictions, or perhaps stopped writing altogether. In any event, contradictions of any depth or seriousness are seldom fully understood by those caught in them; that is part of what makes them contradictions, and indeed, the novels are arguably the richer precisely for those contradictions. The question of conscious self-reflexivity, like that of conscious self-positing, would not contribute much to appreciating these texts even it if could be adequately answered. Suffice it to say that insofar as these texts are rhetoric addressed to a public, they bear the traces of that enabling and constraining circumstance; and that a careful look at the narrative and thematic logic of the novels analyzed leads readily to reflection on that logic's implications (usually compromising) for the rhetorical situation of the novels themselves. For this reader, those implications—even if they undermine the specific fictional project—make it even more significant. It is doubtful in any case whether completely specular self-reflexivity is either attainable by an author, discoverable by a reader, or necessarily admirable in a text; and to make a text's degree of self-awareness a central issue may run the risk of installing a kind of idealism that would not be very helpful, finally, in discerning literature's importance and meaning. What a work of art does is more vital than what it knows; and like people, texts undoubtedly end up imparting a great deal of wisdom the authors never knew they had.

All the same, some wisdom probably bears more closely on a work's urgency than other wisdom; the historical emphasis suggested in these pages is directed to focusing on those contradictions that are most likely to inform the novel. The "phantom audience," after all, is a specific press of generic, cultural, and political forces; and there can be little doubt that Flaubert and Conrad, serious men who were apprised of their time, felt that press of circumstance as writers, whether or not they consciously formulated it at all times. And, if one has no audience in mind—a difficult condition to imagine in using language—the work of one's text, whether "ordinary" or "poetic" language, is likely to reveal symptoms of the ideological travail of one's time and place, if only because they are one's time and place. What has been presented here can be argued to be another form of thematic criticism: a just characterization as long as it notes that not only the works' "themes" but also their role as persuasion—their potential use—have been in question in this analysis; it has often been in that of Flaubert and Conrad. It is for this reason that the theme of legitimation has deliberately been one that cannot avoid referring to the persuasive, rhetorical role of a given novel as well as to the subject of that novel.

And what is the polemical backdrop within and against which this study is undertaken? What "expectation norms" does it work through and work to compromise? Where does it seek for its own legitimacy?

One of the polarities that has seemed long most in need of revision or extirpation is that between intrinsic and extrinsic criticism. It recurs in various registers, but is most often used as a defense of formalist critical method against the depradations of sociologizing or politicizing approaches. In its mild form, this polarity works to uproot thematic or semantic textual material from a determinate situation by essentializing some stratum of meaning or by making it metaphysical in some way. The assumption underlying many of these ways of establishing a sacredness or quarantine for the literary text is that, as a practical matter, there is an irreconcilable divergence between the necessity to attend carefully to a text—"close reading," as it is often called—and the irresponsible desire to make relays between a work of literature and its cultural moment. As mentioned in chapter 6, these two agendas, pursued properly, are compatible.

Rather the opposite—it has come about that as the readings of Flaubert's and Conrad's novels have developed in complexity and detail, those novels have proven ever more, rather than less, complicitous with their "outside" contexts in thematic ways that determine elements of their content and more importantly by their status as rhetorical objects, language with a persuasive dimension.

It could be replied that the novels selected, with the explicitly political content and thematics, make it easier to adapt a politicizing reading to a work of literature. Let us presume, then, for argument's sake, that there is no necessary convergence between "intrinsic" and "extrinsic" approaches; let us assume the polarity that does not hold up very well in this instance is true for other instances of critical reading. It may then be that to deal with both the "text itself" (whatever that may be) and the larger context sometimes risks slighting both. That risk must be taken. It is no longer possible to rest secure within the covers of the book one analyzes, comforted that a cozy fit between the author and the critic suffices for analysis. What I have been aiming at is the development of literally a "meta-language": a side-discourse that operates across the space separating the words of novelists from the larger "text" of their time and place. And can that time and place ever fully be known by our time and place? A negative answer does not relieve one of the responsibility to pursue the clues one has, especially concerning writers who operated in a social order not so very different, in many fundamentals, from one's own.

The gesture of looking back to embrace a past is as incomplete, as untotalizable, when it is done to secure an analytical point as when it is done to legitimate or authorize some present claim to recognition by an audience. (In the case of a critical text, of course, the two gestures are identical.) The bourgeois era, for all its alterations, still holds sway much as it did when Flaubert and Conrad wrote; and even if that only goes to prove that the terms of our entanglement confuse us as they confused our supposedly modernist predecessors, still to map the contours of that perplexity and that entanglement is to engage more profit-ably with the usable, and not just the authorizing, past. The interplay between the text of a given work and its literary and historical pre-text (the cultural "already said" that works to form the phantom audience) has been the focus of this study; and its own legitimacy could reside only in the extent to which it has brought out, rendered, and complicated that interplay.

Notes

Introduction: Readership into Audience

1. Cf. Burke, *Rhetoric of Motives,* especially pp. 37–39, "Rhetoric of 'Address' (to the Individual Soul)."

2. Booth made this challenge years ago in *Rhetoric of Fiction*, especially in the section entitled "Art Ignores the Audience," pp. 89–116.

3. This term is Alvin Kernan's, from *Imaginary Library.*

4. There is some similarity between the concept of the phantom audience sketched here and Sartre's theory of the "virtual public" as opposed to the "real public" in *What Is Literature?* (see especially the section "For Whom Does One Write?" et passim). The crucial distinction is that Sartre's virtual public, actually far more class-bound and specific than the phantom public, is the proletariat, based to some extent on the extension of literacy to a statistically greater pool of readers: "The objective aspect of the conflict may express itself as an antagonism between the conservative forces, or the real public of the writer, and the progressive forces, or the virtual public" (p. 82). I doubt the phantom audience I describe, shifting as it must from text to text, could ever hope for the kind of political fixity that Sartre's virtual public seems here to possess.

5. Sartre, for example, describes one outstanding exemplar of such an audience: "society" within seventeenth-century France. Cf. Sartre, *What Is Literature?*, pp.86–94.

6. This curious anonymity of the readership is discussed by Sartre, who employs the interesting term *passive* to describe the nineteenth-century reading public (ibid., p. 100). Benjamin also explores this contrast between folktale audience and novel readership in an essay I use more fully in introducing Conrad, "The Storyteller" in *Illuminations*, ed. Hannah Arendt, trans. Harry Zohn.

7. Flaubert to Maxime du Camp, 26 June 1852, *Letters of Gustave Flaubert, 1830–1857*, p. 161.

8. Sartre, for one, makes much of Flaubert's susceptibility to the blandishments of the Second Empire of Napoleon III. Cf. Sartre, "Nevrose et program-

mation chez Flaubert: Le deuxième empire,'' in *L'Idiot de la famille*, vol. 3. This section explores what Sartre asserts is a psychological synchrony between Flaubert's own aspirations and those of his age.

1. Heirs and Usurpers: Legitimation as Rhetoric

1. The distinction between origins and beginnings is discussed by Said in *Beginnings*. The approach in these pages to the specific relation between the growth of the novel and the search for origins owes much as well to chapter 3 of that text, ''The Novel as Beginning Intention,'' and especially to pp. 81–100.

2. *The Compact Edition of the Oxford English Dictionary*, 1971, s.v. ''legitimate, adj.''

3. Freud, *Totem and Taboo*.

4. Wilden, ''Lacan and the Discourse of the Other,'' in Jacques Lacan, *The Language of the Self*, pp. 263–64.

5. Ibid., p. 264.

6. This difficult speaking (and, later, writing) situation has an emblem for Freud in the word ''Signorelli,'' which in Freud's personal experience became for him what Wilden calls ''the discourse of the Other; in its simplest form, it was a message saying on the one hand: 'You want to kill your father and sleep with your mother' . . . ; and on the other: 'Do not kill your father and sleep with your mother''' (ibid., p. 266).

7. The persistence of the metaphor of fatherhood in the political legitimation of nation-states is a central concern of Freud in his later works. Here, for example, is Sennett's distillation of late Freud from Sennett's fine book *Authority*: ''The picture presented to us in his late works like *Moses and Monotheism* and *Civilization and Its Discontents* is of images of authority which are formed in childhood and which persist in adult life. . . . His vision is, at its most extreme, one in which the moral content of adult controls is like pretext, or like strategic weaponry in a game of psychological chess begun the moment every human being was born '' (pp. 22–23, 24). The Freud represented here is not far in his view of authority from Friedrich Nietzsche.

8. The attempt on the part of poets to father themselves, so to speak, is explored most famously by Bloom in, for example, *Anxiety of Influence*.

9. Yet his insistence upon their separateness is itself the result of a tendency on the part of others to blur the two realms. Sennett discusses this in ''Evolution of Paternalism,'' in *Authority*, pp. 52–62.

10. Burke, *Rhetoric of Motives*, p. 38.

11. Ibid., p. 39.

12. Ibid., p. 38.

13. Ibid., p. 39. The result of this state of affairs is that one's own dreams, for all their real or imagined uniqueness, are often surprisingly similar to everyone else's, as Gustave Flaubert's hero, Frédéric Moreau, finds out to his chargrin in *L'Education sentimentale*. His innermost desires differ little from most other people's and in fact seem interchangeable with theirs at time— a condition he does not wish to acknowledge.

14. Ibid., p. 269.

15. Ibid., pp. 269–70.

16. Ibid., p. 274.

17. Ibid., p. 23.

18. Ibid., p. 20, p. 22.

19. This aspect of rhetorical activity is elaborated as well by another theoretician of language, Foucault, in *Archaeology of Knowledge*, p. 120. The political economy of discourse Burke describes is quite akin to Foucault's insight that the capacity of statements for "circulation and exchange" makes them very valuable "not only in the economy of discourse, but, more generally, in the administration of scarce resources." Discourse, in this view, becomes something very like "an asset—finite, limited, desirable, useful—that has its own rules of appearance, but also its own conditions of appropriation and operation; an asset that consequently, from the moment of its existence (and not only in its 'pratical applications'), poses the question of power; an asset that is, by nature, the object of a struggle, a political struggle." For our purposes as students of literary language, the operative clause here may well be the parenthetical one; Foucault strongly argues that the political and contestatory status of language does not begin and end with its narrow deployment for one or another specific goal or purpose, so that even "useless" discourse (which is how some would characterize literary or aesthetic language) cannot escape a struggle for appropriation and power.

20. Burke, *Rhetoric of Motives*, p. 205.

21. Wittgenstein's theory of language, in many cases, relies upon a political notion of discourse as command. In *Philosophical Investigations*, for instance, especially in sections 1–18, Wittgenstein generalizes the power relationship involved in the giving of an order to apply to the enunciation of discourse *tout court*; the ideal locus of enunciation is thus that of command.

22. Weber, *Economy and Society*, vol. 3, p. 946.

23. Sennett, *Authority*, pp. 25–26.

24. In Gramsci, *Selections from the Prison Notebooks*, passim. Gramsci makes frequent use of this term. One instance should suffice to show its moral resonance. In addressing the rise of the late nineteenth-century Moderate party in Italy, Gramsci writes: "A social group can, and indeed must, already exercise 'leadership' before winning governmental power. . . . It seems clear from the policies of the Moderates that there can, and indeed must, be hegemonic activity even before the rise to power, and that one should not count only on the material force which power gives in order to exercise an effective leadership" (pp. 57–59). The term *hegemonic*, applied to a specific party and emphasizing leadership, stressess two things: moral or psychological as well as practical ascendancy (legitimacy), and the existence of rival, but subjugated, forms of civic philosophy.

25. The theoretician of recognition is Hegel, whose *Phenomenology of Mind* has a section in "Lordship and Bondage" which famously relies on this notion.

26. Sennett, *Authority*, p. 193.

27. Ibid., p. 192.

28. Weber, *Economy and Society*. vol. 3, p. 953.

29. Indeed, this is one of the definitions of the adjective *legitimate* given in

the *O. E. D.*: "Sanctioned by the laws of reasoning; logically admissable or inferrible." In other words, following a line of causal development or logical succession.

30. Discussed in Pocock, *Ancient Constitution and the Feudal Law*. What is of interest here is not so much that William had these laws forged—a genuinely cynical and self-serving act, it would seem—as that many subsequent generations were so ready to credit the laws as having existed. It is almost as if there were an unspoken conspiracy among all subjects to ground the monarchical line in an earlier, less disruptive lineage than that of William. Pocock even points to "the insertion [by William] in the coronation oath—where it remained until 1688—of a promise to observe the laws of St. Edward" (p. 43). It stayed there, apparently, despite considerable suspicion and some evidence that these laws had been made up by William.

2. The Bourgeois State: Remembrance of Legitimacy Past

1. Weber, *Economy and Society*, vol. 3, p. 954.

2. Oliver Cromwell and Adolf Hitler, two charismatic leaders, short-circuited traditional hierarchies (Cromwell—monarchy, Hitler—parliamentarism). But retrograde appeals are still the norm for them: Hitler's "blood and soil" ideology is the obvious case. Specifically, charismatic rulers most often find the primitive mask of the patriarch the most congenial one. Furthermore, even though Weber insists that "charismatic and patriarchal power" are "very different" in their respective bases (ibid., p. 1117), nonetheless he admits that in practice "the two basically antagonistic forces of charisma and tradition regularly merge with one another" (ibid., p. 1122).

3. Nietzsche, *Genealogy of Morals*, p. 209, section 12 of second essay.

4. Ibid., pp. 209-10.

5. Ibid., p. 210.

6. Cf. Foucault, *Discipline and Punish*.

7. Gadamer, *Truth and Method*, pp. 21-22.

8. Ibid., p. 26.

9. Ibid., p. 23.

10. This fact provides the basis for Tom Nairn's thesis that Great Britain's political troubles today stem from the historical absence of a genuine bourgeois revolution. Cf. Nairn, "The Decline of the British State," *New Left Review*, no. 101-102 (1977), pp. 3-61.

11. Habermas, *Legitimation Crisis*, p. 105.

12. Ibid., p. 110.

13. Ibid., p. 30.

14. Polanyi, *Great Transformation*, passim, especially chapters 12 and 13. He remarks: "While *laissez-faire* economy was the product of deliberate state action, subsequent restrictions on *laissez-faire* started in a spontaneous way" (p. 141). Polanyi goes to great lengths to show that what classical liberals have often called a "collectivist conspiracy" to hinder the growth of unbridled trade in the latter nineteenth century is a "myth" that is "contrary to all the facts" (p. 150).

15. The United States may be an exception, though even in that instance frequent appeals are made to those quasi-patriarchal, aristocratic figures known as the Founding Fathers.

16. Cf. Sennett's "Evolution of Paternalism," in *Authority*, pp. 52–62, and especially the discussion of corporate paternalism as practiced in New Lanark, Waltham, and Pullman, Illinois.

17. Ibid., p. 55.

18. Ibid., p. 57.

19. In fact, Sennett "squares off" Weber's view of legitimacy against Freud's vision of authority in late texts such as *Moses and Monotheism* and *Totem and Taboo*. To Sennett, Weber's view is too rationalistic, for authority is "a belief in legitimacy, measured by voluntary compliance" (ibid., p. 22); and Sennett is concerned that such a notion slights the dangers of "infantilization" Freud saw as built into the structure of large-scale institutional authority. I am not sure that Weber, with his notion of "charismatic" legitimacy, does not account for this emotional or psychological element, nor do I feel that there is usually a marked divergence between the moral principles said by Weber to be always necessary to legitimacy and the strong paternalistic figure said by Freud to be capable of swaying the masses. Even a Hitler may be lionized by his people not merely because he is perceived by them as strong, "apart from the [moral] content of what they perceive" (ibid., p. 22), but because it is felt that he will do right by Germany—which may involve evildoing toward other nations and to those not "true Germans," perhaps.

20. Ibid., p. 43.

3. The Case of the Novel: The Fatherless Genre

1. See Lukács, *Theory of the Novel*; Benjamin, "The Storyteller"; Robert, *Origins of the Novel*; and Fletcher, *Novel and Reader*.

2. Robert, *Orgins of the Novel*, p. 16.

3. Cf. ibid., pp. 21–40.

4. Tanner, *Adultery in the Novel*, p. 97.

5. Ibid., p. 52.

6. Ibid., p. 371. Tanner even points out that these nineteenth-century novels, *Madame Bovary* is one instance, often have few children, and that when one is needed, the novel generally "turns to the unplaced or misplaced child rather than to the secure and protected child of a legitimate union" (p. 370).

7. Cited in ibid., p. 373.

8. Ibid., p. 371.

9. Ibid., pp. 369–70.

10. Robert, *Origins of the Novel*, p. 18.

11. Reed, *Exemplary History of the Novel,* p. 5.

12. Ibid., p. 264.

13. Ibid., p. 14.

14. Ibid., p. 265.

15. Ibid., p. 27.

16. Ibid., p. 20.

17. The French philosopher Derrida generalizes this condition of orphan-hood to writing per se, and so discourse as a whole, in his essay "La pharmacie de Platon": "L'Ecriture est le fils *misérable* . . . de toute façon un fils *perdu*. Dont l'impuissance est bien celle d'un orphelin, autant que d'un parricide persécuté, et parfois injustement" (in *La Dissémination* pp. 167–68). All writing is, in a sense, fatherless discourse; but this observation, to the extent true, reveals also the limitations of the metaphor of parentage for either writing or for discourse in general: limitation that Derrida's own project works to expose.

18. Watt, *Rise of the Novel*, p. 206.

19. Sennett, *Fall of Public Man*, pp. 128–29.

20. Ibid., p. 60.

21. Watt, *Rise of the Novel*, p. 62.

22. Foucault, *Order of Things*. See especially the chapter entitled "The Prose of the World."

23. Even the coincidences for which Victorian novelists such as Dickens were so often chided for can be read as one perverse means of holding the elements of a fictive universe in horizontal relation, even at the expense of verisimilitude, narrowly conceived. Beyond that, Dickens will often justify the interweaving of disparate narrative strands as testifying to a larger verisimili-tude. Thus, in *Dombey and Son*, Dickens remarks: "In this round world of many circles within circles, do we make a weary journey from the high grade to the low to find that they lie close together, that the two extremes touch, and that our journey's end is but our starting-place?" (p. 517). Dickens is often given to philosophical reflections on the secret or unseen ties linking the unlikeliest of individuals or groups—not only, as here, to make a point about the linking of classes but also to justify the often audacious linkages he himself will make. (And, not incidentally, to give the reader the pleasant suspense of wondering which will be forged in the text.)

24. Watt, *Rise of the Novel*, p. 42.

25. Conrad, *Great Short Works*, p. 57.

26. Ibid., p. 58.

27. Ibid., p. 59.

28. Ibid., p. 60.

29. Of course, the appearance of painstakingly self-conscious novelist-craftsmen after Flaubert has also caused to appear, as if in a gestalt picture, the ground of the unselfconscious, gloriously instinctive artist—Leo Tolstoy, Honoré de Balzac, Charles Dickens, Victor Hugo—who turned out genius as though without reflection, to whom rewriting and introspection were alien notions. While this opposition has a certain positional value—no doubt these figures are instinctive compared to Flaubert and Conrad, at least in their work—it is probably owing to larger ideological and economic currents that this relative ease of production was acquired. For one thing, the novelist and the bourgeois reader were more spontaneously "in tune" in the early nineteenth century, in part perhaps because the bourgeoisie and its point of view were in the ascendant. For another thing, the economics of publishing itself—from the newspaper serials to the triple-decker novels that the lending libraries encour-aged—may have placed a greater value on prolixity than was later the case.

Nonetheless, Conrad himself eventually become rather prolific—though Flaubert, with an inheritance, had less reason to concern himself with these matters.

On the increasingly distant relations between nineteenth-century novelists and their reading publics, Roland Barthes said: "Between the third person as used by Balzac and that used by Flaubert, there is a world of difference (that of 1848): in the former we have a view of History which is harsh, but coherent and certain of its principles, the triumph of an order; in the latter, an art which in order to escape its pangs of conscience either exaggerates conventions or frantically attempts to destroy them" (*Writing Degree Zero*, p.38). On the economic strictures enforcing new modes of writing, see Watt, *Rise of the Novel*: "Once the writer's primary aim was no longer to satisfy the standards of patrons and the literary élite, other considerations took on a new importance. Two of them, at least, were likely to encourage the author to prolixity: first, to write very explicitly and even tautologically might help his less educated readers to understand him easily; and secondly, since it was the bookseller, not the patron who rewarded him, speed and copiousness tended to become the supreme economic virtues" (p. 56).

4. The Muse and the Marketplace in Early Flaubert

1. Flaubert, *Oeuvres complètes*, vol. 1. Translation mine. All subsequent references are given in the body of the text.

5. *L'Education sentimentale*: The Political Economy of the Sign

1. Benjamin, *Charles Baudelaire*, p. 39.

2. Flaubert, *Sentimental Education*, p. 128; p. 127.

3. Prendergast, "Flaubert's Writing and Negativity," *Novel* 8, no. 3 (1975); 204.

4. Proust, *A la recherche du temps perdu*, vol. 3, p. 899. Proust said "Chaque personne qui nous fait souffrir peut etre rattachée par nous à une divinité dont elle n'est qu'un reflet fragmentaire et le dernier degré." Marcel's art constructs a divinity from the fragments of his loves.

5. Benjamin, *Baudelaire*, p. 97.

6. Ibid., p. 172.

7. Quoted in Cogny, *L'Education sentimentale de Flaubert*, p. 188. Translation mine.

8. Benjamin, *Baudelaire*, p. 34.

9. Frédéric's may be a "commodity fetishism" even in the specific way Jean Baudrillard appropriates the term. He states: "It is not the passion . . . for substances that speaks in fetishism, it is the *passion for the code* [i.e., for the culturally determined code of values itself]" *For a Critique of the Political Economy of the Sign* (p. 92).

10. Bachelard, *Poetics of Space*, pp. 85–86.

11. Culler, *Flaubert: The Uses of Uncertainty*, p. 149.

12. Benjamin, *Baudelaire*, p. 62.

13. Of course, the absence of class lines characteristic of nineteenth-century crowds, and which thinkers as early as Gustave LeBon had remarked before Benjamin, became a positive aspect of the crowds to the people of 1848, for many believed that class had been transcended (they were incorrect). LeBon's text, *The Crowd,* is an early study of the phenomenon of cross-class crowds in the last century, and particularly of their role in the accession to power of Louis Bonaparte.

14. Cf. Hegel, *Phenomenology of Mind*, especially pp. 599–610. He argues there that the "universal freedom" every participant in a revolution becomes imbued with is only the effect of a unified act of destruction. Once positive acts have to be accomplished, the division of social labor reasserts itself and solidarity recedes. Hegel speaks here of the French Revolution; but the same dynamic seems to have applied to 1848, except that instead of terror there followed only the onset of privatization.

15. Mehlman discusses the way this mass feeling can become excessive and beyond political recuperation in the phenomenon of "Bonapartism" in *Revolution and Repetition*, especially pp. 5–41.

16. Flaubert's technique in presenting his marketplace recalls Northrop Frye's mode of Menippean satire, in which the characters are presented primarily as representatives of various moral or ideological positions. See Frye's *Anatomy of Criticism*, especially pp. 309–12. Though he does not mention *L'Education*, Frye does note Flaubert's "encyclopaedic approach" to *Bouvard et Pécuchet* as "marking an affinity with the Menippean tradition" (p. 311).

17. Brombert has noted the persistence of the "bazaar of ideas" in Flaubert's *oeuvre* and has linked it with the feast, in his analysis of the banquet scene in "Hérodias," which he compares to Montesquieu's *Les lettres persanes* and to Voltaire's *Candide*. In *Novels of Flaubert*, he also discusses satiety of the mind as well as the body; see pp. 250–52, 215.

18. Baudrillard, "Beyond Use Value," pp. 130–42.

19. This charge—that nothing happens—is constantly leveled at the novel as a whole. The difference is that in the story of the visit to la Turque the "nothing" that happens is a paralysis at the point of realizing a dream, whereas the novel also chronicles the disillusionment with dreams in their realized form (always other, certainly, than the form in which they are anticipated).

20. Culler, *Flaubert: The Uses of Uncertainty*, p. 155.

21. The famous passage from his 16 January 1852 letter to Louise Colet is rendered in English as follows: "What seems beautiful to me, what I should like to write, is a book about nothing, a book dependent on nothing external, which would be held together by the strength of its style, just as the earth, suspended in the void, depends on nothing external for its support" (*The Selected Letters of Gustave Flaubert*, p. 127).

22. Further, although his letters reveal the stray sign of discomfort here and there at the thought of publishing at all, they also show concern with the published products. He writes to his friend Roger des Genettes: "Vous me parlez de *L'éducation sentimentale*. . . . Pourquoi ce livre-là n'a-t-il pas eu le succés que j'en attendais?" (*Préface à la vie d'écrivain*, p. 288).

23. Barthes notes of "Sarrasine," in which a man agrees to tell his mistress the truth about a mysterious portrait in "exchange for a night of love," that the story is so antipathetic that it ends "by contaminating the lovely listener and, withdrawing her from love, keeps her from honoring the contract" (*S/Z*, pp. 212-13). Flaubert's novel honors its contract to communicate up to a point (it is still a readerly novel), but it tries to find escape clauses.

24. This concern grows with the writing of Flaubert's unfinished novel *Bouvard et Pécuchet*, although for our purposes it may be somewhat less interesting since there the game is already over—cliché becomes the only possibility.

25. *Agoraphobia* in its standard psychoanalytical meaning is the fear of open spaces. Etymologically, it derives from the Greek term *agora*, marketplace, thus making it a doubly appropriate concept here. In its final chapters, this novel certainly displays an inward-turning tendency, a desire to reject the great world and specifically to reject its *agora*, its political economy.

26. It appears Flaubert was highly conscious of the egregious historical moment within which he was writing, a fact made clear by the knowledge that his original intention for *L'Education* was to conclude with a chapter on Louis Napoléon at Sedan. Sartre discusses this in his *L'Idiot de la famille*, vol. 3. He mentions the abortive chapter on Napoleon III at several junctures; see, for example, p. 642.

6. Phantom Publics and Imaginary Libraries

1. Starkie, *Flaubert the Master*. For the years following *Salammbô*, see pp. 103-14, "The Man about Town." Pp. 135-39 recount Flaubert's hurt and bewilderment at the critics' vituperation, especially that of Barbey d'Aurevilly, and of many of his friends' unwillingness, given the tense political situation of the empire's wane, to acknowledge copies he had personally sent them.

2. Sartre has emphasized this "vassalage," as he calls it, in Flaubert's connection with the Court. But Barnes suggests that his relation to the Second Empire, despite his kowtowing, was not "wholly synchronic," as Sartre argues it to be. See Barnes, *Sartre and Flaubert*, pp. 297-99.

3. Barnes, *Sartre and Flaubert*, p. 298.

4. Sartre, *L'Idiot de la famille*, vol. 3, p. 333. As Sartre's commentator Barnes puts the thesis, "By his disaffiliation with his own class and by his refusal to communicate, the writer won for himself the very readers he rejected" (*Sartre and Flaubert*, p. 286).

5. Ibid., p. 287.

6. Ibid., p. 286.

7. Ibid., p. 283. Cf. Sartre, *L'Idiot de la famille*, vol. 3, pp. 244-45, on self-hatred and self-sacrifice.

8. Barnes, *Sartre and Flaubert*, p. 248.

9. In this regard see Felman, *La Folie et la chose littéraire*, especially "Gustave Flaubert: Folie et cliché," pp. 157-213. Felman examines Flaubert's horror of the cliché chiefly as it is manifested in "Un coeur simple," *Novembre*, and *Memoires d' un fou*. In the section "Prostitution et lieu commun," she makes very apposite relays between the two as Flaubert's *Memoires* views them. She

writes: "Le paradoxe de cette histoire d'initiation, de ce récit de perte de la virginité du narrateur, c'est qu'il apprend au narrateur qu'il perd précisément ce qu'il n'avait jamais eu: la virginité. Dans le langage, on ne peut etre vierge, on ne l'a jamais été, puisqu'on habite le lieu commun" (p. 202). *L'Education* exfoliates this dual theme of cliché and whoredom.

10. Sartre discusses the curious nature of Flaubert's connections with the eighteenth-century philosophers. The "inherited imperative" that "reason be employed to make comprehensible the totality of man in the world" was looked at with less optimism. Even that Catholicism despised by Voltaire was the object of "nostalgic longing" for Flaubert's generation of writers: "They blamed Voltaire for being right," says Barnes (*Sartre and Flaubert*, p. 257). This is linked to the fact that in speaking to universal reason, Voltaire was also speaking to the interest of the coming universal class, the bourgeoisie. Flaubert had no use for such a mode of address: "For whom was one to write if the universal class was the despised bourgeoisie?" (ibid., p. 258). Paradoxically, though, if *Bouvard et Pécuchet* is an ironic reinscription of the clichés of Enlightenment optimism, it can be seen as another species of the ever-prevalent "black humanism," which retains the notion of universal human nature and merely reverses the valorization of the terms. In poking fun at Bouvard and Pécuchet's optimism, Flaubert may be right in step with the late nineteenth-century bourgeoisie, if Sartre's model is correct.

11. Kernan, *Imaginary Library*. See chapter 1, "The Actual and Imaginary Library: Literature as a Social Institution," pp. 12-36. Kernan crisply establishes with admirable clarity both the era and the world view that spawned a separate "literature" institution: "The transformation we know the most about is that of the middle to late eighteenth century when 'poetry' became 'literature' and the orientation shifted from service to the established aristocratic order to a reaction against a newly dominant middle-class order" (p. 30). Unqualified, this is suspiciously sweeping, but it states the case succinctly.

12. Barnes, *Sartre and Flaubert*, p. 261.

13. Watt, *Conrad in the Nineteenth Century*, pp. 50-55.

14. Ibid., p. 51; Karl, *Joseph Conrad: The Three Lives*, p. 70.

15. The following gush from Ford is typical. Referring to the aspiring writer, Ford says that "if he is a prudent man, he will read that book [*Madame Bovary*] and *Education Sentimentale* and *Bouvard et Percuchet* [*sic*] a great many times, over and over again, with minute scrutiny, to discover what in Flaubert's methods is eternal and universal in appeal" (*Critical Writings of Ford Madox Ford*, pp. 63-64). Cf. the section entitled "Technique," pp. 56-71.

16. See for instance McClure, *Kipling and Conrad*, p. 82. McClure's argument is interesting because it points out that Conrad's experience would not have led him to unambiguously denounce all imperialist oppression. He writes of the Malay novels: "In the archipelago of Conrad's day, as in the Ukraine, three parties were competing for power: various indigenous peoples, more or less closely related groups of warrior-rulers, and the Europeans. Of these three, the group that most closely corresponds to Conrad's own in the Ukraine is not the Europeans but the warrior-rulers, who are threatened both by the Europeans and by the people they have been accustomed to rule" (p. 87). One thinks

in this respect of the *blancos* in *Nostromo*'s Costaguana, positioned between the indigenous Indians they rule and the newer "material interests" represented by Charles Gould's Concession. Given McClure's argument, it is not too surprising that the *blancos* come off so comparatively well—though any similarity between Latin America and the Ukraine must be taken under advisement.

17. Quoted in Arac, "Romanticism, the Self and the City: *The Secret Agent* in Literary History," *Boundary 2* 9 (Fall 1980): 82.

18. See for instance Karl, *Joseph Conrad: The Three Lives*, p. 270.

19. Arac points out this feature of Conrad as it operated in *The Secret Agent*, and in addition to the perceptive link to Benjamin's "storyteller," makes much of the origin of that novel in a story drawn by "his 'casual and omniscient' friend Ford out of the urban oral tradition" ("Romanticism, the Self and the City," p. 82).

20. Books that have dealt with the impact of Conrad's early years include Meyer, *Joseph Conrad: A Psychoanalytic Biography*, and Najder, ed., *Conrad's Polish Background*. A classic study of nationality as an influence on Conrad is Morf's *Polish Heritage of Joseph Conrad*. His analysis of *Lord Jim*, where Jim's abandonment of the *Patna* is seen as a figure of Conrad's own guilt at having left Poland, is especially intriguing and ingenious (pp. 149–66).

21. Conrad, *Notes on Life and Letters*, p. 112.

22. At the same time, the nature of Conrad's objections to empire, based as they are on something like an organicist notion of legitimacy, also hints at a certain nostalgia for monarchy: "The revolutions of European States have never been in the nature of absolute protests *en masse* against the monarchical principle; they were the uprising of the people against the oppressive degeneration of legality" (ibid., p. 101).

23. Cf. ibid., for example, "Well Done" and "Tradition," pp. 179–93, pp. 194–201.

24. Of course, such denunciations tended to concern empires other than Britain's. On Conrad's contribution to the undermining of King Leopold's Belgian empire in the Congo, see Hawkins, "Joseph Conrad, Roger Casement, and the Congo Reform Movement," *Journal of Modern Literature* 9, no. 1 (1981–1982): pp 65–80, especially Conrad's 21 December 1903 letter (pp. 69–70).

25. Jameson, *Political Unconscious*, p. 264.

26. Cf. ibid., pp. 278–80.

27. Ibid., p. 274.

28. Ibid., p. 207.

29. Jameson, making Flaubert his "privileged locus of this development," sees the "depersonalization of the text, the laundering of authorial intervention, but also the disappearance from the horizon of its readership" as all part of a process of "reification" (ibid., pp. 220–21).

7. The Kernel and the Enveloping Haze

1. Ford, *Return to Yesterday* p, 293. Ford relates that "every now and then . . . Conrad would launch into a frightful diatribe against the English lan-

guage. It was a language for dogs and horses. It was incapable of conveying human thoughts."

2. McCarthy, *Writing on the Wall*, pp. 42 ff.

3. Lukács, *Theory of the Novel*, passim.

4. Benjamin, "Storyteller," p. 83. All subsequent references to this essay are given in the body of the text.

5. The seriality encouraged by industrial capitalism has affected every other mode of our older social relations, and so has not left our narratives intact either. For a discussion of seriality, a term used by Sartre, see Jameson's "Sartre and History" in *Marxism and Form*, pp. 206-305. See especially pp. 247-50.

6. Cf. Conrad, *Great Short Works,* p. 213.

7. Says Marlow: "After all, this was the expression of some sort of belief; it had candour, it had conviction, it had a vibrating note of revolt. . . . It was an affirmation, a moral victory paid for by innumerable satisfactions. But it was a victory!" (ibid., pp. 284-85).

8. Watt, *Conrad in the Nineteenth Century*, p. 212.

9. Eagleton, *Criticism and Ideology*, pp. 137-38.

10. Conrad, *Great Short Works*, p. 270.

11. Ibid., p. 213.

12. This no doubt is what leads Barthes, discussing linguist Roman Jakobson's dichotomy between *metaphor* and *metonymy*, to place "popular novels" in particular on the side of metonymy. They share that distinction, by the way, with only one other form, according to Barthes, "newspaper narratives." Cf. Barthes, *Elements of Semiology*, vol. 2, p. 60.

13. Sherry discusses the Jeddal incident as the founding moment for the narrative of Jim in "That Scandal of the Eastern Seas" in *Conrad's Eastern World*, pp. 41 ff. In his companion volume, *Conrad's Western World*, Sherry reveals the accounts of Simon Bolívar's Colombian revolution, among other sources that Conrad used in *Nostromo* from contemporary records, on pp. 137-201. Also, Fleishman's book, *Conrad's Politics*, deals with his sources for *Nostromo* (pp. 167-71). As to Conrad's account of *Secret Agent's* origin, cf. "Author's Note" to *Secret Agent*, pp. 9-11.

14. One might argue that the newspaper itself contains implicit admonitions, such as the execution account that inscribes itself in Winnie Verloc's consciousness. But even if this were true, it is counsel that she fails to heed—until after she commits her own crime.

8. Paragon and Enigma: The Hero in *Lord Jim*

1. Conrad, *Lord Jim* (New York: Doubleday, Page & Co., 1924), p. 78. All subsequent references to this work are noted in the body of the text.

2. Lee makes a similar argument in *Conrad's Colonialism*, pp. 35-39. Curiously, though Lee isolates the "us" of "one of us" quite precisely, he still seems anxious to conclude that Conrad's essential view of the "us" is affirmative.

3. See Conrad's article "Tradition," which attacks a British M.P. for intimating that the merchant marine lacked a tradition of courage, despite the

generally eulogistic character of the remarks as a whole. Cf. *Notes on Life and Letters*, in *Collected Works*, p. 195.

4. A figure who ignores the social and material conditions of his own work and who views himself as the hero in a book could well be interpreted as the carrier of ideology, and this is indeed the way Jim's character is encoded. If Louis Althusser is right to say that ideology, like the Freudian ego, is a *fonction de méconnaissance*, then Jim is the ideological character par excellence, the man whose image of his own mission—and, by extension, that of his nation and race—is a noble fiction, subtended by the social and material elements it strains always to ignore. On Althusser's relay between the Freudian ego and ideology as two forms of the *fonction de méconnaissance*, see *Lenin and Philosophy*, p. 172, pp. 218–19, et passim.

5. Guerard, *Conrad the Novelist*, pp. 155–56.

6. Roussel, *Metaphysics of Darkness*, p. 100.

7. Fleishman, *Conrad's Politics*, pp. 58–59.

8. Lee emphasizes the "subtle appeal to their common blood" that Brown allegedly makes to Jim in *Conrad's Colonialism*, p. 105. Guerard, despite his earlier belief that race is the decisive factor, comes to decide that Brown's role is a kind of *semblable* for Jim: a mirror-image that brings forth memories of Jim's own disgrace on the *Patna*. Discussing this theory in *Conrad the Novelist*, p. 150, he credits it to Gustav Morf.

9. Roussel, *Metaphysics of Darkness*, p. 101.

10. Tanner, "Butterflies and Beetles—Conrad's Two Truths," *Chicago Review* 16, no. 1 (1963): 123–40. Tanner recognizes the contaminating role played by Cornelius, Chester, and Brown, although he ignores the subtler but more effective contaminating agent that Stein becomes.

11. Fleishman, *Conrad's Politics*, p. 111.

12. Roussel, *Metaphysics of Darkness*, p. 93. Just as Jim relies on the people of Patusan for his own sense of worth—just as "they possessed him," rather than the reverse—so he now relies upon the community for the opportunity to display his gesture of "exalted egotism," although undoubtedly he sees the community as somehow his creation. To the end, Jim apparently ignores the bonds of dependence which make his great gesture possible.

13. Watt, *Conrad in the Nineteenth Century*, p. 356.

14. This ambiguity in Jim's line of legitimacy is at least sensed by Watt when he remarks that "Jim cannot possibly reconcile all the just claims upon him" during his tenure on Patusan (ibid., p. 348).

15. Ibid., p. 347.

16. Heilman, in his introduction to *Lord Jim* (New York: Rinehart, 1957), suggests this line of interpretation on p. xxiii. This shift from subjective psychology to ineffable fate is partly attributable to an increased tendency in the narrative for Jim's tale to be told not by himself but by other witnesses: "It is through the eyes of others that we take our last look at him," says Marlow (p. 339). It is partly owing to the larger ritual setting of Jim's final fall from grace, as well. Both modes for evoking ambiguity are retained throughout, though, and both elide much that the narrative logic itself has built up. The imagery surrounding Jim's story alternates between subjective motive and public, inevitable fate—both shrouded in the Marlovian mists of inscrutability.

9. Lost in Azuera: The Fate of Sulaco and Conrad's *Nostromo*

1. Conrad, *Nostromo*, p. 11. All subsequent references to this work are noted in the body of the text.

2. Conrad to Cunninghame Graham, 31 October 1904: "Costaguana is meant for a S[outh] Am[eri]can state in general" (*Joseph Conrad's Letters to Cunninghame Graham*, p. 157).

3. Cf. Barthes, *Mythologies*, especially "Myth Today," pp. 109-58.

4. Said, *Beginnings*, p. 110.

5. The reader interested in exploring the process by which Conrad transforms contemporary accounts of Latin America into his narrative is advised to read Sherry's study, *Conrad's Western World*, especially the section on *Nostromo* (pp. 137-201).

6. Derrida, *Of Grammatology*, p. 101.

7. The necessity and desire for record keeping throughout the text of *Nostromo* have been dealt with by Said in *Beginnings*, pp. 101-2.

8. Sherry, in the chapter entitled "Costaguana and Sulaco" in *Conrad's Western World*, shows the extent to which Conrad's rendering of the persona of Captain Mitchell is indebted to the style of Edward Eastwick, whose travelogue *Venezuela* was an obvious source for *Nostromo*:

> For most of the details given here [in Mitchell's tour] Conrad drew upon Eastwick's account . . . Conrad took not only topographical detail from Eastwick but also the whole conception of Captain Mitchell and his conducted tour. . . . Eastwick's interpolations and forceful directives to his friend—"Now, mark me," "You see the large house on the right hand"— are very like Captain Mitchell's "We enter now . . .," "Observe the old Spanish houses," and both men make use of white-covered umbrellas. (Pp. 199-200)

When one realizes that Captain Mitchell's character—right down to little fatuities of personal style—is taken largely from Eastwick, the edge in Conrad's portrayal of this spokesman for civilization becomes even sharper. (Eastwick's reason for visiting Venezuela, by the way, was to ascertain "whether Venezuela, could keep up the payments" of an "immense loan" that his employer, the General Credit Company, had floated for the country [ibid., p. 172].)

9. Among the critics to remark on this increasing hollowness has been Guerard in his book *Conrad the Novelist*, where he says that the third part of *Nostromo* "is for the most part good intelligent popular fiction on a quite different level from the first two parts" (p. 204).

10. Jenkins, "Conrad's *Nostromo* and History," *Literature and History: A New Journal for the Humanities* 6 (1977): 175.

11. Ibid., p. 165.

12. Ibid., p. 176.

10. The Structure of Suspicion in *The Secret Agent*

1. Miller, *Poets of Reality*, p. 51.

2. Foucault, *Discipline and Punish*, pp. 195-228.

3. Ibid., p. 201.

4. Conrad, *Secret Agent*, p. 23. All subsequent references to this work are noted in the body of the text.

5. Miller, *Poets of Reality*, p. 47.

6. Fleishman, *Conrad's Politics*, p. 212.

7. Foucault, *Discipline and Punish*, p. 204.

8. Sennett, *Fall of Public Man,* p. 161.

9. Ibid., p. 261.

10. Ibid., p. 169.

11. Foucault, *Discipline and Punish*, p. 201.

Conclusion

1. Jameson makes this point in *The Political Unconscious* in comparing Conrad's setting here to Ford Madox Ford's in his tetralogy: "Conrad's work finally becomes contiguous to the elaborate presentation and self-questioning of the British aristocratic bureaucracy in Ford's *Parade's End*, and uses much the same anecdotal form of social *scandal* to deconceal social institutions otherwise imperceptible to the naked eye" (p. 265).

2. Ibid., p. 217.

3. This does not mean that reading *Secret Agent* teaches nothing; the attentive reader learns a great deal. But the purposeful valorization of this teaching—literature as a cultural institution that teaches that little bit of truth for which the reader forgot to ask, to paraphrase Conrad's preface to "Nigger of the *Narcissus*"—that valorization is given over, suppressed.

4. Pocock's fascinating text, *Ancient Constitution and the Feudal Law* provides superb examples of this reflexive positing in the seventeenth-century debates by which the British Whigs attempted to limit the powers of kingship by invoking an immemorial law that preceded monarchy: "The content of the concept [of this ancient constitution] differed from time to time (as also from man to man): as parliament laid claim to new powers these were represented as immemorial and included in the fundamental law" (p. 49). In other words, these new claims were posited as prior. Many common-law supporters, troubled by the Norman Conquest that was in fact responsible for "an indelible stain of sovereignty upon the English constitution," resorted to a notion that the constitution emerged from "an altogether fabulous antiquity . . . and denying, in effect, that its origin could ever be discovered by the historian" (p. 53). In any event, to the typical "educated Englishman" of the seventeenth century, "a vitally important characteristic of the constitution was its antiquity, and to trace it in a very remote past was essential in order to establish it securely in the present" (p. 46). Throughout his account, Pocock stresses the antiquarian justification the Whigs generally gave for any fresh seizure of power from the monarchy, in the form of this constitution. See "The Common-law Mind: Custom and the Immemorial," pp. 30-55.

5. Iser speaks of "expectation norms," dividing them into "two categories. (1) The repertoire of social norms and literary references . . . against which the text is to be reconstituted by the reader. (2) . . . The social and cultural conventions of a particular public" (*Act of Reading*, p. 89). These categories roughly correspond to "historical" and "generic" constraints.

6. Barthes, *Writing Degree Zero*, p. 9.

7. Ibid., p. 10.

8. Ibid., p. 16.

9. Eagleton, *Criticism and Ideology*, p. 62.

10. Pratt discusses this matter in *Toward a Speech Act Theory*. She makes a striking case for including literature among other forms of discourse from an American pragmatist standpoint:

> Far from being autonomous, self-contained, self-motivating, contextfree objects which exist independently from the "pragmatic" concerns of "everyday" discourse, literary works take place in a context, and like any other utterance they cannot be described apart from that context. Whether or not literary critics wish to acknowledge this fact—and sometimes they have not, a theory of literary discourse must do so. More importantly, like so many of the characteristics believed to constitute literariness, the basic speaker/audience situation which prevails in a literary work is not . . . the result of a use of the language different from all other uses. (P. 115)

It is curious, by the way, that an heir to Grice and John Searle approaches conclusions to the status of a literary text similar to those so often attributed to poststructuralist thinkers like Derrida.

11. Jameson is especially good on this aspect of modernism. In reference to Theodore Dreiser, Jameson shows how the point of view in *Sister Carrie* represents Carrie's desire "as a private wish or longing to which we relate ourselves as readers by the mechanisms of identification and projection, and to which we may also adopt a moralizing stance, or what amounts to the same thing, an ironic one" (*Political Unconscious*, p. 160). This privatized and relativized desire is contrasted to the sort of desire he sees encoded by earlier novelists such as Balzac: a form of "wish-fulfillment" where "the working distinction between biographical subject, Implied Author, reader, and character is virtually effaced" (p. 155). Desire, instead of this stable social encoding, gradually becomes fragmented and privatized for Jameson, a process which, following Lukács, he calls "reification." He sees "point of view," that exemplary tool of modernist narrative, and Henry James, its "inventor" in some eyes, as key to this withdrawal of desire from a common social sphere into a more isolated idiosyncratic realm (pp. 221–22). He does acknowledge, however, as do I, that "the effects of reification . . . also determine the opening up of whole new zones of experience and the production of new types of linguistic context" (p. 160). In many ways, then, the modernists did make it new, as has been suggested.

12. These processes include the convention that more literal forms of truth value are normally suspended, that the diction is normally elevated (this less certain now but still often true), that the discourse is contained between covers, promising a kind of self-sufficiency, even that the *passé simple*, in the case of French narrative until recently, is preferred.

For the close-ended, "comprehending" nature of the book, cf. Derrida's chapter entitled "The End of the Book and the Beginning of Writing," in *Of Grammatology*, especially pp. 15–18. Pratt discusses the institutional status of the book—as opposed, for instance, to conversation—in her chapter entitled "The Literary Speech Situation," in *Toward a Speech Act Theory* ("In the literary speech situation, the book itself as *object* symbolizes [a certain] selection and ratification procedure" [p. 118].) Barthes describes the preterite among other things as "part of a ritual of Letters" in *Writing Degree Zero*, p. 30.

Bibliography

Althusser, Louis. *Lenin and Philosophy*. Translated by Ben Brewster. New York: Monthly Review Press, 1971.

Arac, Jonathan. "Romanticism, the Self and the City: *The Secret Agent* in Literary History." *Boundary 2* 9 (1980): 75–90.

Bachelard, Gaston. *The Poetics of Space*. Translated by Maria Jolas. New York: Orien Press, 1964.

Barnes, Hazel. *Sartre and Flaubert*. Chicago: University of Chicago Press, 1981.

Barthes, Roland. *Mythologies*. Translated by Annette Lavers. New York: Hill & Wang, 1975.

———. *S/Z*. Translated by Richard Miller. New York: Hill & Wang, 1974.

———. *Writing Degree Zero and Elements of Semiology*. Translated by Annette Lavers and Colin Smith. 2 vols. Boston: Beacon Press, 1970.

Baudrillard, Jean. *For a Critique of the Political Economy of the Sign*. Translated by Charles Levin. St. Louis: Telos Press, 1981.

Benjamin, Walter. *Charles Baudelaire: A Lyric Poet in the Age of High Capitalism*. Translated by Harry Zohn. London: New Left Books, 1973.

———. "The Storyteller." In *Illuminations*, edited by Hannah Arendt, translated by Harry Zohn. 83–109. New York: Schocken Books, 1969.

Bloom, Harold. *The Anxiety of Influence*. New York: Oxford University Press, 1973.

Booth, Wayne. *The Rhetoric of Fiction*. Chicago: University of Chicago Press, 1961.

Brombert, Victor. *The Novels of Flaubert*. Princeton: Princeton University Press, 1966.

Burke, Kenneth. *A Rhetoric of Motives*. Berkeley and Los Angeles: University of California Press, 1950.

Cogny, Pierre. *L'Education sentimentale de Flaubert: Le monde en creux*. Paris: Librairie Larousse, 1975.

Conrad, Joseph. *Great Short Works of Joseph Conrad*. New York: Harper & Row, 1966.

———. *Joseph Conrad's Letters to Cunninghame Graham*. Edited by C.T. Watts. Cambridge: Cambridge University Press, 1969.

————. *Lord Jim*. New York: Doubleday, Page & Co., 1924.

————. *Lord Jim*. Introduction by Robert B. Heilman. New York: Rinehart, 1957.

————. *Nostromo*. Baltimore: Penguin, 1975.

————. *Notes of Life and Letters*. New York: Doubleday, Page & Co., 1924.

————. *The Secret Agent*. Garden City, N.J.: Doubleday & Co., 1953.

Culler, Jonathan. *Flaubert: The Uses of Uncertainty*. London: Paul Elek, 1974.

Derrida, Jacques. *La Dissémination*. Paris: Editions du Seuil, 1972.

————. *Of Grammatology*. Translated by Gayatri C. Spivak. Baltimore: Johns Hopkins University Press, 1976.

Dickens, Charles. *Dombey and Son*. New York: New American Library, 1964.

Eagleton, Terry. *Criticism and Ideology*. London: Verso Editions, 1978.

Felman, Shoshona. *La Folie et la chose littéraire*. Paris: Editions du Seuil, 1978.

Flaubert, Gustave. *The Letters of Gustave Flaubert, 1830–1857*. Edited and translated by Francis Steegmuller. Cambridge, Mass.: Belknap, 1980.

————. *Oeuvres, II*. Paris: Pléiade, 1952.

————. *Oeuvres complétes*. Paris: Editions du Seuil, 1964.

————. *Preface à la vie d'ecrivain*. Edited by Genevieve Ballème. Paris: Editions du Seuil, 1963.

————. *The Selected Letters of Gustave Flaubert*. Edited and translated by Francis Steegmuller. New York: Farrar, Straus, & Cudahy, 1953.

Fleishman, Avrom. *Conrad's Politics*. Baltimore: Johns Hopkins Press, 1967.

Fletcher, John. *Novel and Reader*. Boston: Marion Boyars, 1980.

Ford, Ford Madox. *Critical Writings of Ford Madox Ford*. Edited by Frank McShane. Lincoln: University of Nebraska Press, 1964.

————. *Return to Yesterday*. London: Gollancz, 1931.

Foucault, Michel. *The Archaeology of Knowledge*. Translated by A.M. Sheridan. New York: Harper & Row, 1972.

————. *Discipline and Punish: The Birth of the Prison*. Translated by Alan Sheridan. New York: Pantheon, 1977.

————. *The Order of Things*. New York: Vintage Books, 1973.

Freud, Sigmund. *Totem and Taboo*. Translated by A.A. Brill. New York: Vintage Books, 1946.

Frye, Northrop. *Anatomy of Criticism: Four Essays*. New York: Atheneum, 1969.

Gadamer, Hans-Georg. *Truth and Method*. Translated by Garrett Barden and John Cumming. New York: Crossroad, 1982.

Gramsci, Antonio. *Selections from the Prison Notebooks*. Edited and translated by Quintin Hoare and Geoffrey Nowell Smith. New York: International Publishers, 1971.

Guerard, Albert. *Conrad the Novelist*. New York: Atheneum, 1967.

Habermas, Jürgen. *Legitimation Crisis*. Translated by Thomas McCarthy. Boston: Beacon Press, 1973.

Hawkins, Hunt. "Joseph Conrad, Roger Casement, and the Congo Reform Movement." *Journal of Modern Literature* 9, no. 1 (1981–1982): 65–80.

Hegel, G.W.F. *The Phenomenology of Mind*. Translated by J.B. Baillie. New York: Harper & Row, 1967.

Iser, Wolfgang. *The Act of Reading: A Theory of Aesthetic Response*. Baltimore: Johns Hopkins University Press, 1978.

Jameson, Frederic. *The Political Unconscious*. Ithaca, N.Y.: Cornell University Press, 1981.

———. "Sartre and History." In *Marxism and Form*, 206–305. Princeton: Princeton University Press, 1974.

Jenkins, Gareth. "Conrad's *Nostromo* and History." *Literature and History: A New Journal for the Humanities* 6 (1977): 138–78.

Karl, Frederick. *Joseph Conrad: The Three Lives*. New York: Farrar, Straus & Giroux, 1979.

Kernan, Alvin. *The Imaginary Library: An Essay on Literature and Society*. Princeton: Princeton University Press, 1982.

Lacan, Jacques. *The Language of the Self*. Translated by and commentary by Anthony Wilden. New York: Dell, 1968.

LeBon, Gustave. *The Crowd: A Study of the Popular Mind*. New York: Macmillan, 1928.

Lee, Robert F. *Conrad's Colonialism*. The Hague: Mouton, 1969.

Lukács, Georg. *The Theory of the Novel*. Translated by Anna Bostock. Cambridge, MIT Press, 1971.

McCarthy, Mary. *The Writing on the Wall and Other Literary Essays*. New York: Harcourt, Brace & World, 1970.

McClure, John A. *Kipling and Conrad: The Colonial Fiction*. Cambridge: Harvard University Press, 1981.

Mehlman, Jeffrey. *Revolution and Repetition*. Berkeley and Los Angeles: University of California Press, 1977.

Meyer, Bernard. *Joseph Conrad: A Psychoanalytic Biography*. Princeton: Princeton University Press, 1967.

Miller, J. Hillis. *Poets of Reality: Six Twentieth-Century Writers*. New York: Atheneum, 1969.

Morf, Gustav. *The Polish Heritage of Joseph Conrad*. London: Sampson Low, Marston, 1930.

Nairn, Tom. "The Decline of the British State." *New Left Review*, no. 101–102 (1977): 3–61.

Najder, Zdzislaw, ed. *Conrad's Polish Background*. London: Oxford University Press, 1967.

Nietzsche, Friedrich. *The Genealogy of Morals*. Translated by Francis Golffing. Garden City, N.J.: Doubleday & Co., 1956.

Pocock, J.G.A. *The Ancient Constitution and the Feudal Law*. Cambridge: Cambridge University Press, 1957.

Polanyi, Karl. *The Great Transformation*. Boston: Beacon Press, 1957.

Pratt, Mary Louise. *Toward a Speech Act Theory of Literary Discourse*. Bloomington: Indiana University Press, 1977.

Prendergast, Christopher. "Flaubert's Writing and Negativity." *Novel* 8, no. 3 (1975): 197–213.

Proust, Marcel. *A la recherche du temps perdu*. 3 vols. Paris: Pléidade, 1954.

Reed, Walter. *An Exemplary History of the Novel: The Quixotic versus the Picaresque*. Chicago: University of Chicago Press, 1981.

Robert, Marthe. *Origins of the Novel.* Translated by Sacha Rabinovitch. Bloomington: Indiana University Press, 1980.

Roussel, Royal. *The Metaphysics of Darkness.* Baltimore: Johns Hopkins Press, 1971.

Said, Edward W. *Beginnings: Intention and Method.* New York: Basic Books, 1975.

———. *Orientalism.* New York: Vintage Books, 1978.

Sartre, Jean-Paul. *L'Idiot de la famille.* 3 vols. Paris: Gallimard, 1972.

———. *What Is Literature?* Translated by Bernard Frechtman. New York: Philosophical Library, 1949.

Sennett, Richard. *Authority.* New York: Vintage Books, 1981.

———. *The Fall of Public Man.* New York: Vintage Books, 1978.

Sherry, Norman. *Conrad's Eastern World.* London: Cambridge University Press, 1966.

———. *Conrad's Western World.* Cambridge: Cambridge University Press, 1971.

Starkie, Enid. *Flaubert the Master: A Critical Biographical Study (1856–1880).* New York: Atheneum, 1971.

Tanner, Tony. *Adultery in the Novel.* Baltimore: Johns Hopkins University Press, 1979.

———. "Butterflies and Beetles—Conrad's Two Truths." *Chicago Review* 16, no. 1 (1963): 123–40.

Watt, Ian. *Conrad in the Nineteenth Century.* Berkeley and Los Angeles: University of California Press, 1979.

———. *The Rise of the Novel.* Berkeley and Los Angeles: University of California Press, 1957.

Weber, Max. *Economy and Society: An Outline of Interpretive Sociology.* Edited by Guenthes Roth and Claus Wittich. 3 vols. New York: Belminster, 1968.

Wilden, Anthony. "Lacan and the Discourse of the Other." In Jacques Lacan, *The Language of the Self.* Translated by and commentary by Anthony Wilden. 157–311. New York: Dell, 1968.

Wittgenstein, Ludwig. *Philosophical Investigations.* Translated by G.E.M. Anscombe. New York: Macmillan & Co., 1957.

Index

THE JOHNS HOPKINS UNIVERSITY PRESS

Modernism and Authority

This book was set in Baskerville text and display type
by BG Compostition, Inc., Baltimore, Maryland.

It was printed on S. D. Warren's 50-lb. Sebago Eggshell paper
and bound in Kivar by the Maple Press Company,
York, Pennsylvania.